Novels and Plays

Novels and Plays

Thirty Creative Teaching Guides for Grades 6–12

Albert B. Somers
Furman University

Janet Evans Worthington
Plattsburgh State University of New York

1997
Teacher Ideas Press
A Division of
Libraries Unlimited, Inc.
Englewood, Colorado

TEACHER IDEAS PRESS
A Division of
Libraries Unlimited, Inc.
P.O. Box 6633
Englewood, CO 80155–6633
1-800-237-6124
www.lu.com/tip

Production Editor: Kevin W. Perizzolo
Copy Editor: Jody Berman
Proofreader: Susie Sigman
Design and Layout: Pamela J. Getchell

Library of Congress Cataloging-in-Publication Data

Somers, Albert B., 1939-
    Novels and plays : thirty creative teaching guides for grades 6-12
/ Albert B. Somers and Janet Evans Worthington.
    x, 221 p. 22x28 cm.
    Rev. ed. of: Candles and mirrors. 1984.
    Includes index.
    ISBN 1-56308-489-9
    1. Literature--Study and teaching (Secondary) 2. Literature--
Study and teaching (Elementary) I. Worthington, Janet Evans,
1942-   . II. Somers, Albert B., 1939-   Candles and mirrors.
III. Title.
PN59.S59 1997
810'.71'2--dc21   97-20283
                                                            CIP

Contents

Grades 8–11

Grades 9–10

Grades 9–12

Grade 11

Grades 11–12

Grade 12

Preface

In 1984, Libraries Unlimited published the first edition of *Candles and Mirrors*, a collection of guides to the teaching of thirty-five novels and plays in middle and high schools. The intent of the book was to provide, in a single volume, suggestions for the teaching of a large number of frequently taught works in English language arts classrooms.

From the outset, our purpose was to offer an array of useful possibilities to the thousands of English language arts teachers in America who are long on talent and commitment but often short on planning time. When we asked ourselves the question "What would be helpful?" our answer for each of the thirty-five guides in the original book was clear: Provide a brief summary of the plot, an appraisal of the work's reputation and its place in the curriculum, lists of the themes and literary concepts most often taught through the work, related titles for outside reading, a section on the reading problems and opportunities the work presents (including vocabulary enrichment), and lists of selected media and print resources. More important, we felt teachers could use a large body of thought-provoking questions for promoting discussion of each book as well as a wide variety of purposeful activities to initiate, accompany, and follow the reading of the book. Teachers would especially want writing activities, we believed, but also some that involved other language arts skills (e.g., role-playing, debating, interviewing) and others that interrelated various components of the curriculum (e.g., history, art, science, and geography).

Novels and Plays: Thirty Creative Teaching Guides for Grades 6–12 presents a revised version of *Candles and Mirrors*. Like the original book, *Novels and Plays* assumes that teachers often look for help, but want a lot of choice. Better than anyone else, they know the needs and interests of their students and the concerns of their communities. Their experience and intelligence enable them to select not only books but questions and activities on the basis of what they believe is important. With this in mind, the collection of guides was never intended as a cookbook with rigid recipes for success but rather as a source-book of possibilities. Good teachers, we knew, would use a given guide as they saw fit—some selecting perhaps an initiating activity they liked, others a sequence of questions, others drawing from the list of resources, and so on. Perhaps a few teachers (especially beginners) might rely on a guide more thoroughly to jump-start a unit and to save time. To whatever extent it is used, we've always envisioned the book being passed around a school from teacher to teacher.

Novels and Plays, then, is a newer version of *Candles and Mirrors*, based on the same concept. In this book (a companion volume is scheduled for later publication), thirty novels and plays are offered. Twenty titles were retained from *Candles and Mirrors*, but the guides have been updated with new suggestions in the Related Readings sections, new Selected Teaching Resources (including, in most cases, appropriate related Internet listings), and revised questions and activities. Ten guides are new—for *Prairie Songs* by Pam Conrad, *Maniac Magee* by Jerry Spinelli, *A Wrinkle in Time* by Madeleine L'Engle, *The Adventures of Tom Sawyer* by Mark Twain, *Roll of Thunder, Hear My Cry* by Mildred Taylor, *Dragonwings* by Laurence Yep, *The Giver* by Lois Lowry, *The Red Pony* and *Of Mice and Men* by John Steinbeck, and *The House on Mango Street* by Sandra Cisneros. Four of these books—*Prairie Songs*, *Maniac Magee*, *The Giver*, and *The House on Mango Street*—were written since *Candles and Mirrors* was published. The titles were selected on the basis of quality, variety, frequency of use, and potential appeal to a wide variety of students.

For the literature we have selected, works were chosen with the potential for "spreading light" within the lives of students; we hope that *Novels and Plays* will help teachers reflect and extend that light in many ways. Ultimately, we hope that by offering questions, activities, and experiences that involve students in the active response to literature, the book will play a part in broadening the influence that literature can have upon our students and increase the likelihood that they will, now and in the future, enrich their lives through reading.

Introduction

Novels and Plays is written for teachers. As former public school teachers, we want the book to be practical, timely, affordable, and easy to use. For this reason, we have chosen works that teachers teach, including both established classics and titles published in the 1990s. We have developed questions and activities that address multiple intelligences, promote critical thinking, and integrate the curriculum. Also, rather than writing and marketing individual guides (two or three of which are often as expensive as this single volume), we have compiled thirty into a single book.

In this revision of *Candles and Mirrors*, we again emphasize the idea of *students responding actively to books*. By offering higher-level questions for discussion and a variety of activities, we hope that teachers will actively engage their students in the works they choose to teach—talking, writing, drawing, debating, role-playing, viewing, exploring the Internet, reporting, interviewing, surveying, creating collages and mobiles . . . the possibilities are almost limitless.

The thirty response guides in *Novels and Plays* use the same format featured in *Candles and Mirrors*. The standard publication information is followed by a brief Summary, an Appraisal that comments on the work's reputation and most common grade placement in the schools, lists of suggested Themes and Literary Concepts for teaching, and an updated Related Reading section. For each book there is also an extensive discussion of Reading Problems and Opportunities. This includes such matters as problems with dialects in a book like *The Adventures of Huckleberry Finn* and challenging subject matter (like the references to mortgages and credit in *Roll of Thunder, Hear My Cry*), but mostly there are lists of vocabulary words that may be useful for study. As we noted earlier, while we don't believe that the teaching of a book should be bogged down in vocabulary work, we do feel that the best way for students to increase their fund of words is through reading. Thus, the lists. We suggest, in particular, that teachers emphasize the words that appear more than once since reinforcement is a key to vocabulary development.

The bulk of the book again consists of questions and activities. The Discussion Questions are simply that—questions that promote not only talk but higher-level thinking. For any given response guide, a few questions may be expressed at the "knowledge" or "recall" level, but the great majority aim higher, urging students to compare, apply, analyze, predict, generalize, evaluate—in other words, to *think*. Every teacher, we realize, will supplement these questions with their own and will use reader-response approaches that capitalize on questions that students themselves ask.

We hasten to emphasize one other point regarding the questions: since the great majority of them require critical thinking, many could be used as essay questions for a unit-ending test. Two examples among many are the final question for *The Scarlet Letter:* "Of the main characters in the novel, who committed the greatest sin and what was it? Justify your answer."—and any one of the three questions that complete the discussion of *To Kill a Mockingbird*: "What are the most important things that Scout and Jem have learned from their father and from the experience with Boo Radley? How much have they changed? How much has Maycomb itself changed—if any?"

The first activities—Initiating Activities—offer opportunities for teachers to involve students in some of a work's ideas and issues *before* they begin reading it. The activities *anticipate* conflicts or themes and thus usher young readers into the work. One initiating activity may promote discussion of, for example, the practice of witchcraft before reading *The Witch of Blackbird Pond*; another might have students complete an opinionnaire on homeless people before reading *Maniac Magee*. Most of the initiating activities, like all the other activities in the book, are addressed to the student.

The Writing Activities are numerous and varied. Some invite a personal response—like asking a student—after reading *A Separate Peace*—to consider writing about a lost opportunity. Many invite rhetorical writing—composing, for example, diary entries from the point of view of Sam Meeker in *My Brother Sam Is Dead* or Mr. Pignati in *The Pigman*. Others call for poems (a diamante contrasting *hope* and *despair* for *A Raisin in the Sun*), research, eulogies or obituaries, letters, ads, stories, critiques, reports, dialogues, myths, slogans, even bumper stickers, wills, and college applications.

As with everything else in these guides, our idea was to offer teachers options, as they, in turn, would offer choices to their students. The Other Activities obey the same rule. For the most part, these offerings reach out to other areas of the curriculum and the culture—to history and music, to science and art, to geography, economics, and sometimes even to mathematics and food (like the activity for *Jacob Have I Loved,* suggesting that a student prepare a pot of she-crab soup for the class to sample).

Finally, the last section presents Selected Teaching Resources. Here are not only cassettes, videos, articles, books, and teaching aids, but also CD-ROMs and even homepages on the Internet. (Just one example of a website: anyone teaching *The Diary of Anne Frank* would surely find the homepage *Anne Frank Online* to be interesting and useful.) Users of *Novels and Plays* will realize, of course, that the Internet is an extremely fluid phenomenon: homepages here today are often gone tomorrow, or at least altered. Most of the ones we've included, however, seem substantial enough to remain in place for more than a few years.

Teachers interested in any of the resources can inquire about or order them from the appropriate companies listed in Appendix B. (Appendix A explains a form of poetry called *diamante*, which we've often recommended as a writing activity.)

We hope that *Novels and Plays* will be helpful. However it is used—by one teacher as the source of a single activity, by another as the first item in an extensive file on the teaching of a favorite work—our purposes will be realized if the book plays a small role in spreading the light that only literature can cast, leading students to find in books the same joy and excitement and heightened awareness that all of us have found.

Prairie Songs

Pam Conrad

New York: HarperCollins, 1985
Available in paperback from
HarperTrophy.

SUMMARY

Louisa Downing and her brother, Lester, live with their parents in a sod house on the Nebraska prairie sometime in the late 1800s. When a new doctor arrives from New York to serve the community, Louisa is fascinated by his beautiful and cultured wife, Emmeline, who is pregnant with their first child. Emmeline is frail and vulnerable, and the demanding life of the frontier with its dirt houses, extreme weather, and primitive Indians leaves her unable to cope. After numerous mishaps, large and small, Emmeline gives birth to a stillborn child and later dies in a blizzard. Louisa witnesses these events with sadness, but with an increased appreciation of her own mother's strengths and of the awesome beauty and power of the prairie.

APPRAISAL

As a transition novel between books for children (e.g., the Laura Ingalls Wilder series) and books for adults (e.g., much of Willa Cather's fiction), *Prairie Songs* depicts a young girl whose unyielding surroundings force maturity upon her at an early age. The novel's sad but hopeful ending will provide many young readers (in grades six and seven, for the most part) with their first taste of realistic fiction. Pam Conrad won the *Boston Globe/Horn Book* Award for this novel, which was also cited by the American Library Association as a Best Book for Young Adults.

THEMES

adapting to change, growing up, survival, family, the frontier

LITERARY CONCEPTS

characterization, setting, plot (foreshadowing), point of view, imagery, figurative language, symbol

RELATED READING

Precocious readers might try one of Willa Cather's works, such as *My Antonia* or *O Pioneers!*, although they are far more demanding than Conrad's book. Other appropriate novels for young adolescents are *Sarah, Plain and Tall* and *Skylark*, both by Patricia Maclachlan, *The No-Return Trail* by Sonia Levitin, *Beyond the Divide* by Kathryn Lasky, *The Homesman* by Glendon Swarthout, and *My Daniel* by Conrad. Among the many worthwhile nonfiction accounts of life on the prairie are *A Pioneer Woman's Memoir* by Judith E. Greenberg and Helen Carey McKeever (written for young adults) and *Women's Diaries of the Westward Journey* by Lillian Schlissel (written for adults).

READING PROBLEMS AND OPPORTUNITIES

Narrated in the third person from Louisa's perspective, *Prairie Songs* is not a difficult book, but it does include numerous words that young adolescents may not be familiar with. These include (chapter numbers are in parentheses):

refined, refinement (1, 7),	*muslin* (4, 11),	*aimless* (9, 10),
taunt (1),	*mottled* (4),	*delicate* (9),
parasol (1),	*startled* (4),	*lure* (9),
spellbound (2),	*expedition* (4),	*lament* (9),
donated (2),	*qualified* (4),	*treacherous* (11),
formalities (2),	*escort* (5),	*derailed* (12),
revive (2),	*vast* (5, 12),	*haggard* (12),
exaggerate (2),	*absurd* (5, 7),	*severe* (12),
gingerly (2),	*engulf* (5),	*hodgepodge* (13),
oblivious (2),	*skeptical* (5),	*mime* (13),
frivolous (2, 4),	*endurance* (5),	*protruding* (13),
edgy (3),	*commotion* (6, 10),	*defiant* (13),
willful (3),	*warily* (6),	*ghastly* (14),
intricate (3),	*sociable* (6),	*grotesque* (14),
flounced (3),	*coddle* (7),	*morsel* (15),
taut (3, 8),	*brittle* (7, 10, 12, 14),	*intent* (15),
stimulate (4, 10),	*sheepish* (8),	*smug* (15), and
	smirk (8),	*riled* (15).

INITIATING ACTIVITIES

1. Have the students discuss moving. Ask them the following questions: How many times have they moved? What was it like? Were there things that they liked about moving? Explain. What was the hardest part about living in a new place? How long did it take for them to adjust?

2. If the movie *Heartland* is available in a local library or video store, play the first several minutes for the class. In the film, after the mother and

daughter have reached the Wyoming prairie and settled in on the ranch, have students write answers to the following questions: How would you feel about moving if you were Mrs. Randall's daughter? How do you think the long train ride would have affected you? What could be hard about living on a ranch out on the prairie without neighbors nearby?

3. Try to get the students to imagine vast distances. Identify a place three miles from the school that they all know. Have them imagine that their house is where the school is, their nearest neighbor is where the identified place is, and there is nothing but open land between the two. Have them write about how they think they would feel living in a place like that.

DISCUSSION QUESTIONS

1. Chapter 1: Where does the story take place? Who is telling it? Do you think she is remembering the story after she has grown up, or is she telling it shortly after it happened? What is Lester like? How is Louisa different? If you could pick one word to describe the prairie setting in the first chapter, what would it be? Why did you choose that word? Whom are the Downings eagerly awaiting that afternoon? When they arrive, why is the welcoming party surprised by Emmeline Berryman? The first picture of Mrs. Berryman that Louisa has "frozen in [her] memory for all eternity" is not a pleasant one. Do you think the second one will be pleasant? Why or why not?

2. Chapter 2: What does the doctor's mustache tell you about him? What do the first words that he speaks tell you? What does his clothing tell you? Besides being ill from the journey, what is Mrs. Berryman like? What is a soddy? How does Louisa see her mother in comparison with how she sees Mrs. Berryman? By the end of the chapter, what do you know about Louisa that you didn't know at the beginning? What kinds of things seem important to her? What seems important to Mrs. Berryman? At this point, what do you know about Mr. Downing? Mrs. Downing? Mrs. Whitfield?

3. Chapter 3: Before going over to the Berryman's, why do you think Mrs. Downing is "edgy"? How does she answer Louisa's question about being pretty? How would you answer Lester's question about being pretty? How would you answer Lester's question, "If you pick pretty, does that mean you can't pick strong?" What do Mrs. Berryman's remarks to Clara about the children being lucky suggest about her? What does Mrs. Downing's story about the Indians tell about her? Is Mrs. Downing's attitude toward them very different from Mrs. Berryman's? Is it surprising to you that Mrs. Berryman is so uninformed about the kind of life she was going to lead on the prairie? Why or why not? How does Mrs. Downing react to Mrs. Berryman's question about Delilah? Why do you think Lester seems comfortable around Mrs. Berryman? What might the incident at the end of the chapter suggest about what may happen later?

4. Chapter 4: What do the table setting—and later the seating arrangement—suggest about the Downings? What do you think Mrs. Downing's plan for the children is? Why does she worry about them? What does this statement indicate about Mr. Downing: "He winked at me and stooped

over a little more"? Why does Louisa say, ". . . apples imported from Philadelphia"? Right afterward, what do the two women's comments about the prairie suggest about them? At this time in the book, how do you feel about Mr. Berryman?

5. Chapter 5: Why does Solomon Butcher introduce himself so playfully to everybody? What is his business? Why is he chosen to do it? Why do the Downings agree to it? Why do you think the author included this incident?

6. Chapter 6: In what way are Mrs. Berryman's instructions to Lester about letters incorrect? Why is she unsatisfied with the first selection she reads to the children? What is she unable to understand about Louisa? How do you think you would like living in a place like the Nebraska prairie at this time, where the nearest house was three miles away? Explain. Why does Louisa like it? How do you feel about Mrs. Berryman? Does she deserve our sympathy? Why or why not?

7. Chapter 7: What does Momma mean when she says, "I think everyone should have something in their life that they need to carry water to. Heavy water. And far"? What is a hothouse flower, and why does Mr. Berryman compare his wife to one? Does her reaction to the broken cradle tell us anything more about her? If so, what? Why does she lose control? What does she see the broken cradle as a sign or symbol of? Is the last sentence in the chapter a sign of anything?

8. Chapter 8: How do Mrs. Downing's reactions to Mrs. Berryman's behavior differ from the men's reactions? Why do you think they differ? Why do you think the author included the incident with Paulie?

9. Chapter 9: Compare Lester's fears with Mrs. Berryman's. Do you think his father is too hard—or too easy—on him? Why was the walk over to the Berryman's so much more important than the walk back? At the end of this chapter, do you have a better idea of what might have caused Lester's shyness and fear? What might it be?

10. Chapter 10: Early in the chapter, what tells you that Mr. Downing is a thoughtful man? Is Dr. Berryman thoughtful? In what ways has Mrs. Berryman changed for the worse since her baby died?

11. Chapters 11 and 12: What does the behavior of Momma and Poppa as it rains tell you about them? Why do you think Mrs. Berryman argues for letting Lester be what he is? Given his wife's difficulty adjusting, why doesn't the doctor return with her to New York? Later, when Momma tries to persuade Mrs. Berryman to go over to the Downings, why does she refuse? What has happened to her books?

12. Chapter 13: As the Indians approach, why does Momma slap Lester and then hug him? How is the visit by the Indians similar to the one described earlier by Mrs. Downing? How is it different? Why does Louisa try to get Lester to come out from under the bed? What do you think the Indian's parting word "Hakahe" means? Do you think Mrs. Downing will eventually remember this incident with the same good humor that she remembered the earlier Indian visit? Why or why not? How will Lester remember it?

13. Chapter 14: Why does Mrs. Downing decide to bring Mrs. Berryman's body inside? Why does she ask Louisa to help? Do you think she was wrong in asking? Why or why not?

14. Chapter 15: Why do you think the author included a family of freed slaves among Solomon Butcher's photographs? Looking at the picture of her family, in what way does Louisa realize that her mother is beautiful? Why is it important for Louisa to recite the Tennyson poem? In what other way does she bring Mrs. Berryman to mind as she and Lester talk to each other on the wagon ride home?

    Overall: Over the course of the book, how have the two children changed? What have they learned about themselves? about other people? about where they live? How much effect do you think the prairie has had on these changes? Was Emmeline Berryman's unhappiness caused by the prairie or by other things? Explain. Why do you think the book is titled *Prairie Songs*?

Writing Activities

1. Write several days of diary entries that you think Emmeline Berryman might have written on her trip west or at several important places in the book—such as at the end of chapter 2 (her arrival), the end of chapter 3, the end of chapter 7, etc.

2. Write an epitaph that Louisa might have composed for Emmeline Berryman's tombstone. Keep in mind her thoughts about Emmeline in the last few pages of the book.

3. It may be hard for us to imagine living in a house made of sod, but the Downings worked hard to make their soddy a home—for example, by growing flowers on the roof and planting cottonwoods where no one thought they would grow. In a paragraph or two, describe how your family has used personal touches to make your house a home.

4. Write a diamante poem with the first and last words being *city* and *prairie*, respectively (see Appendix A). Or, have as the first and final words *Emmeline* and *Momma*—as Louisa might have written the poem.

5. Lester's experience with the Indians in chapter 13 is clearly one he will remember forever. Write the account as you think he might write it fifty years later for his own grandchildren.

6. At the end of the book, Louisa sees her mother as beautiful "in a way that made me feel good inside." Write about how your own mother is beautiful in ways besides being pretty.

7. Read "Can the Tallgrass Prairie Be Saved?" in the January 1980 issue of *National Geographic* or "The American Prairie" in the October 1993 issue of the same magazine. Using one of these articles and at least one other source (see Internet listing further on), write a paper on what the prairie is like today. Include the following: how much original tallgrass prairie is left, where it is, and efforts being made to preserve it.

OTHER ACTIVITIES

1. Act out a scene among the Downing family as they discuss whether they think the Berrymans should leave Nebraska and return east after the experience in chapter 7. Keep in mind the community's need for a doctor.

2. Read about one of the following topics mentioned in (or suggested by) the book. Then write a one- or two-page paper using at least two sources. Topics: Indians on the prairie, especially the Lakota Indians; animals on the prairie (prairie dogs, coyotes, hawks, buffalo, rattlesnakes, etc.); prairie wildflowers; prairie grasses; the overland journey; the Oregon Trail; doctors and medicine on the prairie frontier; prairie fires.

3. Read about sod houses. Then, using at least two sources, write about how they were built and what they looked like. Try to include at least one photocopy of a sod house in your report. Explain why they were "cool as an icehouse" in the summer and "warm as a barn" in the winter. Also explain how the "prairie bricks" were cut out of the earth and held together.

4. Although we are not told exactly when the story takes place, there is a clue early in chapter 2 (paragraph 8) that indicates it was not before 1867. What is this clue? Are there others that help to narrow down the time? Using a resource like *The Historical Atlas of the United States* (National Geographic Society), draw a time line of important dates in the history of the American prairie. Include at least ten dates, including the invention of the mechanical reaper and the Homestead Act.

5. As she gathers buffalo chips with Lester, Louisa sings pieces of the old song "Buffalo Gal." Try to find a songbook in the library that has the lyrics to the song. Find out when the song was written. Copy the lyrics and share them with the class. If possible try to locate a recording you can play for the class.

6. Prepare an oral reading of passages from the book to accompany the playing of *The Plow That Broke the Plains* by Virgil Thomson (which may be available in your local library). One useful passage for this might be Louisa's remembrance of walking on the prairie in chapter 9.

7. Make a "split-screen" collage with one side representing Mrs. Downing as Louisa sees her at the beginning of the book and the other as she sees her at the end.

8. The Time-Life book *Pioneers* by Huston Horn includes several recipes for such American frontier foods as buffalo jerky, soda bread, and Mormon johnnycake. With help from your parents, prepare one of these simple dishes and bring it to the class for sampling.

9. Based on what the book tells you (especially in chapters 1, 2, and 13) and using an atlas, draw a map of Nebraska that includes places mentioned in the book and your best guess as to where the Downing farm was. Keep in mind that the men made the trip to Grand Island and back in about a day, and that a horse and farm wagon could travel about five miles an hour.

SELECTED TEACHING RESOURCES

Media Aids

Internet

Robertson, Kenneth R. 1995. *The Tallgrass Prairie in Illinois.* Available: http://www.prairienet.org/tallgrass (Accessed March 1, 1997.)

Although this site features a prairie in Illinois instead of Nebraska, it is perhaps the most useful prairie homepage. It includes sections on What Is a Prairie?, Settlements, and Prairie Plants, among many others.

Printed Materials

Article

Conrad, Pam. "Telling the Historical Story." *Book Links* 5 (January 1996): 31.

Teaching Aid

Prairie Songs. Novel-Ties. Learning Links.

Maniac Magee

Jerry Spinelli

New York: Little, Brown, 1990
Available in paperback from HarperTrophy.

SUMMARY

After running away from his emotionless guardians, Jeffrey Magee finds himself living off the streets. He ends up in the town of Two Mills, where an African American family invites him to live with them. Jeffrey's unequaled ability on the ball field, his penchant for running, his misty past, his fearlessness, and his refusal to attend school—all earn him the nickname "Maniac." When racial tensions in the town and other problems cause him to flee Two Mills, Maniac joins with a lonely old groundskeeper at a zoo to create a loose version of a family. The groundskeeper's death, however, forces him to flee again. Throughout the book, Maniac remains on the run, invariably naive, good-hearted, and irrepressible. In the end, he finally finds the home and loving family he has long been searching for.

APPRAISAL

Because of its short chapters and humor and the tall-tale exploits of its main character, *Maniac Magee* has become a favorite among many early adolescents. It has also become a frequent choice among teachers, who appreciate the opportunity it affords for involving students in the discussion of issues like prejudice and social and family values. The novel is most often taught in grades six and seven. *Maniac Magee* won the 1991 Newbery Medal.

THEMES

family, friendship, prejudice, homelessness, running away

LITERARY CONCEPTS

legend and tall tales, characterization, setting, plot, point of view, imagery, simile and metaphor, personification, hyperbole, foreshadowing, symbol

---

NOTE: This response guide was prepared, in part, by Susannah S. Hogan, who teaches reading and literature at Hillcrest Middle School in Simpsonville, SC.

RELATED READING

Books with similar subjects or themes include *The Meantime* by Bernie MacKinnon, *The War Between the Classes* by Gloria D. Miklowitz, *Speeding Bullet* by Neal Shusterman, and *Peace, O River* by Nancy Garden. An excellent nonfiction title is *The Diary of Latoya Hunter: My First Year in Junior High* by Latoya Hunter. Other novels about homeless young adults are *Slake's Limbo* by Felice Holman, *Monkey Island* by Paula Fox, *The Beggar's Ride* by Theresa Nelson, and *Street Child* by Berlie Doherty.

READING PROBLEMS AND OPPORTUNITIES

Maniac Magee is divided into three parts, each concerning a different family situation to which Maniac must adapt. Most young adolescents will find it easy to understand and identify with Maniac's difficulties, although some explanation of the causes and complexities of racism may be called for, especially in part 3. The book can lead to lively, thoughtful discussion on the causes and effects of prejudice, homelessness, and general social ills. Although the novel is not difficult, many words may need defining and are thus appropriate for vocabulary study (chapter numbers are in parentheses):

legacy (Before the Story),	*ranting* (17),	*stoic* (32),
scraggly (2, 7, 8, 9),	*gawking* (17),	*careening* (33),
crusade (3),	*eons* (19),	*stark* (33),
infamous (5),	*contortions* (19),	*desolation* (33),
misfortune (5),	*foresight* (20),	*replicas* (33),
hoisted (5, 11, 22),	*distraction* (20),	*gaunt* (33),
maw (5),	*leering* (21),	*beseeching* (33),
clamoring (5),	*mosey* (22),	*bedeviled* (33),
mirage (5),	*lugging* (22, 39, 42),	*retaliated* (34),
hallucination (5),	*claptrap* (22),	*warily* (34),
emanations (5),	*dumbfounded* (24),	*gaped* (34),
phantom (5, 33),	*grizzled* (24, 26),	*bickered* (34),
carcass (5),	*frayed* (25),	*lambasting* (35),
reeled (6),	*robust* (25),	*autopsy* (35),
flinched (7, 21, 35),	*sleazy* (25),	*carrion* (35),
slithered (7, 18),	*repertoire* (26),	*ambled* (35),
pandemonium (7, 38),	*flaunting* (26),	*nonchalantly* (35, 37, 41),
lumbered (7, 22),	*gingerly* (27),	*swaggers* (35, 41),
lurching (7, 35),	*preposterous* (28),	*portal* (36),
befuddled (10),	*polka* (29),	*devour* (36),
lingered (10),	*proclaimed* (29),	*perilous* (37),
finicky (11),	*dispersing* (30),	*scoffing* (37),
solitude (14),	*languished* (30),	*exuberance* (38),
converged (14),	*pungent* (30),	*forlorn* (38),
unbeknownst (15),	*filigreed* (31),	*marooned* (38),
veering (15, 44),	*meandering* (31),	*compromise* (38),

hysterical (38),	*goaded* (40, 41),	*gauntlet* (42),
ecstatic (39),	*fortified* (40),	*sauntered* (42),
ludicrous (39),	*frenzied* (40),	*diverged* (44), and
marauding (39),	*chaotic* (40),	*amplified* (45).

INITIATING ACTIVITIES

1. For each of the following survey statements, have students indicate whether they *strongly agree, agree, disagree,* or *strongly disagree*. Then tally the answers and discuss the results. Afterward, students could be asked to choose one statement to defend in a paragraph or two.

   a. Children are not as prejudiced as adults.

   b. People who are homeless have only themselves to blame.

   c. Black people and white people have more differences than similarities.

   d. In order to be a family, there must be more than two persons included.

   e. It is better to be part of a group than to be alone.

2. Show the class several news articles or perhaps a video on the American civil rights movement of the 1960s. Then engage the students in a discussion of racism and segregation, "Jim Crow" laws, and what progress, if any, has been made since that time.

3. Have the students imagine what life would be like if they had no home. Discuss the differences they would find between their own lives and their lives if they lived "on the street." Have them write several diary entries from the point of view of a homeless person.

DISCUSSION QUESTIONS

PART 1

1. Before the Story: When does this "prologue" take place? What do you know and think about Maniac Magee after reading it? Why do you think the girls have a jump-rope rhyme about him?

2. Chapters 1–5: What must life with Jeffrey's aunt and uncle have been like? Why did Jeffrey start screaming during the school performance? Is the person telling the story remembering it a few days after it happened, or years later? How do you know? Why has Jeffrey created such a lasting impression? What is Amanda Beale like? What do you know about the town of Two Mills? What do you learn about Finsterwald? What is a one-way boomerang? What are "finsterwallies"? At this point, what do you think the narrator of the story thinks about Maniac Magee?

3. Chapters 6–10: Who are the Pickwells? What are they like? Why was Jeffrey called Maniac? Do you think this is an appropriate nickname? Why or why not? How does Maniac feel as he is running away from the Cobra gang? Why do you think the faces in the windows stand out to him? What one word causes Maniac and Mars Bars' misunderstanding? What is Maniac unaware of?

4. Chapters 11–15: What do you know about the Beales? Why does Maniac look at the house numbers so carefully? What does Maniac's allergy suggest about his background? Why does he love his life? How is it different from his past? Would you like such a life? Why or why not? How does Maniac feel about his nickname? Why?

5. Chapters 16–21: Why do you think Mrs. Beale does not like trash talk? What is Maniac blind to? What happens at the block party? Is the old man prejudiced? Is he ignorant? Is ignorance an excuse for being prejudiced? Why or why not? Why do some people not like Maniac? Why does Maniac feel bad for the Beales? What do you think they feel? Why does Amanda want Maniac to untie Cobble's Knot? Why does Maniac leave? Is this a good idea?

PART 2

6. Chapters 22–26: What kind of person is Grayson? What does the narrator mean when he says that Grayson thinks "the fish he had caught might be the same one he had caught before"? How does Maniac feel about school? Why won't he go to school? Does Grayson agree with him? Is Grayson prejudiced? Is he ignorant or stupid? Is there a difference? Do you think Grayson is happy? Why or why not? Describe his past. In what ways is Grayson "not what you see"?

7. Chapters 27–32: What are Grayson and Maniac doing together? Why is *The Little Engine That Could* an appropriate book for Grayson to read first? How do you think he felt after reading it? Why is this Maniac's best Thanksgiving? Why does he paint "101" on the door? What Christmas gifts do you think were Maniac's favorites? Grayson's? Why? How does Maniac react to Grayson's death? Why does he run while waiting for the minister?

PART 3

8. Chapters 33–37: Why does Maniac go to Valley Forge? How do Piper and Russell help him? Compare and contrast the McNabs' home to the Beales'. What details tell you that the McNabs are preparing for something? Why does Maniac become important to Piper and Russell? What does this do for him? How does Maniac keep Piper and Russell in school?

9. Chapters 38–42: Why does Maniac race backward when he is racing Mars Bar? Is this okay? Why or why not? How do you feel about the McNabs? Why? Do they have any redemptive qualities? Discuss. Why are they afraid? What are they doing about it? What does Maniac "smell"? Is this a real odor? What smells would you assign to other emotions? Who does Maniac bring to Piper's party? Why does he do this? How does Mars Bar feel about the situation he is in? How do the McNabs respond to Mars Bar?

10. Chapters 43–46: What does Maniac like about Two Mills in the morning? Why do you think Maniac and Mars Bar run together? Is it accidental or not? Why does Maniac leave Russell on the trestle? Why does Mars Bar look for Maniac? What do Russell and Piper tell Mars Bar about playing Rebels with them? What does this tell you about them? At the end of the book, why does Maniac believe he has found a home at last? How has Maniac changed by the end of the book? What has contributed to these changes? Does Two Mills change? How? How do you think Maniac will be remembered? Why do you think Jerry Spinelli wrote this book?

WRITING ACTIVITIES

1. Write a second stanza to the jump rope rhyme on page 2. Your version should also add to the legend of Maniac Magee. Or, write a rap song about Maniac, including at least ten lines.

2. Write an obituary for Grayson. Look in the newspaper for ideas. You will have to invent some of the details that were not given in the book.

3. Write a letter that Maniac may have written to Amanda explaining his experiences with Grayson in part 2.

4. In chapter 14, we are told what Maniac loves about his new life: "He loved his new sneakers . . . the sound of pancake batter hissing on the griddle . . . the colors of the East End, the people colors." Write a list poem entitled "The Things I Love." Try to include specific images and experiences that represent each of the five senses.

5. Write a newspaper report complete with a headline about either the experience Maniac has with McNab and the frogball, or the experience with Cobble's Knot. Be sure your article is descriptive and informative.

6. Pretend you are writing a sequel to *Maniac Magee*. Write a paragraph telling what you would have happen to Maniac in the chapters that would take place after the end of the book. Do you think he will remain with the Beales? What will happen concerning his education? Will he remain friends with people from both sides of town?

7. Conduct some research on the homeless people in your community. Write a report on what your city or state does to help the homeless.

8. You are a newspaper reporter assigned to interview Maniac Magee. (You may interview him when he is a child or as the adult he later becomes.) List at least ten questions you would ask him, as well as his responses.

9. "Maniac loved trash talk." In chapter 15, Hands Down gives an example. Write a dialogue of lively trash talk that might occur between two basketball players. Like Hands Down, avoid any use of curse words.

OTHER ACTIVITIES

1. Draw a map of Two Mills and the surrounding area. Be sure to include the East and West Ends, the Schuylkill River, the trestle, and Cobble's Corner.

2. Pretend that you work for the Two Mills Chamber of Commerce. Create a travel brochure for someone who might wish to visit the town. Include a description of the town, events someone might want to attend (like the block party), people important to the town's history (like Maniac), and places one might want to visit. Make sure it is colorful and attractive.

3. With another student, role-play a discussion between Maniac and McNab in which Maniac tries to dissuade McNab from building the pillbox in his home.

4. Write and illustrate a picture book that Maniac might have written for Grayson about an incident in Maniac's life. Be sure to write it so that someone with limited reading skills could enjoy and understand it.

5. There are several different families in the book—Magee, Aunt Dot, and Uncle Dan; the Pickwells; the McNabs; the Beales; perhaps even Grayson and Maniac. Create a collage that depicts one of these families—or your own family. Use print, pictures, and found objects to represent interests, values, abilities or talents, relationships, and the like.

6. Hold your own Cobble's Knot contest. Using heavy-duty rope that's fairly easy to work with, create several different knots for individual students to try to untie. Award a small prize or privilege to the winner.

SELECTED TEACHING RESOURCES

Media Aids

Internet

Hurst, Carol and Rebecca Otis. 1996. *Carol Hurst Children's Literature: Maniac Magee.* Available: http://www.crocker.com/~rebotis/titles/maniacmagee.html (Accessed March 1, 1997).
   This site features a teaching guide with a review of the book and sections on Characters, Things to Notice and Talk About, Activities, and Related Readings.

National Coalition for the Homeless. 1997. Available: http://nch.ari.net (Accessed March 1, 1997).
   This site is one of several homepages on the issue of homelessness, with a Facts About Homelessness section that leads to information on children, the elderly, education of the homeless, mental illness and the homeless, How You Can Help, Legislative Alerts, and links to other Internet resources.

Videos

A Class Divided. 60 min. PBS Video, 1985. Examines the long-term effects of racial stereotyping in schools and offers suggestions for improving the situation.

Good Conversation: A Talk with Jerry Spinelli. 20 min. Rainbow Educational Media.

Maniac Magee. 30 min., animated, color. Aims Media, 1992.

Printed Materials

Article

Spinelli, Jerry. "Newbery Medal Acceptance." *The Horn Book Magazine* 68 (July/August, 1991): 426–432.

Teaching Aids

Maniac Magee. Novel-Ties. Learning Links.

Maniac Magee. Novel Unit Guide and Student Packet. Perma-Bound.

Maniac Magee. Portals to Reading series. Perfection Learning Corporation.

A Wrinkle in Time

Madeleine L'Engle

New York: Farrar, Straus & Giroux, 1962
Available in paperback from Laurel Leaf. *

SUMMARY

Hoping to rescue her father from a mysterious fate, Meg Murry—along with her precocious brother, Charles Wallace, and their friend Calvin O'Keefe—travels through time to the planet Camazotz with the assistance of three strange but kindly helpers, Mrs. Whatsit, Mrs. Who, and Mrs. Which. There they confront IT, the planet's intimidating force for conformity. Helped by her father and the gentle creatures led by Aunt Beast, the impetuous Meg overcomes frustration and disillusionment, triumphing by using the one power IT cannot comprehend—love.

APPRAISAL

A Wrinkle in Time is a challenging, thought-provoking book, beautiful in theme as well as style. Winner of the Newbery Medal in 1963, it has become a standard work for teaching in grades six and seven, especially among gifted students. Although the book is read independently by many students, it will bear much classroom discussion.

THEMES

love, individuality versus conformity, courage, good versus evil, appearances

LITERARY CONCEPTS

plot, foreshadowing, suspense, characterization, setting, symbol, irony, allusion, analogy, sonnet

---

*NOTE: Some of the material in this section first appeared in *Response Guides for Teaching Children's Books* (NCTE, 1979). Reprinted with the permission of the National Council of Teachers of English.

RELATED READING

Madeleine L'Engle has written two sequels involving the Wallace children: *A Wind in the Door* and *A Swiftly Tilting Planet*. Many young adolescents would also find some of her other novels equally provocative, such as *Ring of Endless Light* and *Many Waters*. Other thoughtful and imaginative works of fantasy/science fiction are *Eva* by Peter Dickinson, the novels of William Sleator (e.g., *Singularity* and *The Interstellar Pig*), *Heartlight* by Thomas A. Barron, The Dragonriders of Pern series by Anne McCaffrey, and *The Giver* by Lois Lowry. *The Giver* considers some of the same questions presented in *A Wrinkle in Time*.

READING PROBLEMS AND OPPORTUNITIES

References to scientific terms (e.g., *tesseract* and *megaparsec*), religious implications, literary quotations and allusions, figurative language, and philosophical issues may make this book difficult reading for some students. Narrated in the third person, the novel also contains advanced vocabulary. Numerous words are available for study, like the following (chapter numbers are in parentheses):

wraith (1),
uncanny (1),
vulnerable (1, 6, 11, 12),
serenely (1, 4, 5),
exclusive (1),
prodigious (1),
repulsive (1),
indignant, indignation (1, 3, 4, 5, 12),
supine (1),
unceremoniously (2),
piteous (2),
dutifully (2),
flounce (2),
belligerent (2, 7),
tractable (2),
inadvertently (2),
placidly (2),
compulsion (2, 6),
raucous (2),
peremptory (2),
assimilate (2),
gamboled (3),
wryly (3, 8),
judiciously (3),
defensively (3),
dubiously (3),

morass (3),
tangible (3, 4, 6, 9, 11, 12),
paltry (3),
authoritative (4),
corporeal (4, 5),
void (4),
inexorable (4, 9, 12),
ineffable (4),
askew (4),
ephemeral (4),
metamorphose (4),
verbalize (4, 5),
disperse (4),
materialize (4, 5, 6, 12),
dissolution (5),
intolerable (5),
plaintively (5),
sonorous (5),
tentatively (5, 9),
writhe (6, 9),
anticlimax (6),
wheedled (6),
unkempt (6),
impersonal (6),
malignant (6),
precipitously (6),

propitious (6),
talisman (6),
resilience (6),
arrogance (6, 7),
aberration (6),
bilious (7),
nondescript (7),
bravado (7),
impressionable (7),
obliquely (7),
chortling (7),
opaque (7, 11),
dilated (7),
menace, menacing (7, 9),
tenacity (7),
hysterical (8),
infuriate (8),
connotations (8),
grimace (8),
coaxing (8),
pedantic (8),
deformity (8),
annihilate (8),
ominous (8, 9),
sadist (8),

emanate (8, 11),   atrophied (10),   reproving (11),
deviate (8),   corrosive (10),   appallingly (12),
placidly (9),   fallible, fallibility (10, 11),   formidably (12),
brusquely (9),   indentations (10),   devouring (12),
gibberish (9),   loathing (10, 12),   imperceptibly (12),
insolent (9),   revulsion (10),   permeating (12),
omnipotent (9, 10),   assuaged (10),   tic (12),
disembodied (9),   trepidation (11),   vestige (12),
miasma (9, 12),   oppressive (11),   catapulted (12), and
revelation (9),   temporal (11),   exuberance (12).
dais (9, 12),   despondency (11),

INITIATING ACTIVITIES

1. In recent years, numerous schools in the United States have adopted a uniform for all students. Everyone wears the same shirt, pants or skirt, and shoes to school. Discuss the pros and cons of such a program.

2. Do you believe in ESP (extrasensory perception) or mental telepathy? What examples of these phenomena have you heard or read about? Try an experiment with a friend: Think of a word or phrase, concentrate on it, and see if your friend can "feel" what it is. Report your findings to the class.

3. Have you ever been to school with other children who are extremely bright, who seem to be years ahead of everyone else in terms of their ability to read and understand difficult subjects? How did you feel about them? Discuss why it might be difficult being such a child.

DISCUSSION QUESTIONS

1. Chapter 1: Mrs. Whatsit: On the basis of what we know in the first few pages, what is the Murry family like? How do the parents relate to the children? Where do you think Mr. Murry might be? How are the children different? Why do outsiders consider Meg and Charles Wallace not "all there"? What is Mrs. Whatsit like? What special abilities does she seem to have? Why do you think Mrs. Murry is so calm about her sudden arrival? How is her calm disturbed at the end? What questions does the author leave the reader with at the end of the chapter?

2. Chapter 2: Mrs. Who: Regarding Sandy's remark about his mother, is it possible to have a great mind but not much sense? Explain. How are Sandy and Dennys different from Meg and Charles Wallace? How would you feel if you were asked the questions that Mr. Jenkins asks Meg? Do you think her response to him is rude? What else do we learn about Charles Wallace in this chapter? Do you agree with him when he says people hate children who are overly bright? Discuss. What is Calvin O'Keefe like? How are he and Charles Wallace similar? Different? In what ways are Mrs. Who's comments mysterious?

What do you think Calvin means by his remark about "coming home" at the end of the chapter?

3. Chapter 3: Mrs. Which: Why does Calvin feel he is lucky to have met the Murry family? When Meg and her mother talk after supper, do you agree with Mrs. Murry's explanation of the "unexplainable"? Why or why not? What does she mean when she says Charles Wallace is different "in essence"?

4. Chapter 4: The Black Thing: Why do you think Meg feels Mrs. Which can be trusted? Mrs. Who and Mrs. Which have problems communicating. Describe their problems and how they try to handle them. Why doesn't Mrs. Whatsit have these problems? In this part of the book, how does the author increase the suspense? During the ride on Mrs. Whatsit's back, what does she try to get Charles Wallace to "translate"? Do you think that the beautiful garden, the flight upward, and the Dark Thing have possibly deeper meanings? Discuss.

5. Chapter 5: The Tesseract: Why have the three children been brought on this journey? Mrs. Whatsit says, "Though we travel together, we travel alone." Can you think of examples of this in our world? What does Mrs. Whatsit mean by a time wrinkle? What does Mrs. Whatsit mean by saying the Dark Thing has been on earth for many years? What does she mean by "some of our very best fighters have come right from your own planet"? Can you think of other fighters that she and the children do not mention?

6. Chapter 6: The Happy Medium: Why is Calvin glad that everyone sees his mother? Why do Mrs. Whatsit and the others want the Medium to be happy? When the group arrives on Camazotz, what does Mrs. Whatsit mean by giving Meg her faults? Why does Mrs. Whatsit warn Charles Wallace of pride and arrogance? In the town that the children approach, what do the bouncing balls and the jump ropes suggest? What else do the children learn about the town? What concerns each individual child the most?

7. Chapter 7: The Man With Red Eyes: What do you think "reprocessing" involves? How do you react to The Man With Red Eyes? Would it be nice to have someone like him "assume all the pain, all the responsibility, all the burdens of thought and decision"? Why or why not? Why does The Man say "the younger the better"? Later, he says, "I am peace and utter rest." What else is he? Would a group of three adults respond differently to this situation? At the end of the chapter, where does Meg think that Charles Wallace has gone?

8. Chapter 8: The Transparent Column: What do we learn about IT in this chapter? What is a sadist? Do you agree with Meg that "maybe if you aren't unhappy sometimes you don't know how to be happy"? Discuss. How does the author create suspense as we proceed from one chapter to the next?

9. Chapter 9: IT: How is Meg able to penetrate the column to reach her father? How does she manage to escape without wearing the glasses? How does IT try to exert control? What are the possible meanings of IT? How does Meg try to combat IT? What happens when people accept authority without question? Can you think of any times this has happened? Are there—or have there been—places where such a situation exists? Through Charles Wallace, IT says, "But that's what we have on Camazotz. Complete

equality. Everyone exactly alike." To this, Meg replies, "*Like* and *equal* are not the same thing at all." Discuss these two positions. How do they relate to life in our own society?

10. Chapter 10: Absolute Zero: How do Meg's strengths and weaknesses reveal themselves in this chapter? Why is Calvin able to approach the three beasts?

11. Chapter 11: Aunt Beast: What does Calvin mean when he says, "We're— we're shadowed. But we're fighting the shadow"? One of the beasts tells Meg, "We do not know what things *look* like, as you say. We know what things *are* like." Which of these would be the more important? Discuss. Why does the beast decide she would like to be called "Aunt"? Do you agree that this is an appropriate word? Why or why not? What point do you think the author is trying to make through including Aunt Beast in the book? There are times when Meg seems unbearable. What are her saving graces? Most of us, like Meg, have combinations of strengths and weaknesses. Can you think of some of your own?

12. Chapter 12: The Foolish and the Weak: What do you think Mrs. Whatsit means by "This is not our way"? Why does Meg believe she must be the one who goes after Charles? Do you believe that Mrs. Whatsit's comparison of the situation with a sonnet is a good one? Explain. How would you summarize Mrs. Who's final quotation to Meg? Who are the foolish and who are the weak? Do you think that the author is saying that love is the most powerful force in the universe? Are there other powerful forces for good? In summary, how has Meg changed during the course of the novel? As she returns to school, will her attitude and behavior be different? Explain.

WRITING ACTIVITIES

1. Obviously, Aunt Beast and the others are not attractive, at least not initially. Think of an ugly, unpleasant creature, perhaps a vulture or a wart hog. Write a few sentences about the animal that reveal its ugliness. Then write a sentence or two about how the creature might be considered beautiful.

2. Imagine you are Charles Wallace under the influence of IT. Write a letter to your mother in which you try to convince her to join you on Camazotz.

3. Write a paragraph in which you describe a sunset to a person who is blind. Be very specific in conveying the colors, especially how they change in the several minutes of the sunset's occurrence.

4. Write a diary of at least five entries that Calvin might have kept during the journey through Uriel to Camazotz.

5. Research the idea of tesseracting, that is, of traveling through time, and report your findings to the class.

6. Compile a booklet of quotations that you might offer to others as examples of humanity's wisdom if you were Mrs. Who. Consult a book of quotations, like *Bartlett's*.

7. Write a one- to two-page paper entitled "Flatland: Twenty-Four Hours in a Two-Dimensional World." (For fun, you might read the book written by Jeff Brown for younger children called *Flat Stanley*.)

8. Write a diamante beginning with *like* and ending with *equal*. (See Appendix A.)

OTHER ACTIVITIES

1. With spools, tabs, buttons, etc. (or perhaps even a computer), create a "number one spelling machine" that would show the spellings of words which follow a particular spelling rule, such as "*i* before *e* except after *c*" or "never a *q* without a *u*." Test your machine with younger children to see how it works.

2. In chapter 9, Meg tries to counteract the force of IT by quoting nursery rhymes and the Gettysburg Address. To see how difficult this task is, try to decide when a minute has passed while your partner attempts to distract you by engaging you in conversation.

3. Using pictures, objects, scraps of material, print, etc., create a collage on the idea of fear, love, or anger as it is reflected in *A Wrinkle in Time*.

4. Design a mobile that illustrates the concept of "a wrinkle in time."

5. With other students, enact the coordinated ball-bouncing and rope-skipping of the Camazotz children referred to in chapter 6. How difficult is it? How would you feel if you were made to do this?

6. Meg experiences many strange sensations as she tesseracts through time and space. Attempt to re-create these experiences by blindfolding each member of a group and providing a unique variety of stimuli for touching, smelling, and hearing. An electric fan, ice cubes, perfume, etc., could be used. After everyone has a turn, try to pantomime the phenomenon of tesseracting.

7. Improvise what might have happened if, in the last chapter, Charles Wallace had responded to Meg's love by saying, "Love is strongest among those who look and live and act alike."

8. Draw a series of cartoons showing Mrs. Whatsit's transition from a funny old lady to a beautiful winged creature.

9. With some other students, debate one or more of the following statements in class:

    a. It was wrong for Mr. Murry to leave home on such a dangerous mission.

    b. Meg was right to blame her father for leaving Charles Wallace.

    c. Mrs. Who, Mrs. Which, and Mrs. Whatsit should not have sent Meg, Charles Wallace, and Calvin into Camazotz alone.

10. With three other students, prepare a reading of the encounter between the three children and The Man With Red Eyes in chapter 7. Be sure to practice so that you capture the spirit and personality of each character.

11. Draw a picture of Aunt Beast based, in part, on the descriptions at the end of chapter 10. Even though the beasts seem ugly in conventional terms, try to depict Aunt Beast in such a way as to capture her essence, goodness, and beauty.

SELECTED TEACHING RESOURCES

Media Aids

Cassettes (4)

A Wrinkle in Time. Unabridged. Listening Library and Perma-Bound.

Video

Good Conversation: A Talk with Madeleine L'Engle. 20 min. Rainbow Educational Media, n.d.

Printed Materials

Article

L'Engle, Madeleine. "The Expanding Universe: Newbery Award Acceptance." *The Horn Book Magazine* 39 (August 1963): 351–355.

Teaching Aids

A Wrinkle in Time. Book Wise Literature Guides. Christopher-Gordon Publishers, Inc.

A Wrinkle in Time. Literature Unit Plans. Teacher's Pet Publications.

A Wrinkle in Time. Novel Unit Guide and Student Packet. Perma-Bound.

A Wrinkle in Time. Novel/Drama Curriculum Units. The Center for Learning.

A Wrinkle in Time. Novel-Ties. Learning Links.

The Adventures of Tom Sawyer

Mark Twain

1876
Available in paperback from several publishing companies.

SUMMARY

Being raised by his strict Aunt Polly does not deter Tom Sawyer from finding opportunities for mischief at every turn, including convincing his friends to take over the chore of whitewashing the fence, showing off in Sunday school, and sneaking out at night with Huck Finn. On one of these night vigils, the two boys accidentally witness Injun Joe's murder of Dr. Robinson, a deed that is attributed to Muff Potter. Tom and Huck keep silent until the trial, when Tom comes forward to free the miserable Potter. In the meantime, Tom falls wildly in love with the new girl, Becky Thatcher, and then runs off with Huck and Joe Harper when his affections are not returned. This trick allows him to return in time for his own funeral. After Becky and Tom are finally united, they become lost in a cave during a picnic, and Tom's pluckiness is all that saves them. Finally, Tom and Huck uncover a small fortune in the cave, and the treacherous Injun Joe dies locked inside its walls.

APPRAISAL

The first novel that Mark Twain wrote entirely on his own, *The Adventures of Tom Sawyer* was not at first the huge financial success that Twain had hoped for. Over the years, however, the novel has become one of the best loved of all his books among general readers, including children. The stories in the book—like the famous episode of whitewashing the fence—are universally known. This novel led Twain on to the other great works of fiction based on his childhood, especially *The Adventures of Huckleberry Finn*. *Tom Sawyer* is most often taught in grades six and seven.

THEMES

growing up, adventure, youthful romance, human foibles, civilization, poetic justice

LITERARY CONCEPTS

multiple plots, foreshadowing, figurative language, stereotypes, setting, mood, local color, realism, humor, deus ex machina

RELATED READING

Students who wish to read more of the escapades of Tom Sawyer will enjoy *Tom Sawyer Abroad* and *Tom Sawyer, Detective*. Students may also wish to read more about Huckleberry Finn in *The Adventures of Huckleberry Finn* and *The Further Adventures of Huckleberry Finn* by Greg Matthews. Twain's other tales of adventure, such as *Life on the Mississippi* and *Roughing It*, will also be appealing. Readers interested in more modern adventures of mischievous boys might consider the Soup stories by Robert Newton Peck and *Harris and Me* by Gary Paulsen.

READING PROBLEMS AND OPPORTUNITIES

For the most part, students should have few problems reading *The Adventures of Tom Sawyer;* however, Twain does at times use lofty diction as he holds human behavior up to ridicule. Further, some words may be unfamiliar because they describe items or behavior from an earlier period in American history. Possible words for study include (chapter numbers are in parentheses):

dander (1),	*smote* (7, 20),	*irresolutely* (18),
Old Scratch (1),	*cogitating* (8, 10),	*skylarking* (18, 19),
guile (1),	*accouterments* (8),	*lethargy* (20),
sagacity (1),	*caterwauling* (9),	*ferule* (21),
pantaloons (1),	*ensconced* (9),	*gesticulation* (21),
alacrity (2, 6),	*sublimity* (10),	*edification* (21),
pantalettes (3),	*lugubrious* (10),	*mesmerizer* (22),
evanescent (3),	*ostentatiously* (11, 27),	*omniscient* (24),
furtive (3, 4, 7, 11),	*miscreant* (11),	*sepulchral* (25),
hypercritical (3, 6),	*phrenological* (12),	*palpable* (26),
pathos (3, 5, 13),	*clandestinely* (12),	*auspicious* (28),
clat (4),	*avariciously* (12),	*stile* (29),
cravat (4),	*succumb* (13),	*brace* (30),
mien (4),	*purloined* (13),	*sinuous* (31),
repining (4),	*conflagrations* (14, 16),	*clamorous* (34), and
restive (5),	*ejaculations* (15, 21),	*magnanimous* (35).
fillip (5),	*inundation* (16),	
expectorate (6),	*soliloquized* (17, 18),	

INITIATING ACTIVITIES

1. Remember a time from your childhood when you did something wrong but managed to escape punishment. Write down as many details of this event as you can remember. Explain how you were able to escape blame or punishment. Compare your story with those of your classmates and later with the adventures of Tom Sawyer.

2. In the book, Aunt Polly is greatly troubled because she fears she is "sparing the rod and spoiling the child." Decide whether you agree or disagree with this old saying. Brainstorm with others in your class who share your opinion about the results of these practices. List your results on the board, and attempt to resolve the differences and come to a conclusion everyone can agree with.

Discussion Questions

1. Chapter 1: How does Tom trick Aunt Polly? Why is Aunt Polly so lenient with Tom? Why does Tom get into a fight? Was he right to do this? Why or why not?

2. Chapter 2: Why does getting water at the town pump seem like a pleasant task? Why does Tom give up the ideas of paying friends to paint the fence? Do you agree that "Work consists of whatever a body is obliged to do, and play consists of whatever a body is not obliged to do"? Why or why not?

3. Chapter 3: What is Aunt Polly's reaction to Tom's whitewashing job? Was Tom's reaction to the new girl realistic? Why or why not? Why does Tom engage in daydreaming? What similar dreams have you had?

4. Chapter 4: Describe Tom's skills in reciting Bible verses. Why is it so difficult to earn a Bible? How is Tom's receiving a Bible ironic? What is Tom's motive in seeking the Bible?

5. Chapter 5: Why is the mayor unnecessary? What effect does the pinch bug have on the congregation? What other events have you seen that destroyed a solemn moment?

6. Chapter 6: What effects does Tom's imagined illness have on Sid? What effects does it have on Tom himself? Why do the parents of St. Petersburg hate Huck Finn? How does Tom react to Huck? What is Huck's method of curing warts? What approach might you use (or have you heard of using)?

7. Chapter 7: What is Tom's relationship with Joe Harper? With Becky Thatcher? What mistake does Tom make in courting Becky? What mistake does Becky make?

8. Chapter 8: How does Tom plan to make Becky feel sorry for the way she treated him? What similar plans have you ever made? What determines the course of the actions in the Robin Hood tale played out by Joe Harper and Tom Sawyer?

9. Chapter 9: Why do Tom and Huck go to the graveyard? At first, what do the three figures appear to be? Later on, who do they prove to be? Why is Injun Joe angry with the doctor? How does Injun Joe frame Muff Potter? Which of Potter's character traits makes it possible for him to do this?

10. Chapter 10: How do Tom and Huck deal with the murder they have witnessed? Why does Huck believe that Muff Potter wasn't killed by the blow he received? What scientific evidence supports or does not support his belief? Why does Tom have to show Huck how to make an "H" and an "F"? What events at the end of this chapter contribute to Tom Sawyer's sorrow?

11. Chapter 11: Why do Tom and Huck believe that Injun Joe sold himself to the devil? What strange actions make Sid suspicious of Tom?

12. Chapter 12: Why is Aunt Polly so taken by miracle cures? How does Tom use the cat to show Aunt Polly the error of her ways?

13. Chapter 13: How do the three "pirates" react, at first, to their lives on the island? How are these reactions affected by their normal lifestyles?

14. Chapter 14: Why do the boys find the food and drink so refreshing in their hideaway? When the boys decide that they are not the objects of the search, they are elated. Why? Why do you think Tom leaves the camp?

15. Chapter 15: What are Aunt Polly and Joe Harper's mother saying about Tom and Joe? Why are they feeling this way? Is this typical human behavior? Why or why not? Why doesn't Tom come forward and make his aunt happy?

16. Chapter 16: Why do Joe and Huck want to leave their island paradise? How is Tom able to convince them to stay? How are the boys able to weather the hurricane?

17. Chapter 17: How does the minister portray the three boys in his funeral sermon? How does the congregation respond to these portrayals? Is this typical? Why or why not?

18. Chapter 18: What games do Becky and Tom play to attract each other's attention? How do these games backfire?

19. Chapter 19: Why does Aunt Polly forgive Tom for running away?

20. Chapter 20: Tom's actions in this chapter illustrate the code for male behavior in school. What are the rules of this code? Does Tom truly behave nobly? Explain.

21. Chapter 21: Based on the author's description of Examination Day, how do you think Twain felt about current educational practices?

22. Chapters 22 and 23: Why is Tom's vacation so unsatisfactory at first? What are Tom's initial reactions to the trial? Why does Tom come forward to testify on Muff Potter's behalf?

23. Chapters 24 and 25: How does Tom react to his hero status? Why is Huck chosen for the treasure hunt adventure? Where does Tom get his information about buried treasures?

24. Chapter 26: How does superstition affect Tom and Huck's progress? What motivates Injun Joe to commit crimes?

25. Chapters 27 and 28: Why doesn't Tom want to be seen with Huck? Why doesn't Huck want people to know he eats with Uncle Jake? Are these hypocritical acts? Why or why not?

26. Chapter 29: Why is the cave the highlight of the picnic? Why was Injun Joe seeking revenge on the Widow Douglas? Why does Huck risk himself to save her?

27. Chapter 30: How does Huck reveal more than he intends to? Why does he insist that his part of the rescue remain a secret? Why is the Widow Douglas incident soon forgotten?

28. Chapters 31 and 32: How does Twain build the mood of fear and hopelessness while Tom and Becky are lost in the cave? Is their rescue from the cave believable? Why or why not?

29. Chapter 33: Why does Tom feel both sympathy and relief at the death of Injun Joe? What prompts Tom to return to the cave? If you were in his situation, would you go back? Why or why not?

30. Chapter 34: How do Huck and Tom benefit from their new-found wealth? How do Huck's views cause you to look differently at civilized living?

WRITING ACTIVITIES

1. Tom Sawyer looks forward to Saturday morning only to be disappointed because he has chores to do. Write a list poem on what Saturday morning means in your life, beginning each line with "Saturday morning is. . . ." Try to include at least ten lines in your poem.

2. Twain observes that "the less there is to justify a traditional custom, the harder it is to get rid of it." Choose a custom you would like to see eliminated, such as a school regulation or a rule at home. Write an argumentative essay in favor of abolishing this custom using Twain's approach that there is little to justify it.

3. Huck Finn is admired by the other boys because of the freedom he enjoys. Write a description of a boy or girl today who would be admired because he or she is allowed to make his or her own choices. The subject may be someone you know, someone famous, or someone who is fictional.

4. Rent the movie *Tom and Huck* at your local video store. Write a review of the film based on how well it portrays the characters and events of the book. Compare your review to one in a newspaper or magazine or check one of the review homepages on the Internet, like *Mr. Showbiz* (http://www.mrshowbiz.com/reviews). In what ways does your review agree with the one you found? In what ways does it disagree? How do you account for the differences?

5. Evaluate the villains in this novel: Injun Joe, Muff Potter, and the Spaniard. Are they well-rounded characters or stereotypes? What characteristics do they share? How is each one different? Write a comparison-contrast essay about the three of them.

6. In several places in the novel, the solution to a dilemma seems to "fall from the sky" (deus ex machina). Choose one of these cases and rewrite the scene with a solution that seems more plausible based on the characters and events in the story. Read both selections for your class-mates and ask them to critique your new solution. Possible scenes could include Tom and Huck's escape from Injun Joe in the haunted house, Tom and Becky's escape from the cave, the rescue of Widow Douglas, or the location of the treasure.

7. The compositions that were presented on Examination Day are satirized by Twain in this novel. Try your hand at a composition on a contemporary topic using a style similar to those presented in chapter 21. Then rewrite

the essay in a more direct fashion. Read your two essays to your classmates. Ask them to evaluate how well you have adhered to the style in the novel and how well you have modified your style in the second piece.

8. Huck complains of the "bars and shackles of civilization." What elements of today's civilization hold us in their grip? After brainstorming with your classmates, write a letter to Huck in which you explain the "bars and shackles of contemporary civilization." In your letter, compare these to the struggles that Huck faced and explain why the shackles today are more—or less—severe.

OTHER ACTIVITIES

1. Tom and Huck often discussed folk remedies, sometimes agreeing and sometimes not. Research home remedies your family uses or members of your community use. Do you find that all people agree on these cures? Prepare a chart of remedies for common maladies, such a warts, colds, fever, hiccups, nose bleeds, etc., that illustrates the differences in beliefs.

2. Analyze the dialect found in chapter 2 in the conversation between Tom and Jim. First, rewrite the conversation in standard English, then write the dialect version directly below it. Note the differences in words, phrases, pronunciation, and word order. Write at least five generalizations about Jim's speech based on your analysis.

3. Much of *The Adventures of Tom Sawyer* is drawn from Mark Twain's own experiences. Locate a map of Hannibal, Missouri, and its surrounding area, and pinpoint specific spots where scenes from the novel could have taken place.

4. Twain diagrams the speech of the minister as he gives his sermon. Choose a poem or short oration and set up a similar diagram for it. Have one of your classmates read the selection using your directions. Ask others in the class to comment on how the diagram changed the meaning of the piece.

5. Huck says that a big secret requires swearing and signing in blood. Survey students in your school regarding the keeping of secrets to determine how, when, and why they would keep a secret. Note differences that may result from the ages of the students or from whether they are male or female. Report to your classmates on your findings.

SELECTED TEACHING RESOURCES

Media Aids

Cassettes (5)

The Adventures of Tom Sawyer. 7 hrs. Recorded Books.

CD-ROM

Twain's World CD-ROM. Windows version. Clearvue/eav.

Internet

Zwick, Jim. 1997. *Mark Twain Resources on the World Wide Web.* Available: http://web.syr.edu/~fjzwick/twainwww.html (Accessed March 1, 1997). This is an extensive homepage with links to others. It includes sections on Exhibits, Complete Texts, Maxims and Quotations, Popular Culture, Biography and Criticism, and Teaching Resources.

Video

The Adventures of Tom Sawyer. 76 min., color. Perma-Bound, 1973.

Printed Materials

Criticism

Blair, Walter. "Tom Sawyer." In *Mark Twain: A Collection of Critical Essays*, ed. Henry Nash Smith. Englewood Cliffs, NJ: Prentice Hall, 1963.

Teaching Aids

The Adventures of Tom Sawyer. Insight series. Sundance.

The Adventures of Tom Sawyer. Literature Unit Plans. Teacher's Pet Publications.

The Adventures of Tom Sawyer. Masterprose series and Portals to Literature series. Perfection Learning Corporation.

The Adventures of Tom Sawyer. Novel Unit Guide, Student Packet, and Perma-Guide. Perma-Bound.

The Adventures of Tom Sawyer. Novel/Drama Curriculum Units. The Center for Learning.

The Adventures of Tom Sawyer. Novel-Ties. Learning Links.

Tests

The Adventures of Tom Sawyer. Essay and objective versions. Perfection Learning Corporation.

Julie of the Wolves

Jean Craighead George

New York: Harper & Row, 1972
Available in paperback from HarperTrophy.*

SUMMARY

Trying to escape an intolerable arranged marriage, a thirteen-year-old Eskimo girl named Miyax (Julie in English) finds herself lost on the Alaska tundra. Despite hunger and bitter cold, she survives through her own resources and her communication with a pack of wolves that provides food, love, and inspiration. Miyax grows to prefer the wilderness of wolves and her own Eskimo heritage to the trappings of civilization, but she sadly concludes that she cannot escape the latter.

APPRAISAL

Julie of the Wolves is a compelling story of survival popular with girls and many boys in grades six through eight. Much of its considerable appeal is attributable to the wolves and their relationship with Miyax, to the beautiful but formidable Arctic setting, and to Miyax's developing understanding of how she relates to her heritage and to her environment. The novel won the Newbery Medal in 1973.

THEMES

survival, courage, the conflict of nature versus civilization, the importance of wild animals and wilderness, differences among cultures

LITERARY CONCEPTS

setting, plot, structure, flashback, foreshadowing, symbolism, characterization, imagery

---

*NOTE: Some of the material in this section first appeared in *Response Guides for Teaching Children's Books* (NCTE, 1979). Reprinted with the permission of the National Council of Teachers of English.

RELATED READING

Jean Craighead George has written a sequel to this novel entitled *Julie*, which was published in 1994. *Never Cry Wolf* by Farley Mowat is an excellent nonfiction study of wolves, depicting them as intelligent, affectionate, and responsible. Another book to consider is *The Company of Wolves* by Peter Steinhart. Other titles of possible interest include *One Man's Wilderness: An Alaskan Odyssey* by Sam Keith, *The Wolf* by Michael Fox, *Wolf Pack: Tracking Wolves in the Wild* by Sylvia A. Johnson and Alice Aamodt, *Dogsong* by Gary Paulsen, and *Island of the Blue Dolphins* by Scott O'Dell, a novel about a young girl's lonely struggle to survive on an island off the coast of California.

READING PROBLEMS AND OPPORTUNITIES

Because of the flashback in part 2 and Miyax's uncertainty at the conclusion of the book, the plot of *Julie of the Wolves* is slightly more demanding than those of many other young adult novels. Although the reading level is not advanced for middle school, a number of the following words may be unfamiliar to many young readers (page numbers are in parentheses):

predicament (6, 10),
immensity (6),
discern (6),
regal (6, 137, 153),
instilled (8),
monotony, monotonous (9, 145),
rigorous (9),
bountiful (9),
versatile (12),
reprimanded (18, 61),
vitality (18),
intimidated (19),
dispelled (20),
aggressively (20, 24, 40),
semaphore (21),
acutely (23),
undulating (23, 54),
soliciting (27),
gaunt (28),
carrion (30),
laborious (30, 45),
ravenously (32, 136),
regurgitate (32),
deference (33),

jubilantly (33),
worrisome (38),
groveling (38),
warily (41),
nomadic (42),
conspicuous (43),
demonic (45),
apogee (49),
quell (49),
incorrigible (51),
immobile (51),
improvise (53, 126),
writhed (57),
impulsively (59),
diligently (60),
menacingly (63),
authority, authoritative (66, 131, 161),
predator (66),
infinitely (76),
taut (77),
derisively (85),
prosperous (88),
pinnacles (90),
mythical (90),

misgivings (91),
intricate (101),
piteous (102),
bestial (110),
brandishing (110, 111),
abeyance (111),
sauntered (114),
gingerly (114),
deft (114, 123),
deviating (116),
bravado (117),
cumbersome (117),
disquieting (118),
desolate (120),
contorted (121),
cowed (122),
cauldron (123),
concave (124),
plaintive (130),
harassing (132),
meandering (139),
constricted (140),
treacherous (156), and
resonant (166).

INITIATING ACTIVITIES

1. With your classmates, listen to a recording of wolves howling. Possible sources are *The Language and Music of the Wolves*, narrated by Robert Redford, and *Timberwolf in the Tall Pines*, either of which may be available in your public library. Discuss your reactions to the sounds of "wolf music" with the rest of the class.

2. If possible, view a film or filmstrip with other students about the Alaska tundra. Together, discuss the nature of such an environment and what it would be like to live there. (The film *The Tundra Ecosystem*, available from the Agency for Instructional Technology, would be excellent for this.)

3. Pretend that your area (perhaps your state or part of the country) has been taken over by outside forces that seek to change or remove your culture (e.g., your ways of speaking, your dress, the kinds of food you eat, your customs) and replace it with their own. Discuss with other members of your class how you think you would react to this.

DISCUSSION QUESTIONS

PART 1: AMAROQ, THE WOLF

How does Miyax feel about being alone on the tundra among wolves? Is she afraid? Why is she there? How would you have felt in a similar situation? What do we quickly learn about how living things have adjusted to the harsh Arctic environment? What is a *gussak*? How do the wolves communicate? How would you describe their relationships? Do you agree with the Eskimos on Nunivak Island that the riches of life are intelligence, fearlessness, and love? Why or why not? What other qualities might you add? Why does Miyax conclude that roughhousing is very important to the pups? How does she finally gain Amaroq's acceptance? How does Miyax feel about the Eskimo ways? About the gussaks? How does she feel about her father, Kapugen? How does he help her in her predicament even though he is absent? How is Miyax finally successful in getting meat? How do you feel about the incident? Why do you think Miyax so easily accepts it? In what ways is the tundra dangerous even to Miyax? Is Miyax intelligent? Are the wolves? Cite examples of each. What are Miyax's feelings toward the wolves? Does she respect them or love them or both? Do her feelings change? If so, how? How does she feel toward Amaroq? Toward Kapu? Toward Jello? Regarding Jello, why does Miyax believe his status as lone wolf is not good? Are your own feelings toward wolves changing as you read the book? If so, how? At the end of the chapter, how does Miyax feel about herself? Why does she reread the letter from Amy? At this point, do you think she still wants to go to San Francisco?

PART 2: MIYAX, THE GIRL

Why was Miyax happy during her years at seal camp with Kapugen? How did she feel about being an Eskimo? What is the attitude of the Eskimos to the Arctic animals? What does Kapugen mean when he says, "We live as no other people can, for we truly understand the earth"? Why was Miyax forced to leave the camp? When she becomes Julie, what are some things she does to reject her previous Eskimo culture? How is Amy different from Julie? What does Julie mean when she says, "Daylight is spelled A-M-Y"? On the plane, why does the man say, "That's not a good question"? What is ironic about the pilot's comment, "We now know a lot about living in the cold"? After the wedding ceremony with Daniel, why does Julie sit for a long time "in quiet terror"? As the weeks and months pass at Barrow, why does Julie spend so much time thinking about Amy? Why do you think Eskimos like Naka give in to alcohol? Why are all of the people, gussaks and Eskimos alike, so affected by the sunrise? After the incident with Daniel, why does Julie think she is doing something wrong? Where does she decide to go—and why?

PART 3: KAPUGEN, THE HUNTER

What does Miyax's response to Jello tell us about her? As she makes her way across the tundra toward Point Hope, why does she think someone is watching her? How does her attitude toward Eskimos change? Why does she feel their accomplishments were equal to "sending rockets to the moon"? Do you agree with her? Why or why not? Why does Miyax often break into song? What purpose do the songs serve? As Miyax nears the coast, why is she not sure she is happy to see the oil drum? Why does she become increasingly concerned for the wolves' safety? Why does Miyax make a carving of Amaroq? Why does Amaroq feel it is important now to teach Kapu to be a leader? When Amaroq is shot, Miyax looks up at the plane and sees "great cities, bridges, radios, schoolbooks . . . the pink room, long highways, TV sets, telephones, and electric lights." What does this mean? Why does she have this vision? Why do the hunters not return for Amaroq? What does Miyax mean when she says, about Amaroq, "the pink room is red with your blood"? Why does she think she has nowhere to go? What conflict begins to appear in her thinking? Why does the comb Miyax has carved become so important to her? When she meets the two Eskimos, why does she refuse to speak English? Why does Miyax become so excited during the conversation with Uma? Why are Atik and Uma brought into the story? Why is Miyax so disappointed when she finds Kapugen? How has he changed? Why does she tell Kapugen that she is going to San Francisco? What does Tornait's death seem to mean to Miyax? At the end, why does she point "her boots toward Kapugen" again? What is the larger meaning of her decision? How do you feel about the ending? What other title might the author have given the book? Why was it not titled *Miyax of the Wolves*? Why not *Julie and the Wolves*?

WRITING ACTIVITIES

1. Early in the novel Miyax lists a number of items she thinks necessary for survival: "a backpack, food for a week or so, needles to mend clothes, matches, her sleeping skin and ground cloth to go under it, two knives, and a pot." Imagine yourself in a similar situation. After visiting a local mountaineering store, determine what items (no more than ten) you would need for surviving two weeks in the wilderness in, say, October. List your items in a paragraph, explaining why each is important.

2. Write a letter that Miyax might have written to Amy after returning to Kapugen at the end of the book.

3. Write a diamante poem contrasting nature and civilization. (See Appendix A.)

4. Try to observe, over a period of time, a dog you're familiar with. Focus on the dog's body language and facial expressions. Jot down notes on how the dog seems to communicate pleasure, fear, uncertainty, anger, and so on. Write up your observations in a report.

5. Write what you think Amaroq's thoughts might be from the time he first sees Miyax in part 1 to the moment she becomes one of the pack.

6. In reference books and other works (see the Internet reference further on), find out more about wolves—their packs, their ability to communicate, their hunting habits, their present range, and especially their chances of survival. Write up your report and present it to the class.

7. A similar book by Jean Craighead George tells how a young boy survives for several months in a wild area in New York State. Read *My Side of the Mountain* and compare it to *Julie of the Wolves*.

8. In recent years, several efforts have been made to reestablish wolves in areas they once inhabited, especially in the West in places like Yellowstone National Park. Using library sources, read several articles on these attempts and write a two- to three-page summary of their results.

OTHER ACTIVITIES

1. Miyax carves a totem of Amaroq from bone and asks him "to enter the totem and be with her forever." Using wood or soap, carve a totem of your own—of an animal whose qualities or spirit you admire and respect.

2. With another student, act out the conversation between Miyax and Kapugen that will take place after the book ends. Keep firmly in mind Miyax's recent decision and her feelings for her father.

3. In the book, the wolves quite obviously communicate with each other. Let the wolves speak as you act out the responses of Kapu, Silver, and Nails to Miyax's command that they not follow her to the village of Kangik.

4. With the descriptions of the tundra and the double-page illustration early in part 1 as guides, paint a mural of the tundra as Miyax sees it in this part of the book. Take particular care to capture the color of the landscape.

5. When Miyax recalls the good years at seal camp (beginning of part 2), she refers to colored memories ("flickering yellow," "a silver memory," etc.). Using colored pencils and watercolors, draw and paint a favorite memory of hers—or yours—in the appropriate color.

6. Pantomime how the wolves communicate the following messages:
   a. "I am the leader."
   b. "I surrender."
   c. "I am angry and suspicious. Lie down."
   d. "We recognize you as our leader."

SELECTED TEACHING RESOURCES

Media Aids

Cassette

Julie of the Wolves. Perfection Learning Corporation.

Cassettes (3)

Julie of the Wolves. 4.5 hrs. Recorded Books, Inc.

Internet

International Wolf Center. *Wolf Homepage.* 1995. Available: http://www.usa. net/WolfHome (Accessed March 1, 1997).

    This is among the best of many homepages devoted to the wolf. It focuses mostly on the wolf in Minnesota, Wisconsin, and Michigan and includes sections on Facts about Wolves, Wolf Communication, Wolf Pups and Family Life, and Wolf Photography.

Video

Good Conversation: A Talk with Jean Craighead George. 26 min. Rainbow Educational Media, n.d.

Printed Materials

Article

George, Jean Craighead. "Newbery Award Acceptance." *The Horn Book Magazine* 49 (August 1973): 337–347.

Teaching Aids

Julie of the Wolves. Book Wise Literature Guides. Christopher-Gordon Publishers, Inc.

Julie of the Wolves. Latitudes series and Portals to Reading series. Perfection Learning Corporation.

Julie of the Wolves. Lift series. Sundance.

Julie of the Wolves. Literature Unit Plans. Teacher's Pet Publications.

Julie of the Wolves. Novel Unit Guide and Perma-Guide. Perma-Bound.

Julie of the Wolves. Novel/Drama Curriculum Units. The Center for Learning.

Julie of the Wolves. Novel-Ties. Learning Links.

The Witch of Blackbird Pond

Elizabeth George Speare

Boston: Houghton Mifflin, 1958
Available in paperback from Laurel Leaf.

SUMMARY

When her grandfather dies in Barbados in 1687, Kit Tyler has no one to turn to except her aunt and uncle in Connecticut. After she sails to Wethersfield to begin life with the Wood family, the active, headstrong Kit begins to have problems adjusting to the stark and rigid lifestyle of the Puritans. She incurs the jealousy of her cousin Judith, who resents Kit's fine clothes and her attractiveness to William Ashby; begins a dame school for small children with her handicapped cousin Mercy; and befriends the lonely Hannah Tupper, an eccentric Quaker woman widely thought to be a witch. At the same time, she develops a romantic interest in the son of a local ship captain, Nat Eaton, who visits her periodically. During the winter, when disease strikes the colony and drives the frail Mercy to the edge of death, the people blame Hannah and initiate a witch-hunt. With the help of Kit and Nat, the old woman escapes, but Kit is forced to come before a magistrate under a similar charge. At her trial, Nat convinces the judge of her goodness and innocence with the story of her and Hannah's success in teaching children to read the Bible. The novel ends with Kit and Nat planning a wedding in the spring.

APPRAISAL

Winner of the Newbery Medal for 1959, *The Witch of Blackbird Pond* has maintained its appeal to adolescents, especially girls, over the years. Its compelling plot and strong characters (especially the headstrong Kit), the authentic depiction of setting, the element of witchcraft, and the presence of romance—all contribute to the novel's success with students in grades six through eight, where the book is most often taught.

THEMES

prejudice and persecution, love, friendship, adjustment to change, independence.

LITERARY CONCEPTS

plot, setting, characterization, historical fiction, symbol, theme

RELATED READING

Students interested in other books about life in Puritan New England, especially the witch trials, might want to read *Tituba of Salem Village* by Ann Petry, *Beyond the Burning Time* by Kathryn Lasky, *A Break With Charity: A Story About the Salem Witch Trials* by Ann Rinaldi, and *The Witchcraft of Salem Village* by Shirley Jackson. A novel with similar content—about a girl who must live with her aunt after the death of her mother and who adjusts to a first romance—is *Up a Road Slowly* by Irene Hunt. Older readers may wish to consider Arthur Miller's play, *The Crucible*.

READING PROBLEMS AND OPPORTUNITIES

Despite a few archaic terms related to colonial life, the vocabulary and syntax of *The Witch of Blackbird Pond* offer few problems for adolescent readers. One readability formula sets the book at the sixth-grade level. Words that could be used for vocabulary study include the following (chapter numbers are in parentheses):

punctilious (2),	*timorous* (6),	*rapturously* (13),
scudded (2),	*incredulous* (6),	*wary* (14),
writhe (4),	*rankled* (8),	*elated* (14),
affront (5),	*ingenious* (9),	*retribution* (16),
auspiciously (5),	*obstreperous* (9),	*premonition* (16), and
undulated (5),	*docile* (11),	*inveigled* (18).
staidness (5),	*propitious* (13),	

INITIATING ACTIVITIES

1. Read the statements below and check those you believe to be true. Compare your responses with those of your classmates. Save them for an activity mentioned later after you read the novel.

   a. People who wear fine clothes are invariably vain.

   b. People should adopt the beliefs, customs, and attitudes of the majority around them.

   c. Persons with physical handicaps make few contributions to society.

   d. A fine house and fine furnishings are essential for a happy marriage.

   e. A child who is reared by people other than his or her parents will not be adequately loved.

2. Discuss witchcraft with other members of your class. Use the following questions as a basis for discussion:

   a. Do witches exist? What proof is available for their existing or not existing?

   b. How can witches be detected? What tests have been used in the past to expose witches? How reliable are these tests?

   c. What special powers have been attributed to witches?

    d. What possible explanations are there for people's belief in witches and witchcraft?

3. Role-play the following scene with several of your classmates: A new student has entered your school, one who comes from another part of the country and who dresses differently. He or she has different ideas about how to behave (e.g., always wears red) and about what is right and wrong (e.g., believes in socialism). In the enactment, the student is approached by several others, who initiate a conversation.

DISCUSSION QUESTIONS

1. Chapter 1: What are Kit's first impressions of the colonies? Why is her behavior so shocking to the others on the ship? Is her decision to jump into the water to save the child's toy a wise one? Why or why not?

2. Chapter 2: What aspects of Kit's background surprise Nat? How does she seem different from other women of her time? How does she feel about Nat? Why does she feel this way?

3. Chapter 3: Was Kit wrong to come and stay with her aunt and uncle without warning? What else might she have done? How might the story have changed if she had behaved differently? What kind of man is Matthew Wood? Why is he so concerned about Kit's trunks?

4. Chapter 4: What are Kit's reactions to the work required of her? What causes these reactions? Do you think her attitude is too negative? Why or why not? What is Judith's reaction to Kit and her finery? What part does jealousy play in Judith's response?

5. Chapter 5: Why does Uncle Matthew react negatively to Kit's attire? Why is Kit unhappy about the church service? Do you ever have similar feelings? What feelings does Judith have upon meeting John Holbrook? What do you think will happen between them?

6. Chapter 6: How does Matthew Wood feel about the king and the government in Connecticut? How does Gershom Bulkeley feel? From what you know of American history, what events occurred as a result of these differences?

7. Chapter 7: How is the courtship of William Ashby and Kit different from courtships of today? How is it similar? Why is Kit unaware of William's intentions?

8. Chapters 8 and 9: Why is Kit pleased about being allowed to teach in the dame school? How are Kit and Mercy's teaching techniques different? Which of the two would you prefer to have as a teacher? Why? Why does Kit like Hannah Tupper right away? In what ways are the two of them alike?

9. Chapter 10: How is Kit able to get her job back? Do you think her decision to approach Mr. Kimberly is wise? Why or why not? How would you have acted in her place?

10. Chapter 11: Why is Prudence afraid of Hannah? What causes her to change her mind about the old woman? Have you ever changed your mind

about someone after you have gotten to know them? What caused you to revise your opinion?

11. Chapter 12: How does the relationship between Kit and Nat continue to grow? What experiences do they have in common? In what other ways are they alike? How does Nat try to come to Kit's rescue?

12. Chapter 13: What is Kit's advice to John regarding his affection for Mercy? Is it good advice? Why or why not? Why has John waited so long to declare his love? Why doesn't he tell the truth when Judith thinks he is asking for her hand in marriage?

13. Chapter 14: How does the reader know that Kit goes down to the *Dolphin* to see Nat? What is Kit's reaction to Nat's questions about her possible marriage to William? Why doesn't she tell him how she feels? Why does Judith say, "The men can take care of the government"? How has the role of women in government changed since colonial times? What effects have these changes had on American society?

14. Chapter 15: Explain where each of the following people stands on the issue of the king versus the colonies: Matthew Wood, William Ashby, John Holbrook. What events cause each of them to feel the way they do?

15. Chapter 16: What crime does Nat commit? How is he punished? Do you think the punishment is fair? Why or why not? Why does Nat warn Kit to get away? What gift does Kit wish to give Prudence? Why will she never be able to give it to her? How has Prudence changed since she has been coming to Hannah's house? Where does John go? How does Judith react to his leaving? Why does she feel this way? What does this reveal about her character?

16. Chapter 17: What events lead to the witch-hunt? Why does Matthew refuse to take part in it? What events cause people to sometimes persecute the innocent today? What qualities, physical and mental, enable Kit to save Hannah? Why does Nat go back for the cat despite the dangers? Do you think he behaves foolishly? Why or why not?

17. Chapter 18: Why is Kit accused of being a witch? Why can't her aunt and uncle prevent the constable from taking her to jail?

18. Chapter 19: Why is it so easy to prove that someone is a witch and so difficult for the accused to prove otherwise? Cite examples of guilt by association and the cause-and-effect fallacy that are used in the trial. How is Prudence able to save Kit? Since women in Puritan times occupied such a low position in society, how do you account for Goodwife Chuff's control over her husband and child? How will the family be changed following the trial?

19. Chapter 20: Why do William and Kit finally agree that they should not be married? How does Judith react to the news of John's capture? What or who helps her to overcome her grief? How are the couples finally united?

20. Chapter 21: What are Kit's plans for the future? How does Nat change these plans? What clues does the author provide throughout the book suggesting that Kit and Nat were fated for each other from the beginning? Is the Kit Tyler of chapter 21 different from the Kit Tyler of chapter 1? If so, in what ways?

WRITING ACTIVITIES

1. You are a reporter. Write a news story of Kit Tyler's trial before the magistrate, which could have been included in a newspaper at that time. Include a headline. Remember that reporters are supposed to remain objective.

2. Write a ballad about the romance of Kit and Nat. Include in each stanza some incident that helped to make their love grow.

3. Develop an outline of a possible sequel to this book. Include what happens to each of the couples (Kit and Nat, Judith and William, Mercy and John) after they are married. What problems do they encounter and how do they solve them? Be sure you keep the qualities of the characters firmly in mind as you prepare your outline.

4. Hannah Tupper is persecuted because of her different religious beliefs and her unusual lifestyle. Write a sketch of someone you know who dresses or behaves differently. (You will want to use a false name to protect the individual's privacy.) Describe the person carefully, explain why you think he or she dresses and behaves differently, and discuss whether or not you think the person is treated fairly.

5. Using encyclopedias and reference books about colonial life, write a process paper on one of the following activities: carding wool, making soap, making corn pudding, or making candles.

6. Write a prayer that Mercy might have offered while John was captured. Don't forget that Judith and John were still engaged at that time. Also keep in mind Mercy's particular qualities.

7. Review Initiating Activity #1. Write a paper in which you address the same questions, explaining whether your responses to them have changed since your reading of the novel. If so, how have they changed?

8. Conduct research on one of the following topics. Check reference books, history books, and the Internet if you have access to it. Write a report that focuses on the human side of the topic you have chosen, and include details that your classmates would want to know. Place your completed report in the media center so that others may check it out.

    a. Anne Bradstreet, the seventeenth century poet (see chapter 11),

    b. the Salem witch trials,

    c. Sir Edmund Andros and the Connecticut Colony.

9. Kit Tyler is one of the strongest female characters in young adult literature. With her name serving as the first line, write a cinquain that captures her vitality and spirit. (A cinquain has five lines: the first, a one-word title; the second, two words to describe the title; the third, three words that express an action; the fourth, four words that express a feeling; and the fifth line, a one-word synonym for the title.)

OTHER ACTIVITIES

1. With several of your classmates, act out the scene when Kit first arrives at her uncle's home. Instead of memorizing the dialogue used in the book, simply try to understand the emotions of each of the characters and respond to the situation as they might have.

2. Prepare a storyboard depicting what you consider to be the most important scene in the novel. To do this, you will have to choose "shots" that convey the essence of the scene and draw these shots either freehand or using a graphics program on a computer. When you finish, show your storyboard to other students as part of a book talk to convince them to read the novel.

3. Prepare a skit that illustrates the differences between a dame school from the time period of the book and an elementary school of today.

4. Dramatize the courtroom scene. First write out the script, adding dialogue and stage directions for the characters. Consider appropriate background music for the scene. Then act out the trial for the rest of the class.

5. Using details provided in the book, draw a map of Wethersfield and the surrounding area. Locate the buildings, fields, and landmarks that play an important role in the story. Place this map on the bulletin board or in another location where your classmates can use it as they read the novel.

SELECTED TEACHING RESOURCES

Printed Materials

Article

Speare, Elizabeth George. "Newbery Award Acceptance." *The Horn Book Magazine* 35 (August 1959): 265–270.

Teaching Aids

The Witch of Blackbird Pond. Book Wise Literature Guides. Christopher-Gordon Publishers, Inc.

The Witch of Blackbird Pond. Latitude series. Perfection Learning Corporation.

The Witch of Blackbird Pond. Lift series. Sundance.

The Witch of Blackbird Pond. Literature Unit Plans. Teacher's Pet Publications.

The Witch of Blackbird Pond. Novel Unit Guide, Student Packet, and Perma-Guide. Perma-Bound.

The Witch of Blackbird Pond. Novel/Drama Curriculum Units. The Center for Learning.

The Witch of Blackbird Pond. Novel-Ties series. Learning Links.

Tests

The Witch of Blackbird Pond. Essay and objective versions. Perfection Learning Corporation.

A Day No Pigs Would Die

Robert Newton Peck

New York: Alfred A. Knopf, 1972
Available in paperback from Random House.

SUMMARY

Rob Peck, a twelve-year-old boy living in rural Vermont during the 1920s, is rewarded with a baby pig when he helps a neighbor's cow give birth to a calf. He names the pig Pinky, and the two of them grow up together through the ensuing year—she into a hefty sow, he into a boy with increasing responsibilities. Rob approaches manhood by "doing what has to be done"—helping his beloved father kill Pinky when the pig is found to be barren, and later becoming the head of the household after his father's death.

APPRAISAL

This graphic, emotional novel was a Book-of-the-Month Club alternate selection in 1972. Rich in details and dialect, *A Day No Pigs Would Die* leaves little to the imagination in its portrayal of the hard, often violent, yet rewarding life of a New England farming family during the 1920s. The book is most appropriate for grades seven and eight, where students will especially appreciate its humor and realism.

THEMES

initiation, growing up, family, duty, death, the importance of tradition

LITERARY CONCEPTS

characterization, figurative language, plot, foreshadowing, dialogue, alliteration, theme, point of view

RELATED READING

Similar novels about the importance of animals and family in a boy's coming of age are Marjorie Kinnan Rawlings's *The Yearling*, Wilson Rawls's *Where the Red Fern Grows*, and Fred Gipson's *Old Yeller*. Both boys and girls will appreciate these books. More recently, *Harris and Me* by Gary Paulsen is also popular with middle school readers because of its rural setting and humor. In 1994, Peck published a sequel to *A Day No Pigs Would Die* titled *A Part of the Sky*.

READING PROBLEMS AND OPPORTUNITIES

Narrated by a rural Vermont farm boy, *A Day No Pigs Would Die* has limited potential for vocabulary study, but it is rich in colloquial words and phrases, offering many possibilities for enriching a unit on dialect. Teachers might ask students to explain some of the following examples and others that appear throughout the book (chapter numbers are in parentheses):

"I got a purchase on him" (1, 15),

"I was feathered if I was going to run away" (1),

"we're beholding to you" (2, 3, 9, 11),

"Papa burdened me upstairs" (2),

"I don't cotton to . . ." (2, 4, 7, 10, 11),

"do you idea how big she'll get?" (3),

"he made a big misdo" (5),

"it gave her the vapors" (6, 11),

"a nevermind of fuss" (6),

"they seemed to be het up" (9),

"enough to give me the all overs" (9), and

"hanker" (12, 15).

INITIATING ACTIVITIES

1. Read "Vermont: A State of Mind and Mountains" in the July 1974 issue of *National Geographic*. Take some notes and be prepared to discuss the special features and flavor of the state and its people. As you read this novel, note the similarities and differences between *National Geographic's* description and the descriptions in the novel.

2. Research the subject of Shakers—their origin, beliefs, customs, numbers, and locations. Refer to at least two sources, perhaps encyclopedias, and report to the class. As you read the novel, check details presented about the Peck family's customs to see how well they reflect what you found in your research. Two helpful sources for this activity are the video *The Shakers: Hands to Work, Hearts to God* from PBS Video and the article "The Shakers' Brief Eternity" in the September 1989 issue of *National Geographic*.

3. Discuss with your classmates a time in your life when a pet died. Tell how old you were at the time, what the circumstances were, how you reacted, and how your parents responded.

4. Write a description of a way in which your family does something differently from most families (e.g., eating meals, taking vacations, observing holidays, or playing games). Describe how you feel about this uniqueness.

DISCUSSION QUESTIONS

1. Chapter 1: Why does Rob run off from school? How does he feel about having run away? Is he happy? Ashamed? Angry? Why doesn't he run off from Apron and her calf? Is what he did courageous—or something else? Discuss.

2. Chapter 2: Rob reacts to different kinds of pain. What are they? How do his reactions vary? Which kind of pain causes greater suffering: physical or mental-emotional? Which kind usually disappears more quickly? Which requires greater courage to endure? Why? Why doesn't Papa give Rob a whipping? What feelings does Rob have for his father?

3. Chapter 3: Why does Papa believe in fences? Why does he not want to accept Pinky as a gift from Mr. Tanner to Rob? Why will he not allow Pinky and Daisy to be kept together? Does his reasoning make sense to you? Why or why not? How do you feel about his reply to Rob's question about stealing the milk? Do you agree with him? Why or why not? Why is Shaker law so important to him?

4. Chapter 4: In what ways does Haven Peck consider himself and his family rich? Do you agree with him? Why can't he vote? How do you think this affects his view of himself and his own worth? What are some of the yardsticks we use to measure people's worth today? Are they always fair? Discuss. Is Haven Peck intelligent? If so, in what ways?

5. Chapter 5: Why does Rob become so attached to Pinky? Do children become more attached to animals than do adults? Why or why not?

6. Chapter 6: How does Rob feel about the hawk? About the rabbit's death cry? Does he resent what the hawk has done? Why or why not? What future does he plan for Pinky? How do he and his father differ in their reactions to the sunset?

7. Chapter 7: The incident involving Mr. Hillman almost seems to disrupt the flow of the novel. Why do you think the author included it? What does it tell you about the idea of family in the book?

8. Chapter 8: How are Mama and Aunt Carrie different? How is Pinky changing? How is Rob changing? What happens to suggest that Papa sees the changes in Rob?

9. Chapter 9: At the Rutland Fair, how does Rob reveal that he is more mature than he had been?

10. Chapter 10: Why does Rob look forward to the weaseling? Why does he change his mind about it? Why do you think the author included this incident?

11. Chapter 11: Why does Rob get so upset over the possibility that Pinky might be barren? Why is Papa so insistent that Rob do things right? How does Papa feel about his work? Why does Rob's mention of a new coat upset him? Do you think it was right for Papa to tell Rob that this might be his last winter? Why or why not?

12. Chapter 12: How does Rob react to Mr. Tanner's effort to get Samson to breed with Pinky? Why is Rob so upset? Is Rob still more of a child than a man? In what ways throughout the book has he shown himself to be a little of both?

13. Chapter 13: We know why the killing of Pinky is such a terrible event. In what way is the incident very important to Rob? What does he learn from it, especially about his father? Do you agree that being a man—or being a woman—is "doing what's got to be done"? Why or why not?

14. Chapter 14: How has Rob changed by the end of the book? How do the reactions of others to him differ now? Is the ending realistic? Why is the book called *A Day No Pigs Would Die?*

WRITING ACTIVITIES

1. Folksy comparisons are common throughout the book (e.g., "true as a taproot," "clean as clergy," and "as pretty as laundry on a line"). Create your own comparisons by completing the following phrases. Try to make some of them alliterative.

   a. as dry as

   b. ornery as

   c. the thunderclouds looked like

   d. as perky as

   e. the rain against the windowpanes sounded like

   f. the willow trees resembled a

   g. as uncertain as

2. Read Robert Frost's poem "Mending Wall." Write a two- or three-page paper comparing the ideas in Frost's poem with the discussion between Rob and his father in chapter 3.

3. Write a letter that Rob might have sent to Aunt Matty after his trip to the fair, keeping in mind Aunt Matty's concern for correct grammar.

4. Although it is a sad book, *A Day No Pigs Would Die* comments frequently—directly or indirectly—on the small but joyous wonders of life, especially rural life (for example, the birth of kittens in chapter 5). For one week, keep a journal in which you focus on your awareness and response to things that are "wondrous . . . to see."

5. An important minor character in the book is Mr. Tanner, whom Haven Peck respects as a good neighbor, a man who "will stand without hitching." Write a one- or two-page paper entitled "What Makes a Good Neighbor." As you write, think about Mr. Tanner's particular qualities.

6. Vermonters are often described as being closemouthed but able to say a great deal in a few words. Compose a eulogy for Haven Peck as a native Vermonter might have written it.

7. Read the chapter on slaughtering hogs in *Foxfire* (ed. by Eliot Wigginton). Write a report, perhaps including illustrations, on the procedure.

8. Write three diary entries (at least one-half page each) that Rob might have written on the following separate occasions:

   a. the night before he left for the fair,

   b. the night before Pinky had to be killed,

   c. a day one year after the book ends.

9. Write a list poem with the title "Being a Man." (Girls may write about "Being a Woman.") Each line of the poem should follow this pattern: "Being a

man is having the courage to admit when you're wrong." Try to include at least eight lines—rhyming is optional.

OTHER ACTIVITIES

1. Role-play a scene in which Haven Peck discusses with his wife and Aunt Carrie his plan to kill Pinky the next day. Aunt Carrie is strongly opposed to the plan.

2. Design a coat of arms for the Peck family, taking into consideration their values, strengths, and way of life.

3. Prepare a taped reading of selections from the novel, perhaps with music from Aaron Copland's *Appalachian Spring* as a background. Appropriate chapters might include 7, 12, 14, and 15.

4. "And in a Shaker household, there wasn't anything as evil as a frill." Many people criticize American society today for its preoccupation with frills—objects and possessions that are decorative but unessential and even wasteful. Make a collage of pictures, printed words, and found objects that represent what you consider to be the frills of Americans in general or American youth in particular.

5. The Pecks were simple people whose income and way of life did not allow for extravagance. Still, they created their own occasional diversions, like the whistle Haven Peck carved from a twig of sumac. Make a whistle or some other toy or object a child could use for amusement. One of many useful sources is *Making Things* by Ann Wiseman, (Boston: Little, Brown, 1973).

6. Rob's father often makes statements that are full of rural wisdom, like "Never miss a chance to keep your mouth shut." Write out two or three of these in calligraphy for posting on the class bulletin board.

SELECTED TEACHING RESOURCES

Media Aids

Cassette

A Day No Pigs Would Die. Middle-Grade Cliffhanger Read-Alongs series. Listening Library, n.d.

Cassettes (3)

A Day No Pigs Would Die. Unabridged. Perma-Bound, n.d.

Internet

Lim, Steve. 24 Nov. 1996. *The Shakers: Inventiveness, Hard Work, and Religion.* Available: http://ctdnet.acns.nwu.edu/skul/shaker/index.html (Accessed March 1, 1997).

This is a beautiful website featuring sections on History, the Shaker Community, Shaker Cooking, the Shaker Farm, Shaker Homelife, and a bibliography. There are numerous photographs and drawings.

Printed Materials

Article

Hipps, G. Melvin. "Male Initiation Rites in *A Day No Pigs Would Die.*" *Arizona English Bulletin* 19 (April 1976): 161–163.

Teaching Aids

A Day No Pigs Would Die. Contemporary Classics series. Perfection Learning Corporation.

A Day No Pigs Would Die. Lift series and React series. Sundance.

A Day No Pigs Would Die. Literature Unit Plans. Teacher's Pet Publications.

A Day No Pigs Would Die. Perma-Guide and Student Packet. Perma-Bound.

A Day No Pigs Would Die. Novel/Drama Curriculum Units. The Center for Learning.

A Day No Pigs Would Die. Novel-Ties. Learning Links.

Tests

A Day No Pigs Would Die. Essay and objective versions. The Perfection Learning Corporation.

The Diary of Anne Frank

Frances Goodrich and Albert Hackett

New York: Random House, 1956
Play: available in paperback from Random House.

SUMMARY

When Otto Frank returns to the top floor of the warehouse that was his family's hiding place for two years during the German occupation in World War II, he finds his daughter Anne's diary and recalls the tremendous fear, anxiety, and tribulation his family experienced there. Fearing the family would be sent to a concentration camp, he moved his wife and two daughters into hiding in the three rooms and an attic space that they shared with Mr. and Mrs. Van Daan and their son, Peter, who was sixteen. With the help of friends who brought them supplies, the families settled into their close quarters and tried to adapt to a lifestyle of confinement and quiet. The outspoken Anne, then a teenager, adjusted with difficulty, seeking comfort by writing in her diary and tormenting the shy Peter. Her problems increased when Dussel, a dentist, moved in and shared her room. Despite the conditions, the families established a routine of work and study with each day highlighted by the gathering for the evening meal. Anne and Peter grew to understand and sympathize with each other and shared evening dates in Peter's cramped room. Finally, however, the families were discovered and taken to camps where all except Mr. Frank were killed. As Mr. Frank finishes Anne's diary, he feels ashamed because she had retained her faith in humanity.

APPRAISAL

This play is based, of course, on *Anne Frank: The Diary of a Young Girl*, the immensely popular book. The popularity of both works can be traced to their portrayal of a young girl's indomitable spirit in the face of the horror and degradation of Jewish persecution before and during World War II. More success-ful than the intimate diary in conveying the tension and terror of the family's situation, the play is most often taught in the seventh and eighth grades, whereas the diary itself has its greatest following among high school students.

THEMES

the strength of the human spirit, fear, survival, family, growing up, friendship and love, persecution

LITERARY CONCEPTS

flashback, characterization, conflict, setting, symbol, stage direction

RELATED READING

A number of books are available for students interested in the lives of young people caught up in the trials of war. These include *I Am Fifteen and I Don't Want to Die* by Christine Arnothy, *When Hitler Stole Pink Rabbit* by Judith Kerr, and *The Endless Steppe* by Esther Hautzig. *The Hiding Place* by Corrie ten Boom, *Hiding to Survive: Stories of Jewish Children Rescued from the Holocaust* by Maxine B. Rosenberg, *Number the Stars* by Lois Lowry, and *The Upstairs Room* by Johanna Reiss are about Jewish families forced to hide from the Germans. *Night* by Elie Wiesel relates the story of a Jewish boy in a German concentration camp. *Summer of My German Soldier* by Bette Greene is the unique story of a friendship between a Jewish girl and a German prisoner of war in Arkansas during World War II.

READING PROBLEMS AND OPPORTUNITIES

Students will need to understand that *The Diary of Anne Frank* is principally a flashback. Otherwise, they should have few reading problems. Words that might be used for vocabulary study occur mostly in the stage directions. They include the following (act and scene numbers are in parentheses):

carillon (1:1),	*indignantly* (1:3),	*inarticulate* (2:1),
capitulation (1:1),	*bickering* (1:3),	*advisability* (2:1),
portly (1:2),	*meticulous* (1:3; 2:3),	*bewildered* (2:1),
conspicuous (1:2),	*finicky* (1:3),	*animation* (2:2),
mercurial (1:2),	*humiliated* (1:3; 2:2),	*intuition* (2:2),
self-conscious (1:3),	*subdued* (1:3),	*gauntlet* (2:2),
intolerable (1:3),	*fatalist* (1:4),	*pandemonium* (2:3),
insufferable (1:3),	*sustenance* (1:5),	*convulsive* (2:3), and
vile (1:3),	*ostentatiously* (1:5),	*ineffectually* (2:4).

INITIATING ACTIVITIES

1. Imagine that you are to leave your home and that you will be gone for an indefinite period of time. What would you take with you if all you were allowed were the things you could carry in your arms? Make a list of these items. Save the list for a later activity.

2. Ask a rabbi or a member of the Jewish faith in your community to visit your class to discuss Judaism. Ask the person to talk in particular about Jewish holidays such as Hanukkah or Yom Kippur and about Hebrew and Yiddish words and expressions such as *mazel tov, menorah,* and *yarmulke.*

3. Conduct research on the Nazi party in Germany and the Holocaust that took place before and during World War II. Present what you find to the class, including information on the causes and effects of this period of persecution.

DISCUSSION QUESTIONS

1. Act 1, scene 1: Why does Mr. Frank say that he cannot stay in Amsterdam? Do you agree that it is difficult to stay in a place that is full of memories? Why or why not? Why does Mr. Frank tell Miep to burn all the papers? Why does he change his mind? Explain the importance of the yellow star. In Mr. Frank's memory, why doesn't Anne mind the yellow star and the other restrictions placed upon her?

2. Act 1, scene 2: Why is Mrs. Van Daan concerned about the ration books? How does Mr. Frank reassure her? How are Mr. Kraler and Miep going to help the Franks and the Van Daans? Why is Mrs. Frank shocked when Anne takes off her panties? Why did Mr. Frank invite the Van Daans to hide with them? Do you think this was too great a sacrifice for him to make? Why or why not? How does Peter's mother embarrass him? Why doesn't Anne remember Peter from school? Why isn't Anne able to throw away the yellow star? Will Anne's imagination be a help or a hindrance during the ordeal of hiding out? Why? What advantages and disadvantages are there for her during this period of hiding?

3. Act 1, scene 3: How does Anne tease Peter? Why does she do this? Is her teasing typical of girls who seek attention from boys? Why or why not? How do you feel about Anne's complaint that her mother is unhappy with her no matter how she behaves? Anne says, "I only want some fun." Should she be criticized for this? Why or why not? How does Peter finally get revenge on Anne for all her teasing? What does Mrs. Van Daan teach Anne about boys? Why is Mr. Frank going to take over Peter's education? Do you think it is typical for other adults to have more influence with young people than their parents do? Why or why not? Is Anne rude or does she merely express her feelings? Why do you think so? Anne tells her mother that "things have changed. People aren't like that any more." Is this true of young people today? Why or why not? Describe the relationship between Anne and her sister, Margot. Do you think parents usually treat second children the way Mr. and Mrs. Frank treat Anne? Why does Mr. Frank agree to allow Dussel to move in with them? Is this wise of Mr. Frank? What else might he have done? How does the Franks' and the Van Daans' view of the outside world change after Dussel's arrival? Why does Anne resent Dussel?

4. Act 1, scene 4: How does Anne hurt her mother? Why does she do this? Anne says, "I can stand off and look at myself doing it and know it's cruel and yet I can't stop doing it. What's the matter with me?" What are some possible answers to Anne's question? What comforts of home does Anne miss? If you were in her place, what would you miss?

5. Act 1, scene 5: How is the Franks and Van Daans celebration of Hanukkah similar to previous celebrations? How is it different? Why doesn't Dussel know about Hanukkah? (The answer to this question may require research into Hitler's persecution of the Jews.) Of the Hanukkah presents Anne devised, which do you think is the most clever? Why? How does Peter expose Dussel's pretended allergy? Is this a dirty trick? Why or why not? What serious mistake does Peter make? Despite Peter's accident, why

does Mrs. Van Daan believe they are safe? When Dussel disagrees with her, who do you think is right? Why? Why can't the families leave under any circumstance?

6. Act 2, scene 1: Anne writes "our life is at a standstill." What does she mean by this? What changes is she undergoing? What are her reactions to these changes? Why is Mrs. Frank concerned when Miep and Mr. Kraler bring the families a cake for the New Year? Are Mr. and Mrs. Van Daan selfish? Cite examples of dialogue to support your answer. Is it selfish of Mrs. Van Daan not to want to sell her fur coat? Why or why not? Why does Margot say, "Sometimes I wish the end would come . . . whatever it is"? Do you think it is fair for Anne to blame the adults for the problems of the world? Why or why not? Why does Peter admire Anne? Why do Anne and Peter begin to understand each other better? Anne says, "We have problems here that no other people our age have ever had." What are these problems? Do you think all of their problems are unique? Why or why not? How does Anne feel about her father? Why does she feel this way?

7. Act 2, scene 2: How do you know that Anne's visits to Peter's room are special to her? Why does Mrs. Van Daan object to these visits? How has Peter's attitude toward Anne changed? What has caused this change? What are Anne's reactions to her first kiss?

8. Act 2, scene 3: Is Mrs. Frank justified in wanting to throw the Van Daans out? Why or why not? How does Mr. Frank try to smooth things over? Cite other examples throughout the play in which he has served as a peacemaker. What does he mean by the statement: "We don't need the Nazis to destroy us. We're destroying ourselves"? Why does Peter choose to go with his parents? Why is Anne so upset that the Van Daans may have to leave? Why don't they leave after all? By July 2, 1944, why is everyone in both families as well as Dussel in low spirits? Anne's wish is that she may go on living after her death. How would this be possible? How did she actually achieve this goal?

9. Act 2, scene 4: Is Mr. Frank right in continuing to do nothing to let anyone know they are in the building? Why or why not? What advice does Anne give Peter? Does Anne continue to hope? How do you know? Mr. Frank says that for the past two years they have lived in fear but now they can live in hope. What does he mean?

10. Act 2, scene 5: How are the Franks and the Van Daans discovered? Why do Miep and Mr. Kraler check to find out who was responsible? Why is Anne happy in the concentration camp? Why was it possible that Mr. Frank survived while the rest of the family was killed? What does Mr. Frank mean when he says, "She puts me to shame"?

WRITING ACTIVITIES

1. Review the list you prepared for Initiating Activity #1. Compare your list with the items that Anne Frank takes with her. Write a three-paragraph essay in which you describe the items you chose in the first paragraph, include Anne's list in the second, and present in the third paragraph the reasons for the similarities and differences in the two lists.

2. Prepare a chart detailing the sources of tension among the characters in the play. List all eight characters across the top of the page and also down the left side. Then write any sources of tension where any two names intersect. List internal sources of tension where the character's name intersects with itself. The same source may be referred to more than once. Note the following examples:

Sources of Tension Among Characters

	Anne	**Mrs. Frank**	**Mrs. Van Daan**
Anne	coping with growing up	Anne's rude behavior	Anne's visits to Peter's room
Mr. Van Daan	stolen food	stolen food	fur coat and cigarettes

3. Rewrite one scene from the play (for example, act 1, scene 5) as it might have appeared in Anne's diary. Remember her attitude toward others in the play and toward herself. Make your entries consistent with these attitudes. If possible, find a copy of *Anne Frank: The Diary of a Young Girl* and compare your entries to the actual entries that Anne wrote.

4. Imagine that it is some occasion where you traditionally give presents to members of your family. Like Anne, you have no money. Decide what presents you could make for your family just as Anne did during the Hanukkah celebration. Write a description of these gifts and explain why each would be appropriate.

5. Write a letter to Anne Frank telling her how her wish has come true—that she is still alive after her death. In this letter explain to her what her story has meant to you.

6. Write an essay in which you compare either Anne's mother or father to your own mother or father or guardian. Compare Anne's concerns, arguments, and problems with her parents to those that you have with yours.

7. Write a list poem that defines *prejudice* by using the "Happiness is a warm puppy" pattern popularized by Charles Schultz in his *Peanuts* books. One example: "Prejudice is hating without knowing." Include at least six others.

8. Write a brief character sketch on one of the following figures in the play: Mr. Van Daan, Mrs. Van Daan, Peter, or Dussel. In your paper, discuss the good and bad qualities of the character, how the character handled stress and tension, and how you think you would respond to the person in a situation similar to the one in the play.

9. Imagine that Anne survived the concentration camp and the war. As a senior citizen today, what would be her "world view"? Would she have retained her faith in humanity through the years since the Holocaust despite the problems that plague the world today? Write a paper expressing her thoughts and feelings from the perspective of the present.

10. Anne's diary is a source of sanity and pleasure for her in a tense and anxious world. Keep a diary for several weeks in which you try to view your writing as a source of insight and solace. In terms of spirit and purpose, model your entries after hers.

OTHER ACTIVITIES

1. Draw a sketch or perhaps a blueprint (or both) of the play's setting to help your classmates visualize the stage. Read the stage directions carefully to determine the details about each room, including the furniture, doors, and important props. You may draw this freehand or use a computer graphics program.

2. Prepare a visual representation of the fear that the Franks and the Van Daans feel throughout the play. Because this strong emotion has no clear shapes or images, fingerpaints or watercolors may be appropriate. Choose colors and lines that reinforce the horror that these families endure.

3. Select three or four portions of scenes that illustrate the rising tension in the hideaway. The first selection should show the group's rapport at the beginning; the second should show the rising tension; the third, the difficulty the families experienced in maintaining their relationships. Act out these scenes for the other members of your class.

SELECTED TEACHING RESOURCES

Media Aids

Internet

Miller, M. F. 1995. *Anne Frank Online*. Available: http://www.annefrank.com (Accessed March 1, 1997).

This is an impressive website containing sections on Anne Frank: Her Life and Times (with a photo scrapbook of her life and family as well as extensive information on the diary), Anne Frank in the Classroom, and the Anne Frank Center USA, which sponsors the site. The mailing address of the Center is 584 Broadway, Suite 408, New York, NY 10012. Another homepage of possible interest is the *United States Holocaust Memorial Museum*. 21 February 1997. Available: http://www.ushmm.org (Accessed March 1, 1997).

Video

The Diary of Anne Frank. 150 min., b & w. Perma-Bound and Sundance, 1959.

Printed Materials

Articles

Mapes, Elizabeth A. "A Drama for Junior High School: *The Diary of Anne Frank*." *English Journal* 57 (December 1968): 1307–1311.

Plotka, Marie, and Arnold Lazarus. "Teaching Interpretive Expository Writing." *English Journal* 57 (January 1968): 59–64.

Book

Van der Rol, Ruud and Rian Verhoeven. *Anne Frank—Beyond the Diary: A Photographic Remembrance.* New York: Viking, 1993.

Teaching Aids

The Diary of Anne Frank. Novel Unit Guide. Perma-Bound.

The World of Anne Frank: Readings, Activities, and Resources. J. Weston Walch, Publisher.

The Light in the Forest

Conrad Richter

New York: Alfred A. Knopf, 1953
Available in paperback from Fawcett Juniper.

SUMMARY

For eleven years, True Son, a white boy abducted when he was four from his parents' farm in Pennsylvania, has lived as the Indian son of Cuyloga, leader of the Lenni Lenape. When Cuyloga reluctantly returns True Son to his real parents to keep the peace, the boy despairs and sullenly rejects everything about his new, alien culture—the food, clothing, language, houses, religion, and especially the prevailing white notion of Indians as primitive savages. Only with Gordie, his young brother, does he manage rapport. After several months, True Son escapes during an Indian scare in which an Indian friend, Little Crane, is killed. He returns to his tribe and then joins others on a raid to avenge Little Crane's murder. When he is asked to lure a flatboat of white settlers into an ambush, however, True Son is struck by the sight of a small boy on the boat and warns the settlers of danger. As a result, he is sadly banished from the tribe by Cuyloga, who sends him back to a world that he cannot accept.

APPRAISAL

This novel of contrasting cultures and conflicting loyalties has been popular with young readers since its publication in 1953 largely because of its portrayal of a young man caught between two disparate worlds and its realistic depiction of the lifestyle and values of an American Indian tribe (the Lenni Lenape or Delaware) in the Allegheny wilderness of the 1760s. The book is short, quite approachable, and most often taught in the seventh and eighth grades.

THEMES

the importance of appreciating different cultures, the importance of personal freedom, loyalty, family

LITERARY CONCEPTS

point of view, setting, conflict, symbol, plot, characterization, theme

RELATED READING

Other books about American Indians, especially their difficulties integrating into the mainstream of American culture, include Hal Borland's *When the Legends Die*, Weyman Jones's *Edge of Two Worlds*, Scott Momaday's *House Made of Dawn,* and Theodora Kroeber's *Ishi in Two Worlds: A Biography of the Last Wild Indian in North America.* Fiction about young people reared as Native Americans but who were returned to their white families include *A Circle Unbroken* by Sollace Hotze, *Where the Broken Heart Still Beats: The Story of Cynthia Ann Parker* by Carolyn Meyer, and *I Am Regina* by Sally M. Keehn (which, like *The Light in the Forest*, is set in Pennsylvania).

READING PROBLEMS AND OPPORTUNITIES

This novel is appropriate for students and teachers in middle and junior high schools. It is easily read (an application of the Fry Readability Scale places it at the fifth-grade level), and it offers readers who may be accustomed to happy endings a work of fiction with an unresolved conclusion. Words appearing in *The Light in the Forest* that might be used for vocabulary study include the following (chapter numbers in parentheses):

loathing (1, 2, 5, 6),
ominous (4, 13),
impassive (4, 6, 7, 13, 14),
grave or *gravity* (4, 9, 14),
constriction (5, 6, 8),
barbarous (5, 12),
ostentation (5),
pallid (5, 7),

presumptuous (5),
aloof (6, 12, 13, 14),
piteous (7, 9, 14),
abhorrence (7),
reproach (8),
formidable (9, 15),
exemplary (9),
brusque (10),
miasma (10),
filial (10),

insidious (11),
reprove (11, 14),
alacrity (12),
exult or *exultation* (13, 14),
appease (14),
stratagem (14),
incredulity (14),
disquieted (15), and
volition (15).

INITIATING ACTIVITIES

1. Read in appropriate reference books about conflicts between white settlers and the various Indian tribes along the Allegheny frontier in the 1760s, including Pontiac's Rebellion of 1763–1764 and Colonel Bouquet's march into western Pennsylvania and eastern Ohio in 1763. Report to the class on causes, campaigns, battles, and results.

2. Imagine that you are notified one day of a strange set of circumstances: Because of a mistake in the hospital where you were born, you were given to the wrong parents. Now your real parents—who have since moved back to their homeland in France—have been identified, and you are to be sent to them. Write a one- to two-page paper describing how you feel and what you think you would do.

3. Referring perhaps to past issues of *National Geographic*, read about a foreign culture whose lifestyle and values seem totally different from those that prevail in the United States. (One possible article: "The Threatened Ways of Kenya's Pokot People," *National Geographic*, January 1982.) Present an objective report on the culture to the class.

DISCUSSION QUESTIONS

1. Chapter 1: Why is True Son upset? Because he is white, why does he not want to leave the tribe? Why does his Indian father deliver him to the soldiers? As Cuyloga leaves, what is True Son's frame of mind?

2. Chapter 2: How do the white troops feel toward the Indians? Why have both groups so reluctantly made an agreement? What is the agreement? How does Del Hardy feel about the Indians? About True Son in particular? Why might Del's feelings be slightly different from those of the other whites?

3. Chapter 3: Why does True Son want to eat the root of the may apple? For him, would it be an act of honor? Why? Would it be an act of honor for someone in our culture? Why or why not? What does this suggest about different cultures? Why do the troops allow Half Arrow to run beside True Son? In what way does Half Arrow lift True Son's spirits? In what ways do the two Indians see themselves as superior to white men?

4. Chapter 4: The three Indians enjoy making fun of the white man's weaknesses. Do some of their criticisms seem more valid than others? If so, which ones and why? What advice does True Son's father send to him? What seems to be his father's hope? How does True Son respond? On the basis of the first four chapters, how would you describe True Son? What is he like?

5. Chapter 5: As he is forced further into the settlements of the white man, what bothers True Son the most? What distinctions does he continue to make between the whites and the Indians? Why does he consider the white man who has come to meet him "presumptuous"?

6. Chapter 6: How do Del Hardy's feelings toward the settlements differ from True Son's? Cite two or three specific issues about which they have opposing opinions. Discuss the reactions of the various members of the Butler family to True Son. Who do you think will have the easiest time getting to know him? Why? Who will have the hardest time? Why? What do you think will be True Son's most difficult adjustments?

7. Chapter 7: How do True Son and his uncles differ in their versions of the "Peshtank story"? Who is right? Why is the incident such a barrier between them? Is either of them more reasonable than the other? In what ways do both True Son and his uncles seem inflexible? In general, why is there so much hatred between the white settlers and the Indians?

8. Chapter 8: How do the Butlers try to "civilize" True Son? Which of their methods do you think will have the greatest impact? Why? Why does Bejance, the basket maker, tell True Son and Gordie that they will both become slaves? Why does True Son want to see Corn Blade? What does he seem to miss most of all? What beckons him?

9. Chapter 9: How does Aunt Kate's attitude toward True Son differ from his mother's? How would you characterize Parson Elder? Does he seem reasonable? Honest? To what extent is he open to True Son's way of seeing things? Is he in any way closed-minded? If so, how? To what extent is True Son open-minded?

10. Chapter 10: What does Dr. Childsley feel is the cause of True Son's illness? Mr. Butler wishes he could talk to True Son to "release the burden long on his breast." What might this be? Why do True Son's few belongings affect his father? What do you think are Mr. Butler's thoughts about the Indian trouble he is warned of? Why does he seem to gain reassurance from tending to his account book?

11. Chapter 11: What does True Son continue to hope for? What does he fear? Do you think his fears are justified? Why or why not? What does he begin to feel will be his only escape? Cite some examples in the chapter of True Son's having begun to adjust to (if not accept) white customs and values. Cite examples of his faithfulness to his Indian background. Why does True Son ask Half Arrow so many questions about Little Crane's death? How had Half Arrow and Little Crane made an error in judgment at the cooperage?

12. Chapter 12: True Son is still weak, but why has his sickness left him? Why does Half Arrow decline to attack the small colony of whites in the clearing? As the two boys move through the forest, what disturbs them? What further evidence is there that some of the white culture has perhaps rubbed off on True Son? Despite this, what are True Son's feelings as he makes his way westward?

13. Chapter 13: For the two boys, what kind of place is the forest glade where they camp for several weeks? Why do they delay the final leg of their journey home? Do you think that the desire for such an experience—"forgetting all else and by all else forgot"—is common to most people at one time or another? Is it more common among boys? Discuss. When True Son and Half Arrow arrive at the Indian camp, why do they restrain their emotions?

14. Chapter 14: Why do the Indians feel compelled to seek revenge for the murder of Little Crane? Why does True Son feel "a savage sweetness he had never known before"? Do you think his pride and excitement are different in any way from the feelings of the others? If so, how? When Thitpan's party returns with the scalps, why does True Son ask the question about children? Why do the Indians disapprove of his question? What kind of revenge is Thitpan apparently seeking? At the river, what might True Son's ill-fitting white clothes and his removal of the war paint represent—beyond their literal meaning? Why does True Son warn the whites on the flatboat? Is it because the small boy reminds him of Gordie, or are there other reasons? Discuss.

15. Chapter 15: At True Son's trial, why does Cuyloga preface his statement by blackening both sides of his face? Why is he not attacked? Discuss the statement that he makes to True Son. Is Cuyloga fair? Is he compassionate? Is he too proud? Does he love True Son? Why does he feel they must part? Do you agree with Cuyloga? Why or why not? What lies ahead for True Son?

WRITING ACTIVITIES

1. "Every day they drop another fine strap around you. Little by little they buckle you up so you don't feel it too much at one time." With these words, Bejance the slave warns True Son and Gordie of the way society will rob them of their freedom. Read the poem "The Man in the Dead Machine" by Donald Hall and write a comparison between the poem and Bejance's words. (The poem may be found in *Some Haystacks Don't Even Have Any Needle* by Stephen Dunning et al., or *Old and New Poems* by Donald Hall.)

2. In chapter 9, Parson Elder closes his emotional discussion with True Son with "a long fervent prayer." Based on what the chapter reveals about the parson, write what you think he says in the prayer.

3. When True Son and Half Arrow linger in the secluded wilderness for weeks before going on to the Forks of the Muskingum, they seem to have found the place of their dreams, a place of incredible beauty and freedom they do not want to leave. Write about a time and place in your life when it seemed "all the world did not exist, had never been."

4. Rewrite the last half of chapter 6 from the point of view of Gordie. Or rewrite the last part of chapter 14 and all of chapter 15 from the point of view of Half Arrow.

5. Considering all you know about True Son by the end of the book (his fierce loyalty to Indian customs, his fondness for Gordie, his ability to speak English, etc.), write two or three more pages that reveal what he does next.

6. In chapter 4, Little Crane argues that the reason the white settlers are weak is that they are not "an original people. . . . Some are light, some are dark, some are in-between. Some have black hair, some have light hair." In contrast, some authorities would argue that the strength of America lies in the diversity of its people—in its variety of ethnic heritages. Write a paper agreeing with or refuting Little Crane's argument.

7. True Son often refers to months in terms of natural occurrences (e.g., the month when the Ground Squirrels Begin to Run, the month of the Shad). Create your own calendar based on similar events in nature. Begin with January, the month the Great Bear Sleeps, and proceed from there.

8. Although he keeps his emotions to himself, Harry Butler surely has strong feelings as he rides toward the village and the reunion with his son who has lived among Indians for eleven years. Write a page or two of interior monologue, revealing the hopes and fears and other feelings of True Son's real father as he approaches the meeting between them.

9. Using one encyclopedia and at least two other sources, read about the history of the Lenni Lenape or Delaware Indians from the beginning of the white settlements on the eastern seaboard to 1800. Write a report of three to four pages.

OTHER ACTIVITIES

1. Draw a map of the important locations referred to in the novel. Include the following within the present-day states of Pennsylvania and Ohio: the Forks of the Muskingum, Fort Pitt, the Allegheny, Ohio, and Susquehanna rivers; and Carlisle and Lancaster, Pennsylvania. By reading chapter 12 carefully, roughly trace the path that True Son and Half Arrow followed on their journey home.

2. With other students, hold a debate or discussion on the treatment of Indians by white settlers and governments during the westward movement in America, particularly in the eighteenth century. Refer to pro-Indian and pro-settler arguments voiced in the novel.

3. You are True Son. After the parting with Cuyloga at the end of the book, you are at an utter loss. Seeing no other choice, though, you spend several days making your way back to your family in Pennsylvania. You arrive under the cover of night and enter the house, where Parson Elder is visiting your parents. With three other students, act out the scene.

4. At one point in chapter 11, Mr. Butler tells True Son, "We do things differently here"—a statement that perhaps embraces the novel's central conflict. Create two artistic representations (e.g., drawings, mobiles, collages) of the idea of land—one as though it were done by True Son, the other by his father.

5. With the values of the Lenni Lenape in mind, draw the beadwork design for the moccasins that True Son's Indian mother sent to him embroidered so that "he would go back to his white people newly shod and remember his mother and sister."

SELECTED TEACHING RESOURCES

Media Aids

Cassette

The Light in the Forest. Perfection Learning Corporation.

Cassettes (3)

The Light in the Forest. 4 hrs. Recorded Books.

Internet

Lenape Information Systems. 1995. *Delaware Tribe of Indians.* Available: http://www.cowboy.net/native/lenape/index.html (Accessed March 1, 1997).

The Lenni Lenape Historical Society and Museum of Indian Culture. 1995, 1996, 1997. Available: http://www.lenape.org/main.html (Accessed March 1, 1997).

Printed Materials

Article

LaHood, Marvin. "*The Light in the Forest*: History as Fiction." *English Journal* 55 (March 1966): 298–304.

Poster

The Light in the Forest. 17" x 22", color. Perfection Learning Corporation.

Teaching Aids

The Light in the Forest. Contemporary Classics series and Latitudes series. Perfection Learning Corporation.

The Light in the Forest. Literature Unit Plans. Teacher's Pet Publications.

The Light in the Forest. Novel Unit Guide, Student Packet, and Perma-Guide. Perma-Bound.

The Light in the Forest. Novel/Drama Curriculum Units. The Center for Learning.

The Light in the Forest. Novel-Ties. Learning Links.

Tests

The Light in the Forest. Objective, essay, and alternative assessment. Perfection Learning Corporation.

Roll of Thunder, Hear My Cry

Mildred D. Taylor

The Dial Press, 1976
Available in paperback from Puffin.

SUMMARY

Nine-year-old Cassie Logan, poor and black in depression-struck rural Mississippi, is blessed with a close-knit family. The family has preserved ownership of some four hundred acres of land for many years despite the persistent efforts of Harlan Granger, a descendant of the former white land-owner, to reclaim it. The Logan's pride and independence have helped protect Cassie and her brothers from much of the prejudice present in their community of cotton farmers and sharecroppers. Unlike many other people, Cassie does not believe that white people are more important merely because they are white. One troubled year shatters Cassie's serene world and shows her that maintaining a secure family environment is a constant struggle against bigotry—a struggle that must continue at all costs.

APPRAISAL

The second in a chronology of books about the Logan family, *Roll of Thunder, Hear My Cry* received the 1977 Newbery Medal for the most distin-guished contribution to literature for children and was nominated for the 1977 National Book Award. Some readers may become impatient with the slow narrative pace, but seventh and eighth graders should find this simply told story easy to follow and its rhythmic dialect pleasant for reading aloud. Moreover, the issues of racism that confront Cassie and her family in the 1930s remain relevant to the contemporary student.

THEMES

freedom, pride, courage, family, society, racism, respect, violent and nonvio-lent conflicts, learning from the past

---

NOTE: This response guide was prepared by Rachael Worthington Walker, who manages special projects for Reading Is Fundamental (RIF) in Washington, D.C.

LITERARY CONCEPTS

characterization, voice and narration, plot (especially foreshadowing), oral history, dialect, imagery, symbolism

RELATED READING

Song of the Trees (1975) begins the Logan family saga that is continued in *Roll of Thunder, Hear My Cry.* More stories about the Logans can be found in *Let the Circle Be Unbroken* (1981), *The Road to Memphis* (1990), and *Mississippi Bridge* (1990). Yoshiko Uchida's trilogy—*Jar of Dreams* (1981), *The Best Bad Things* (1983), and *The Happiest Ending* (1985)—about a depression-era Japanese American family in California provides an interesting comparison.

READING PROBLEMS AND OPPORTUNITIES

Although the protagonist's perspective is that of a nine-year-old girl, the story is told from a distance and includes numerous words appropriate for vocabulary enrichment, including the following (chapter numbers are in parentheses):

meticulous (1),
exasperation (1, 9),
admonished (1, 7),
raucous (1),
pensively (1),
emaciated (1),
jauntily (1, 10),
undaunted (1),
absently (1, 4, 6, 9, 10, 12),
morosely (1, 7),
quizzical (1, 3),
dubious (1),
monotonous (1),
appalled (1),
temerity (1),
indignant, indignation (1, 6, 8),
maverick (1),
imperious (1),
formidable (2),
gusto (2),

resiliency (3),
dutiful (3),
inaccessible (3),
humiliation, humiliated (3, 5),
flippantly (3),
conspiratorial (3),
oblivious (3, 12),
careened (3),
gingerly (3, 5),
disgruntled (3),
listless (3, 4),
adamant (4, 10, 12),
precarious (3),
haughtily (4, 5),
authoritative (4),
gravely (4, 8),
aloof, aloofness (4, 5),
obnoxious (5, 7),
malevolently (5, 7),
audible, inaudible (6, 7, 9),

ominously (6),
interminable (7, 11),
collateral (7),
placid (7, 11),
candidly (7),
insolently (7),
sauntered (8),
soberly (9, 10),
amenities (9),
ashen (9),
agitated (9),
despondently (10),
lethargically (10),
reproachfully (10),
wistfully (10),
condescending (10),
despicable (11),
vulnerability (11),
akimbo (11),
crescendo (11),
affirmation (11), and
transfixed (12).

Students may also need definitions for certain regional words, like

chiffonier (chapter 2),
gullies (3),

tenant farming (4),
verandas (5),

Uncle Tomming (8),
and *persnickety* (9).

Finally, some students may need a brief introduction to the nature of credit, mortgages, bank notes, taxes, and other terms related to the purchase of property mentioned in the book.

INITIATING ACTIVITIES

1. Make a list of people you respect and why you respect them. What characteristics or values do these people exhibit? With other classmates, develop a master list of characteristics and values on a blackboard or bulletin board. As you read the novel, keep track of which characters display these attributes and which do not.

2. Throughout history, nearly every cultural group has experienced some sort of oppression. Monitor the news for a couple of weeks and keep a journal about the clashes that arise between different cultures of the world. As you read *Roll of Thunder, Hear My Cry*, compare the characters' plight to that of a currently oppressed group in real life. Based on what you learn from Mildred Taylor's story, make predictions about conflict resolutions in today's society.

DISCUSSION QUESTIONS

1. Chapter 1: How do the Logan children feel about school? How do their feelings differ from T. J.'s? What news does T. J. have to share? How do the Logan children react to T. J. and his news? What is your reaction to T. J.'s news? How does Little Man feel about the textbook he is issued? How would you feel if a textbook were issued to you in that condition? What does Mama do in response to Little Man's reaction?

2. Chapter 2: Why did Papa bring Mr. Morrison home? How does the rest of the community react to the actions against the Berrys? In our society today, how would your community react to such an incident? Why doesn't Papa want the children to go to the Wallace's store?

3. Chapter 3: What problem does the rain create for the Logan children? How do they solve their problem? Why doesn't Jeremy ride the bus with the other white children? Why does Mr. Avery's visit alarm everyone?

4. Chapter 4: Cassie's feelings of guilt about the bus are compounded by her fears of the night men. Do you think what Cassie and her brothers did to stop the bus was wrong? Why or why not? Should they be punished? If Mama knew what they had done, would she punish them? How does Mama "punish" them for visiting the Wallace's store? What was their reason for visiting the store? What does Mama hope to accomplish by encouraging people to patronize another store?

5. Chapter 5: What is Cassie's initial reaction to Strawberry? Why is Cassie unprepared for the realities she faces there? Was Cassie right to demand to be treated equally by Mr. Barnett? Why do Cassie's comments make Mr. Barnett so angry? Could Cassie expect a similar reaction in this day and age? Would you stick up for Cassie or try to silence her? Explain what Stacey means by "I know it and you know it, but he don't know it, and that's where

the trouble is." Why isn't a simple apology enough for Lillian Jean and her father? Why does Big Ma make Cassie apologize to Lillian Jean? What is the significance of making Cassie add the "Miz" to Lillian Jean?

6. Chapter 6: Why does Big Ma try to prevent Cassie from telling Hammer about her day in Strawberry? Why does Hammer laugh about what Cassie said to Mr. Barnett? How does his reaction differ when he hears of her encounter with Lillian Jean and Mr. Simms? Mama tells Cassie that Mr. Simms is "one of those people who has to believe that white people are better than black people to make himself feel big." Have you ever been confronted by a similar prejudice? Did you feel like Cassie did?

7. Chapter 7: What happens to Stacey's new coat? Is Hammer right in preventing Stacey from retrieving his coat from T. J.? What kind of person is T. J.? How would you characterize his relationship with Stacey? Why is it important that the Logan children hear Mr. Morrison's Christmas story? Why are books such treasured gifts? Why is Little Man obsessed with keeping his book clean? Why do you think Jeremy chose to bring Stacey a gift? Do you agree with Papa's assessment of friendships between blacks and whites? When Papa says, "You see blacks hanging 'round with whites, they're headed for trouble," what event is foreshadowed? If you were Stacey, would you be better friends with Jeremy or with T. J.? Why is Mr. Jamison willing to sign the credit so that people can get goods from Vicksburg? Why does Mr. Granger feel threatened by this? What threats does he make in retaliation?

8. Chapter 8: What is Cassie up to by pretending to be nice to Lillian Jean? How is she able to keep her promise to her father and still get even with Lillian Jean? Why does Mama get fired from her teaching job? Why doesn't Stacey believe T. J. when he says he's not responsible for Mama's getting fired? How is T. J. punished for betraying his friends?

9. Chapter 9: How does Jeremy feel about his own family? How does his family life differ from the Logan's? Do you agree with Mama's explanation for T. J.'s friendship with R. W. and Melvin Simms? Why can't Mr. Avery and Mr. Lanier continue to participate in the shopping in Vicksburg? Why do they have to give up when the Logans do not? Why does Papa compare the Logan family to a fig tree? Why is it important that the trip to Vicksburg still be made? Is Stacey right to blame himself for Papa's broken leg? Why or why not? What would you have done if you were in Stacey's situation?

10. Chapter 10: Why is Mama afraid for Mr. Morrison? Why didn't Kaleb Wallace try to hurt Mr. Morrison when they met on the road? Why do you think Jeremy is anxious for the Logan's friendship? Why does Stacey refuse Jeremy's offer to visit his tree house? Why is the bank no longer honoring the Logan's credit? What does Harlan Granger have to do with calling up the bank note? What happens to Hammer's car? Why is land more valuable than the car? Think about your own family's possessions. Are the things you own symbols of your status in the community or for practical use? Why is the pearl-handled pistol so important to T. J.? Why does he bring R. W. and Melvin to the revival?

11. Chapter 11: Why is this chapter prefaced with a spiritual? What does the spiritual foreshadow? Why does T. J. turn to Stacey for help? Why does Stacey feel a sense of responsibility for T. J.? Considering everything that T. J. has done to Stacey, if you were Stacey would you help T. J.? Why or why not? How does the justice that Kaleb Wallace plans to administer to T. J. differ from that of the justice Mr. Jamison would administer? What sometimes enables a single person to stand up to a group of people? What do the Logan children hear that prompts Cassie to return home?

12. Chapter 12: Why is Papa willing to risk his own life to prevent T. J.'s death? Mama asks that Papa not use his gun to stop the hanging. If he had, what might have been the outcome? What is Papa's solution to diffuse the situation? Why does Mr. Jamison advise that Papa not go into town? What's going to happen to T. J.? Does he deserve this fate? How does Cassie feel about what has happened, not only to T. J. but to her own family? In the course of the book, what has Cassie learned?

WRITING ACTIVITIES

1. Consider the following as symbols: trees, mud, land, books, school bus, pearl-handled pistol. Select two or three of these symbols and discuss the ideas and values each represents as well as which characters are identified with them.

2. In the time and place where Cassie lives, the county does not provide school buses for its black students and gives them only discarded textbooks to learn from. Imagine that you are Cassie. Write a letter to your congressional representative about the condition of Great Faith Elementary and Secondary School.

3. In presenting her realistic picture of life in the rural Mississippi of the 1930s, Mildred Taylor often has white characters refer to Cassie or members of her family as "niggers." Cries of "Nigger! Nigger! Mud eater!" are heard from inside the Jefferson Davis school bus, and an enraged Mr. Barnett asks, "Whose little nigger is this!" when Cassie loses her patience in his store. Today society considers the use of the word *nigger* extremely offensive. Research the origins and use of the word. Present your thoughts on why Taylor uses it in her dialogue. Without resorting to profanity, keep a list of other taboo words you find in literature. Write about the different emotions the use of such words evokes in characters you've read about. Compare that to how you feel when you hear words like *nigger* used in everyday language. (*Note:* Teachers should obviously use this activity with tact and sensitivity.)

4. Cassie's sheltered view of life is changed after her visit to Strawberry. She feels she has been wronged by Mr. Barnett and has trouble understanding why he acted as he did. Stacey is just as angry as Cassie, but not confused by Mr. Barnett's words. Rewrite the story of their visit to Mr. Barnett's store from Stacey's point of view.

5. At just nine years of age, Cassie is strong willed and often defies conventional expectations. She does not accept her white neighbors' beliefs that white is better than black simply because it is white. The growth of all society depends on challenges to such beliefs and convictions. Research historical

figures who have questioned the judgments of society, like Martin Luther King Jr., Margaret Mead, Mahatma Gandhi, Rachel Carson, Booker T. Washington, or John T. Scopes. Discuss in an essay how their own beliefs changed those of society. Or, talk with your parents, grandparents, or other adults to find out what social conventions have changed in their lifetimes. Have these changes been for the better? Share your findings with your classmates. Or, make a list of changes you would like to see in your own lifetime. Discuss your ideas with your classmates. As a group, come up with ideas for implementing one or more of these changes.

6. Although Big Ma's son Hammer is very close to his family, he does not live with them on the family land. He misses the events of the evening of the fire. Knowing what you do about Hammer's temper, pretend you are Big Ma and write him a carefully worded letter explaining the loss of part of the cotton crop and T. J.'s imprisonment.

7. At the end of the book, the events of the past year have changed Cassie's view of the world around her. Select an event in your own life that changed the way you perceive your surroundings. Write a brief story in which you develop a character who can relate such an event and its impact on the character's life.

OTHER ACTIVITIES

1. With slavery, black Americans created the spirituals—songs that reflect the feelings of the black community. Grounded in the musical heritage of Africa, spirituals combine the tradition of folk songs with religious themes or inspirational motifs. The title of the book *Roll of Thunder, Hear My Cry* is taken from the spiritual which begins Chapter 11. Find and listen to recordings of spirituals. As you listen, determine which songs would offer appropriate thematic beginnings to other chapters in the book. Or, with other classmates, identify a theme in your culture that has caused suffering or disharmony in your community. Write and perform your own folk song or spiritual about that theme. Discuss why it is important to include such issues in literature and music.

2. Cassie and Big Ma are distraught about the trees that have been chopped down near the pond. The spot is a sacred one that draws many members of the family to it for private discussion or reflection. Is there a place where you or your family go when you want privacy or peace or when you need time to think and reflect? Describe, draw, or paint a picture of this place.

3. Pretend that you are Cassie as a grown woman taking part in the civil rights movement in Mississippi during the 1960s. Write and develop a brochure or flyer that explains the issues at hand and inspires others to join the movement.

4. The book begins in October with the Logan children heading off to school and ends in late August with a summer thunderstorm. Design a calendar that follows the events of the year. Using any medium, illustrate each month with a corresponding scene from the book. For September, illustrate what you think happens to T. J.

5. In Cassie's community, the Logan family name stood for many things to different people. Some whites felt the name meant trouble from blacks who owned their own land and "stirred the colored folks out of their place." For others, like T. J., it meant "all y'all Logans think y'all so doggone much with y'all's new coats and books and shiny new Packards!" But to Cassie and her family and friends, the name stood for hard work and standing up for your beliefs. Create a needlepoint design or a coat of arms that might be framed by the Logan family that includes the name as well as small symbols of what it represents. Or, create a similar design for your own family.

SELECTED TEACHING RESOURCES

Media Aids

Cassettes (6)

Roll of Thunder, Hear My Cry. 8 hrs. Recorded Books.

Video

Roll of Thunder, Hear My Cry. 116 min., color. Perma-Bound and Sundance, 1978.

Printed Materials

Articles

Bontempo, Barbara T. "Exploring Prejudice in Young Adult Literature Through Drama and Role Play." *The ALAN Review* 22 (Spring 1995): 31–33.

Scales, Pat. "Book Strategies: *Roll of Thunder, Hear My Cry* by Mildred Taylor." *Book Links* 4 (January 1995): 12–15.

Taylor, Mildred. "Newbery Award Acceptance." *The Horn Book Magazine* 53 (August 1977): 401–409.

Teaching Aids

Roll of Thunder, Hear My Cry. Book Wise Literature Guides. Christopher-Gordon Publishers, Inc.

Roll of Thunder, Hear My Cry. Literature Unit Plans. Teacher's Pet Publications.

Roll of Thunder, Hear My Cry. Novel Aids series. Sundance.

Roll of Thunder, Hear My Cry. Novel/Drama Curriculum Units. The Center for Learning.

Roll of Thunder, Hear My Cry. Perma-Guide and Student Packet. Perma-Bound.

Roll of Thunder, Hear My Cry. Novel-Ties. Learning Links.

Tests

Roll of Thunder, Hear My Cry. Essay, objective, and alternative assessment versions. Perfection Learning Corporation.

Dragonwings

Laurence Yep

New York: Harper & Row, 1975
Paperback available from HarperTrophy.

SUMMARY

In 1903, Moon Shadow, an eight-year-old Chinese boy, travels to California to meet his father for the first time and help the company with its laundry business. He soon learns of his father's passion for flying and sacrifices greatly to help his father achieve his dream of building a flying machine, *Dragonwings*. With directions and support from the Wright brothers, his father completes and flies his machine. This book is based, in part, on an actual report of a Chinese American who improved on the early planes with his 1909 model. In addition to exploring the close relationships between father and son, this novel also examines Chinese culture and mythology and graphically portrays the problems related to prejudice that plagued the Chinese immigrants in the early twentieth century.

APPRAISAL

A 1976 Newbery Honor Book also cited by the American Library Association as a Notable Book, *Dragonwings* presents a warm picture of a son's dedication to his father's dream. In the afterword to this book, Yep explains that he "tried to make some of these dry historical facts become living experiences" and "show that Chinese-Americans are human beings upon whom America has had a unique effect." Clearly, he is successful on both counts as he shows the reader the demons and the "demonland" through the eyes of the innocent young protagonist and presents dramatically such historic events as the San Francisco earthquake. The book is most often taught in grades seven through nine.

THEMES

father-son relationships, cross-cultural understanding, Chinese culture and values, initiation, myth, men and machines

LITERARY CONCEPTS

point of view, characterization, figurative language (metaphors, similes, symbols), mythology, analogy, historical fiction, multiculturalism, foreshadowing

RELATED READING

Laurence Yep has written and edited a wide variety of books that focus on Chinese culture and the Chinese American experience, including *The Rainbow People* (a collection of twenty Chinese folktales), *Tongues of Jade* (seventeen Chinese American folktales), *The Lost Garden* (a memoir), novels like *The Star Fisher*, *Thief of Hearts*, and *Child of the Owl*, and folklore like *The City of Dragons* and *The Junior Thunder Lord*. Other authors have produced exciting views of Chinese culture and Chinese Americans, notably Pearl Buck, Ruthann Lum McCunn (*A Thousand Pieces of Gold*), and Rumer Godden (*Fu-Dog*). Special interests that could develop from reading this book might lead students to a wide variety of nonfiction, such as *The Geography of China* (Zhao Songqiao) or *Chinese in America: Stereotyped Past, Changing Present* (Loren Fessler, ed.).

READING PROBLEMS AND OPPORTUNITIES

Students may require some preliminary explanations of the point of view of the novel and how this point of view affects the language used. Terms such as *demons, white demons, demonland, Land of the Golden Mountain,* and *Jade Emperor* (all found in chapter 1 and throughout the novel) may require explanation for some; for others, these terms will become clear through context clues. Vocabulary related to aviation includes *horizontal rudder, elevators, vertical rudders,* and *banking* (chapter 11). Other vocabulary words that may require study include the following (chapter numbers are in parentheses):

phoenix (1, 7),	*wizened* (5),	*undulate* (9),
protrude (2),	*celluloid* (6),	*querulous* (9),
queries (2),	*turret* (6),	*shanghaier* (9),
poultice (3),	*stereopticon* (6),	*fastidiously* (9),
malleable (3),	*greengrocer* (7),	*ethereal* (10),
queue (4),	*dime novels* (7),	*sardonically* (10),
ratchety (4),	*junk* (7),	*bristling* (12), and
abacus (5),	*mumblety-peg* (8),	*cantankerous* (12).

INITIATING ACTIVITIES

1. Imagine that you are going to move to another country where you are unfamiliar with the language or the customs of the people. Make a list of your concerns about the move and beside each one write a sentence or two about how you will prepare yourself to handle these potential problems. As you read *Dragonwings*, check off the difficulties that are common between you and Moon Shadow and compare your methods of preparation to his. Why are they the same or different?

2. With a group of your classmates, prepare a presentation for the rest of your class on the traditional customs and values of southern China at the beginning of the twentieth century. You may want to divide the topic into subtopics such as the following: religious beliefs and their importance;

role of parents and elders in society; the value of work, ownership and sharing; relationships with nature; the value of friendship; and evil and retribution. Use large sheets of chart paper to present your findings. As you read *Dragonwings*, list events on the sheets that illustrate these values.

DISCUSSION QUESTIONS

1. The Land of the Demons: Why haven't Moon Shadow and his mother joined Moon Shadow's father in the Land of the Golden Mountain? Where do you think Grandmother got her tales and ideas about the Land of the Golden Mountain? Why was Hand Clap returning to America? Why did Moon Shadow decide to join his father there?

2. The Company: How does Hand Clap view and describe the world around him? Was this a dangerous practice? Why or why not? Why did Moon Shadow feel that he had arrived home? What specific objects or activities attracted Moon Shadow's attention? Why were these particularly important to him?

3. The Dragon Man: How many names could a Tang man have? Should one be able to change names as he or she grows older? Why or why not? How does Moon Shadow view the items in his father's room? How does Moon Shadow react to his father's tale of the dragons? Would you have reacted in a similar way? Why or why not? Why doesn't Moon Shadow tell anyone about his uncle's gift?

4. Tests: What was the purpose of the company? What kind of schooling did Moon Shadow receive? Why was Moon Shadow afraid to go out with his father? Do you think that Moon Shadow's grandfather died for a worthy cause? Why or why not? Do you think the man with the horseless carriage behaved in a typical way in responding to Windrider? Why or why not? Why didn't Uncle believe the stories of aeroplanes? How does Windrider show his courage in finding and rescuing Black Dog?

5. Windrider's Claws: Why do White Deer and Hand Clap insist on helping to pay for Black Dog's crimes? Why does Black Dog return to the opium dens? Why does he hate his life in the Demon Land? Why did the Tang people take care of their own affairs? Why did Windrider and Moon Shadow have to move? What other alternatives did they have? What made the gifts that Windrider and his son received special?

6. The Demoness: At first, how does Moon Shadow like his new home? How does his father help him to feel at home? What is his initial response to the demoness and her home? Why does Moon Shadow think of the landlady as "the demoness who kept the dragon fire locked inside a window"? What causes Moon Shadow to speculate on the demoness's past lives?

7. Educations: What does Moon Shadow learn from the lessons his father provided? What does he learn from the demoness? From Robin? How does Moon Shadow react to the attack by the demon boys? Do you think he handled the situation well? Why or why not? How does Moon Shadow feel about Robin's accompanying them on the trial of the glider? Why does Moon Shadow decide to write to the Wright brothers? Why is Windrider angry at

first about the correspondence with the Wright brothers? Why does he change his mind?

8. Earth, Wind, and Water. Why does Father cut the string and let his glider float away? How does Robin help Moon Shadow deal with the demon gang of boys? Moon Shadow realized that beating up the toughest boy would win him respect within the Demonland or in the Middle Kingdom. Is such an attitude true where you live? Why or why not?

9. The Dragon Wakes: How do Father and Moon Shadow celebrate the new year? Why was Moon Shadow pleased with Robin's participation in the celebration? How does Father greet his uncle? Is this the way you would greet someone you had not seen for a long time? Why or why not? Was Miss Whitlaw a heroine after the earthquake? Why or why not? What different types of behavior do people exhibit during and after the earthquake? Why is martial law necessary? What is Father's view of Miss Whitlaw? Do you agree with him? Why or why not?

10. Aroused: What roles do the soldiers play in the aftermath of the earthquake? How is Uncle convinced to leave his building? Why is Miss Whitlaw able to get along so well with the Tang people? What lessons do the Tang people learn from the earthquake? Why does Miss Whitlaw leave San Francisco? Why does Windrider leave the company?

11. Exile: Why is the Esperanza estate a good place for Windrider and Moon Shadow to live? Father says that Mother had the difficult part because she had to live in the village. Do you agree? Why or why not? What roles does Moon Shadow play in the household? What is Moon Shadow's mountain of gold? Why does he call it that? Why was the plane named Dragonwings? Why does Black Dog seek out Father and Moon Shadow and steal their money?

12. Dragonwings: What motivates the company to come to Father's aid? What do you notice in Uncle's attitude? What brought about these changes? How are Red Rabbit and the members of the company able to pull Dragonwings to the top of the hill? Why does Moon Shadow say that the flying belonged as much to Miss Whitlaw and Robin as to his father? Why is Father so willing to give up his flying career after his first attempt? Given what you know about Windrider, Moon Shadow, Miss Whitlaw and Robin, what do you think they were doing ten years after the end of the book?

WRITING ACTIVITIES

1. Throughout the novel, Moon Shadow sees the world in relation to his life and culture. As he describes what he sees, he uses similes that reflect his worldview, such as "lively as a cricket," (p. 7), "studied me as he would a flatiron," (p. 15), and "the wooden houses seemed like shells of wood which terrible monsters had spun about themselves" (p. 18). As you read the book, make a list of at least ten other uses of figurative language. Then try your hand at rewriting each of them using your life and your culture as points of comparison. Present these to your classmates and explain how and why they are different.

2. At the beginning of chapter 3, Moon Shadow explains that the Tang culture permits a man to change his name. Write a paragraph in which you explain why you would or would not like to change your name at some time during your life. If you would like to change your name, explain what name or names you might choose and why. Compare your ideas with your classmates' and post your new names on the bulletin board.

3. When Moon Shadow first comes to America, he is startled by inventions such as the electric light. He describes it as an "insect within the globe [that] shone with a light that was so bright and intense it hurt my eyes." Imagine that you are seeing a modern invention like the telephone or computer for the first time. Write a description of it, explaining it in terms of an animal or other object with which you are familiar.

4. When Windrider meets Moon Shadow, he admits that he does not know much about being a father. Write a set of instructions for Windrider, including at least twelve rules that a good father should follow. As you read the rest of the novel, list examples of ways Windrider fulfills the items on your list.

5. Windrider notes that "in machines there's a language common to us all." Think about other objects, movements, or signs that communicate to people of all languages. Brainstorm with a group of your classmates and then select one of the ideas that appeals most to you. Write an explanation of why it is possible for this communication to take place.

6. During and following the earthquake, people in San Francisco helped each other to survive. Find three news stories in your local paper about how an individual or individuals helped others in time of emergency. Rewrite each as a short story, adding details to increase the excitement of the scene. Compile your three stories into a book, bind this book, and place it in your school library for other students to enjoy.

7. Throughout the novel, Uncle refers to "the superior man." Try your hand at writing wise sayings completing the sentence "The superior man is. . . ." You may use ideas from *Dragonwings* and your own personal experience to prepare these sayings. Select your best one and prepare a calligraphy or computer-generated sign to hang in your classroom.

8. Conduct research on some of the historical events mentioned in the novel, like the first flight by the Wright brothers in 1903 or the 1906 earthquake in San Francisco. Use more than one source and write up your findings in a report to present to the class.

OTHER ACTIVITIES

1. Research the years 1903–1909 in your library and on the Internet. Make a list of the ten most important events in the United States and the ten most important events in China. Draw a diagram to show how these events were related or not related and what effects they had on Windrider and Moon Shadow.

2. Recreate one of the kites or gliders that is described in the novel. Review the principles of flight so that you can show your kite to your classmates and explain to them how it is able to fly.

3. Check your library for books on the Chinese language, particularly how it was derived from pictures that represented words. Or find in your community a person who is a native speaker of Chinese and ask him or her questions about how the Chinese language was derived and how it is written today. Copy signs in Chinese that Windrider and Moon Shadow would have seen in the Tang area. Provide translations and explanations with each sign.

4. Make a list of the ways that the white demons mistreated the Chinese immigrants. Brainstorm with your classmates the reasons for this treatment. What are the sources of prejudice that existed then and that exist today? Write slogans to explain prejudice and to offer solutions for eliminating it. Submit these slogans to your school newspaper.

5. Investigate the calendars used by the Chinese people. Compare these calendars to those used in the United States. How are they different? How do these differences affect the behavior of the people who use them? Prepare a Chinese calendar to hang in your classroom. Explain the holidays, how the Chinese celebrate them, and when they appear on the calendar.

6. When the earthquake hit San Francisco, its inhabitants had to choose very quickly which of their possessions they would take with them. If your home were struck by a natural disaster, what two items would you rush to save? Write a rationale for your choices, explaining why these items are valuable to you and what they show you about your own value system.

7. Using the novel and scientific and historic textbooks, draw a sketch (free-hand or with the computer) or prepare a model of Dragonwings. Display this creation for your classmates and ask them to evaluate its authenticity.

8. When Uncle and the others were pulling Dragonwings up the hill, they used chants to make their work go faster and smoother. Write a chant that could be used today for repetitive tasks such as stamping letters or folding papers. Try it with a group of your friends to see how effective it is in speeding up the task at hand.

Selected Teaching Resources

Media Aids

Internet

East Asian Studies Center at Indiana University. March 1997. Available: http://www.easc.indiana.edu (Accessed March 1, 1997).

This homepage includes several sections that might be of interest to teachers of the novel: K–12 Resources on Asia, a Geography of the Chinese People, an East Asian Studies Guide, and links to other related sites.

Video

Dragonwings. 15 min. Read On: Cover to Cover series. PBS Video, 1994.

Printed Materials

Article

Yep, Laurence. "Writing *Dragonwings*." *The Reading Teacher* 30 (January 1977): 359–363.

Teaching Aids

Dragonwings. Latitudes series. Perfection Learning Corporation.

Dragonwings. Lift series. Sundance.

Dragonwings. Novel Unit Guide and Perma-Guide. Perma-Bound.

Dragonwings. Novel-Ties. Learning Links.

The Giver

Lois Lowry

New York: Houghton Mifflin, 1993
Available in paperback from Bantam Doubleday Dell.

SUMMARY

Jonas lives in a world that seems perfect, a world where no ones suffers from pain or fear. But his world is also one where no one has choices—no one chooses his or her mate, children, or job because all decisions are assignments from the Committee of Elders. As Jonas approaches his twelfth birthday, he anxiously awaits his "assignment" in the adult world. The assignment, however, proves to be unique, for he is chosen to be the Receiver of Memories for the community. These memories are both beautiful and painful: the joys of sledding as well as the horrors of war. Jonas also learns the horrible truth about the practices of his own community and decides to flee with the newchild, Gabe, who is about to be "released," that is, killed, because of his uniqueness. Although Jonas and the baby escape, it is not clear whether they reach a land full of warmth, hope, and music or perish in their attempt.

APPRAISAL

One of the most highly acclaimed recent novels for young adults, *The Giver* has received numerous awards, most notably the Newbery Medal for best children's book in 1994. It was also a *Boston Globe/Horn Book* Honor Book, an American Library Association Best Book for Young Adults, an American Library Association Notable Book for Children, a *Booklist* Editors' Choice, a *School Library Journal* Best Book of the Year, and winner of the Regina Medal. Critics have emphasized the author's use of detail to present a strong narrative that stimulates discussion on a variety of important issues. Because of the depth of ideas in the book, it could be taught in a wide range of grades, perhaps most effectively seven through nine.

THEMES

utopia, life in the future, human feelings and emotions, learning from the past, freedom, security, survival, manipulation, conformity, euthanasia, ways of knowing, interdependence

LITERARY CONCEPTS

characterization, plot, foreshadowing, utopian fiction, symbol, point of view, mood, metaphor

RELATED READING

Many prominent writers have portrayed their visions of life in the future, most notably Ray Bradbury in *Fahrenheit 451*, George Orwell in *1984*, Aldous Huxley in *Brave New World*, Edward Bellamy in *Looking Backwards*, Frank Herbert in the Dune series, and John Christopher in his Tripod trilogy. In addition, many noted writers have envisioned life in an ideal society, such as Thomas More in *Utopia* and Jonathan Swift in *Gulliver's Travels*.

READING PROBLEMS AND OPPORTUNITIES

The Giver presents some new vocabulary words that may need study. These include (chapter numbers are in parentheses):

ironic (1),
palpable (1),
defiant (1),
chastise, chastisement (3, 7, 20),
humiliation (3),
remorse (3),
nondescript (3),
mystified (3),
rehabilitation (4),
tabulated (4),
tunic (4),
disquieting (5),
irritably (6),
designated (6),
interdependence (6),
indulgently (6),
reprieve (6),
exuberant (6),
transgression (6),
buoyancy (6),
meticulously (6),
scrupulously (6),
exasperated, exasperation (7, 17),
aptitude (7),
acquisition (7),

crescendo (8),
jaunty (8),
reassuring (8),
successor (8),
indolence (8),
exemplified (9),
excruciating (9),
unintentioned (9),
apprehensively (10),
torrent (11),
exhilarating (11),
conveyance (11),
perceive (11),
quizzically (11),
admonition (12),
flustered (12),
furred (12),
vibrant (12),
relinquished (12),
irrationally (13),
sinuous (13),
assimilated (13),
invigorating (14),
unendurable (14),
assuage (14),
distended (14),
wry (14),

ominous (14),
placidly (14),
carnage (15),
imploring (15),
ecstatic (16),
luxuriating (16),
exempted (17),
permeated (17),
dejected (18),
luminous (18),
sarcastic (20),
rueful (20),
stealthily (21),
understatement (21),
frazzled (21),
emphatically (21),
languid (21),
hypnotically (21),
taut (21),
hone (21),
perils (22),
exquisite (22),
imperceptibly (23),
agonizingly (23),
lethargy (23), and
incision (23).

Students will also learn that many common words are used in new ways in this book, including *released, learning community, assignment, newchildren, birth mothers, nurturer, naming, comfort object, bikeports, elsewhere, caretaker, telling,* and *collection crew.* Most of the definitions for these words can be determined through context clues. In fact, the novel provides excellent opportunities for students to hone their skills in defining words through inference.

INITIATING ACTIVITIES

1. Everyone must live by rules, some of them necessary and some arbitrary. Make a list of ten rules that you feel would improve our society. Do not be concerned if you don't think these rules could be enforced; write them down anyway. Then in a short paragraph, explain why these rules would be good for our society and how they would help human beings get along better. Share your list with your classmates and discuss the similarities and differences between your ideas and theirs. Keep your list on hand as you read *The Giver* to see how many of your rules were the same as those in Jonas's world. When you have finished reading the book, review your list to see if you would like to change or omit any of these rules and explain why you want to do so.

2. Make a list of standard phrases that people often say to one another without even thinking about them or really meaning what they say, such as "How ya doin'?" As you read *The Giver*, make another list of the same kinds of words and phrases used in Jonas's world. Are there more of these in Jonas's world? Write a one-page essay for your school newspaper in which you argue that we need more standard phrases to be used in social situations—or fewer of them.

3. Think about a time when you faced an important upcoming event. How did you feel? Were you afraid of how you would perform or what the outcome might be? How did you prepare yourself for this event? How did your family and friends help you to cope with your concerns? Write notes on your feelings or record them on a tape recorder. After you read the first eight chapters of *The Giver*, compare your experiences to those of Jonas as he anticipates his assignment. How were your experiences similar to his? How were they different?

DISCUSSION QUESTIONS

1. Chapter 1: How important are rules in the lives of Jonas and his family? Cite two examples from this chapter. Why is Jonas apprehensive? What do you think "released" means? Who gets released and why? What are Asher's problems? How do the after-dinner activities in Jonas's home differ from those at your home? Which would you prefer? Why?

2. Chapter 2: How are children identified? What does this method of identification say about society's view of the individual? When is the child named? Who names the children? How do families get new children? What is an "assignment"? To what events in our lives today might the assignment be compared? When is a comfort object removed? Is this reasonable? Why or why not?

3. Chapter 3: Why don't people speak of physical differences among citizens? What are the advantages of being a birth mother? What are the disadvantages? What occupations in our society today have many early advantages but few later advantages? Why do people choose these types of jobs? How are children reprimanded for wrongdoing? Is this practice used in our society today? Cite examples to support your answer. How effective is this practice?

4. Chapter 4: Why does Jonas value his volunteer work? How important is volunteer work in the lives of the children 8–12? Jonas notices that bathing the elderly is much like his father bathing a newchild. In what other ways are infants and older people similar? Larissa implies that Edna's life is not meaningful. In your opinion, what makes someone's life meaningful today? What does Jonas's treatment of Larissa tell you about the relations between young and old people? How do these relations compare to those you have with elderly relatives and friends?

5. Chapter 5: Why does Jonas recount every detail of his dream? What different kinds of feelings does he have about his dream and his parents' reaction to it? What are the "stirrings"? In Jonas's world, what is the cure for the stirrings? In our society today, what is the cure for stirrings? In each case, what is the objective of the cure and why is it put into place?

6. Chapter 6: Why are children given to families? How is Gabe's situation special? Why did Jonas's family have to sign a pledge? Do you think signing a pledge could control emotional responses? Why or why not? How is "release" different from "loss"? How does the community treat each one? What rule do the nines usually break? Why aren't they chastised for this? What alternatives are possible if a twelve does not like his or her assignment? Why do matches, placement of children, and assignments usually work so well?

7. Chapter 7: How are children trained to behave during their first eleven years? Why is an instructor of threes an important job? What problems did Asher have at three? What is Jonas's reaction to being skipped in the assignments? What else might he have done?

8. Chapter 8: Why is Jonas's assignment given last? How does Jonas react to his assignment? What characteristics must the Receiver of Memory have? What inspired Jonas to accept the assignment even though he was not sure he had the necessary characteristics?

9. Chapter 9: How was Jonas treated after his assignment? Why? In what way are his instructions startling?

10. Chapter 10: What are Jonas's first reactions to the Receiver? Why does Jonas have trouble understanding "the whole world" and "generations before him"? What similar kinds of things do you have trouble understanding?

11. Chapter 11: Jonas experiences new objects and sensations. How does he find words to describe them? How are words assigned to objects and actions? What does the old man asked to be called? Do you think this is a good name for him? Why or why not?

12. Chapter 12: In his dream, Jonas feels there is a destination beyond the sled. What do you think the destination is?

13. Chapter 13: Jonas observes, "We really have to protect people from wrong choices." In what ways does Jonas's community provide this protection? In what ways does our society today protect people from wrong choices? Why would it be difficult for Jonas to apply for a spouse? Why are the services of the Receiver rarely needed?

14. Chapter 14: Why does Jonas's pain linger? Why can't he take any medication for this pain? Why does he have to abide by this rule? How does the Giver use his memories to solve problems brought by the Elders? Why can't Jonas and the Giver share painful memories with others in the community? Why is Gabriel moved into Jonas's room? Why does Jonas decide not to tell about giving a memory to Gabriel?

15. Chapter 15: Why does the description of the battlefield contain so many references to color? Why does the Giver ask Jonas to forgive him?

16. Chapter 16: What is the Giver's favorite memory? What does Jonas learn from this memory about family and love? How does Jonas explain the risks and dangers in the family scene? What other risks or dangers might he have been searching to describe? How do Jonas's parents respond to his question, "Do you love me?" Why does Jonas stop taking his pills?

17. Chapter 17: How has Jonas's view of the world around him changed? What does he mean by "new *depth* of feeling"? What are Jonas's feelings as he watches Asher, Fiona, and the other children playing? What do you think is going to happen to the smaller twin? What do you think happens when he is "released to Elsewhere"?

18. Chapter 18: Why was Rosemary's training a failure? What happened to the memories she had received? Why wasn't the Giver able to help the community cope with her memories? What problems does Jonas foresee if he were to leave the community?

19. Chapter 19: Why does Jonas want to see the release? How is it possible for him to view it? How do Jonas's feelings about release change after he views one? How do you think his feelings have changed toward his father?

20. Chapter 20: What are Jonas's first reactions to the release? What person(s) and/or groups does he blame? How does the Giver respond to his anger? What is the Giver's plan to change the community? Do you think it will work? Why or why not? Why does the Giver feel he must stay behind? Why do Jonas and the Giver need to care about the rest of the community? Where does the Giver ultimately want to go?

21. Chapter 21: Why do the plans for the escape change? What hardships do Jonas and Gabriel face? How are they able to cope? Why does Jonas fear the planes?

22. Chapter 22: What new experiences does Jonas have on his journey? What new dangers does he face? Jonas begins to question his decision to leave. Do you think he has made the right decision? Why or why not?

23. Chapter 23: What continued deprivations do Jonas and Gabriel face? What gives Jonas hope in the face of these hardships? Jonas's experiences in the snow are similar to his first memories from the Giver. How are they different? What do they symbolize? What do you believe happens to Gabriel and Jonas at the end of the novel? What words, phrases, and images support your ideas?

Writing Activities

1. In Jonas's community, children progress into adulthood through a number of visible signs, including certain clothes, haircuts, toys, and finally certain volunteer and job assignments. Compare this progression with what goes on in our society today. Consider the following questions: Can a child's age and sex be determined by his or her clothing or haircut? If not, what signs do indicate certain ages and sexes? Are all children given toys and privileges at a particular age? If not, how are these allotted? What are the most common signs indicating that a child has reached adulthood? Prepare a chart that compares and contrasts behaviors in Jonas's society with those in contemporary American society.

2. In the Giver's community, being different is avoided and differences are not discussed. Choose one of these statements—our differences make us stronger *or* our differences make us weaker—and write an argument to support your position. Use specific examples from your school, neighborhood, city or town, and your state to support your ideas about differences. Read your argument aloud to your classmates and ask someone who chose the other side to read his or her argument in rebuttal.

3. In Jonas's community, children are classified according to their ages. They are expected to behave in a particular way and to follow particular rules based on these age groups. Compare this system of raising children to America's public education system. How are they the same? Are children in kindergarten expected to behave differently from those in first grade? Are those in first grade expected to behave differently from those in second or third grade? Observe children in the elementary grades and discuss with them the rules they have in their classes. Draw a picture of a kindergartner, a first-grader, a second-grader, or a third-grader and beneath the picture write a description of "what a kindergarten child does," "what a first-grader does," etc. Explain why you think this is a good way for children to learn or whether you feel that our educational system is like Jonas's community—forcing children to behave in a certain way because of their ages.

4. When Jonas is given his instructions, he is told that he can lie. Examine the lies that you find in *The Giver*, and classify them as unintentional (the character doesn't realize he or she is lying), white lies (the character lies to protect someone without hurting others), and bald-faced lies (the character lies and knows it will hurt others). When you have finished, compare your list with the lists made by others in your class and discuss the differences you have in classifying lies. Try to determine why it is difficult to classify lies.

5. Jonas's community allows humans to take the lives of other human beings under certain conditions (e.g., an infant who does not make satisfactory progress). Make a list of these conditions. Our own society also allows humans to take the lives of other human beings under certain conditions (e.g., an assailant who is threatening someone's life). Make a list of these conditions. Compare the two lists and then make your own list of conditions under which you think taking another life is justified. For each condition on your list, write down your reasons for including it.

6. The Giver explains that memories need to be shared. Choose a happy moment from your life that you would like to share with Jonas. Before you begin to write, close your eyes and relive the event in your mind's eye. Then describe it for Jonas in detail, remembering to include details such as colors, smells, and sounds that might not be familiar to him. How has writing this memory helped you to remember it more clearly and even to understand it better? On the back of your paper, list ways that writing this memory helped you to keep it close.

7. Write a description of an everyday activity (e.g., eating lunch in the cafeteria, walking or riding the bus to or from school, or watching television) as though you were Jonas and were experiencing these sights, sounds, and smells for the first time. Remember that you may not always know the exact words for objects or sensations, so you will have to try to describe these events and how you feel about them. Share your descriptions with others in your class and ask them to comment on your accuracy in presenting these activities.

8. In *The Giver*, older people are treated with kindness and respect until they are "released." Compare the treatment of older people in the novel with the treatment of older people in your community. What types of facilities are available for them and who is available to care for them? What attitudes do younger people have toward older people? How do these attitudes affect their behavior toward these senior citizens? Write an essay comparing the treatment of the elderly and at the end of the essay present your ideas for the ideal treatment of senior citizens.

9. The Giver explains Fiona's behavior toward the old by saying, "Feelings are not part of the life she has learned." Examine your daily life to determine what events and/or technology may be leading members of our society into ignoring or suppressing their feelings. Some areas to examine include television, movies, computer technology, video games, huge corporations, and fast-food restaurants. Write an editorial for the school paper on the dangers of an unfeeling society.

10. The individuals in Jonas's community tried very hard to follow the rules and to conform to the patterns set by the Elders. Write a letter to Asher, Fiona, or Lily and explain the advantages of being unique and special. Encourage the character to break out of his or her daily routine to find new joys in being an individual rather than a number.

11. Devise a plan for your school that will help make everyone the same. Prepare a chart of this plan with three columns: (a) change to achieve sameness (e.g., everyone will eat exactly the same lunch), (b) positive results (e.g., cafeteria workers prepare only one menu), (c) negative results (e.g., some students will be hungry because they cannot eat the food that has been prepared). Post your chart on the bulletin board and ask others to add their ideas. Discuss whether the gains will outweigh the losses or vice versa.

12. Lois Lowry does not answer questions about the end of *The Giver*. Instead she responds, "For me to EXPLAIN everything from my own viewpoint limits that experience for the reader" (see Internet reference at the end of this section). Using your own experiences and preferences, explain what happens after Jonas and Gabe reach the bottom of the hill.

OTHER ACTIVITIES

1. In Jonas's community, husbands and wives are matched by the Committee of Elders. Research the practices of matchmaking once common in China, Japan, Russia, and other countries to find the basis for this custom and the factors that were considered in making a match. (You may find information in history or sociology texts.) Write a report on these practices, including, at the end, your own opinion of how effective planned matches can be.

2. Review your history textbook to find a certain event that you would like to receive as a memory from the Giver. Write a brief paragraph explaining why you chose that event and what you hope to experience from receiving this memory.

3. Jonas's community had solved the problem of hunger and starvation by limiting the number of children that each family unit could have. In the library, review the latest population projections for the next ten years and examine the effects population growth will have on hunger and starvation worldwide. Also research the effects that limiting the number of children has had on countries such as China. With other interested students, prepare a proposal to solve the problems of hunger and starvation. After you have carefully reviewed your research and your proposal, send your ideas to an individual or an organization working to solve this problem, such as the World Health Organization.

4. In *The Giver*, the people in Jonas's community have avoided the risks of uniqueness and chosen to forego the rewards that could be gained. For example, Jonas notes that the candles and fireplace are fire hazards but that they provide a comforting warmth. For the following list of modern devices we use, write down beside each item the risks or dangers involved and the benefits gained. Then indicate whether the risks and dangers outweigh the benefits or vice versa.

   a. automobile
   b. computer
   c. airplane
   d. telephone
   e. refrigerator

5. Prepare a "split-screen" collage of Jonas's life—one side reflecting his life and worldview before he is named the new Receiver and the other side showing how he changes. Keep in mind that his early years reflect life without color, pain, or a past.

6. According to the Giver, remembering the suffering of the past gives us wisdom. Skim your history textbook for examples of the truth and lack of truth in this statement. Write an essay in two parts. The first part should provide an example of how humans learned from their past mistakes and appropriately dealt with a new similar situation. The second part should provide examples of how humans did not learn from their past mistakes and repeated them. At the end of the essay, try to explain why these differences occurred.

7. In Jonas's community, the Receiver keeps all the memories of pain and evil to protect others from the discomfort they cause. How are memories of pain and evil presented in our society? Do these memories have an impact on those who see them? Are they presented often enough to guide people on the right path? If not, what techniques could be used to help people relive the past and learn from it? Write your plan in outline form.

8. Write and perform a skit in which the members of your class act out the sameness of Jonas's class. Include the standard responses that students and instructors were required to give, as well as inventing some of your own.

SELECTED TEACHING RESOURCES

Media Aids

Cassettes (4)

The Giver. Unabridged, 270 min. Bantam Doubleday Dell Audio Publishing.

Internet

The Internet Public Library. n.d. Available: http://ipl.sils.umich.edu/youth/Ask Author/Lowry.html (Accessed March 1, 1997).
   The Lois Lowry file of Ask An Author features a photograph, brief biography, and the answers to seventeen questions from readers.

Printed Materials

Articles

Campbell, Patty. "The Sand in the Oyster." *The Horn Book Magazine* 69 (November/December 1993): 717–721.

Lowry, Lois. "Newbery Medal Acceptance." *The Horn Book Magazine* 70 (July/August 1994): 414–422.

Teaching Aids

The Giver. Literature Unit Plans. Teacher's Pet Publications.
The Giver. Novel/Drama Curriculum Units. The Center for Learning.
The Giver. Novel Unit Guide, Perma-Guide, and Student Packet. Perma-Bound.
The Giver. Novel-Ties. Learning Links.

Jacob Have I Loved

Katherine Paterson

New York: Thomas Y. Crowell, 1980
Available in paperback from HarperTrophy.

SUMMARY

Growing up on tiny Rass Island in the Chesapeake Bay during World War II, Louise Bradshaw suffers from perceiving herself as inferior to her twin sister. While her family sacrifices to provide music lessons for her talented sister, Caroline, Louise feels unappreciated and unloved—and even betrayed by those she holds in high esteem. Only after Caroline leaves for further training and Louise is left to help the family does she begin to realize her parents' gratitude and love and emerge as her own person, fulfilled and whole.

APPRAISAL

This novel won both the Newbery Medal and the National Book Award for children's literature in 1981. Its author, Katherine Paterson, is one of the most highly acclaimed writers of books for young adults, having also won the Newbery Medal for *Bridge to Terabithia* in 1978 and the National Book Award for *The Master Puppeteer* in 1977 and *The Great Gilly Hopkins* in 1979. *Jacob Have I Loved* is appreciated especially by girls, who respond to its sensitive portrayal of a young woman who grows up feeling unloved and unlovable. The novel is most appropriate for grades seven through nine.

THEMES

the importance of self-worth, family (especially sibling) relationships, growing up

LITERARY CONCEPTS

setting, symbolism, recurrent plot motif, biblical allusions, simile and metaphor, foreshadowing, structure, theme, characterization

RELATED READING

The relationship of sisters or twins is explored in several other novels, ranging from the classic *Little Women* by Louisa May Alcott to young adult novels like *Me Too* by Vera and Bill Cleaver, *Stranger with My Face* by Lois Duncan, *The Empty Sleeve* by Leon Garfield, and *The Pistachio Prescription* by Paula Danziger. On a much lower literary level, the books in the Sweet Valley Twins series by Francine Pascal could also be recommended.

READING PROBLEMS AND OPPORTUNITIES

Narrated by a well-educated woman recalling her past, *Jacob Have I Loved* presents few reading problems for students in grades seven through nine. Much opportunity exists, however, for worthwhile vocabulary study. Among the many words that may be new to students and that may be taught in context are the following (chapter numbers are in parentheses):

deceptive ("Rass Island"), *delusion* (1), *precarious* (1, 4), *undaunted* (1,9), *cajoled* (2), *lugubriously* (2), *affluent* (2), *rankle* (2), *machinations* (3), *quibble* (3), *petulant* (3, 18), *discomfited* (3), *mediate* (3), *indignation* (3), *reprimand* (3), *purge* (3), *pretentious* (3), *diminish* (3, 12), *caricature* (4), *robust* (4), *unaccountably* (5), *feign* (5), *indict* (6), *shard* (6), *rivulet* (6),

exultation (6), *remorse* (6), *fickle* (6), *squander* (6), *allusion* (6), *malicious* (8), *proscribed* (8), *interloper* (8), *irreverent* (8), *aberrations* (9), *writhe* (9), *befuddled* (9), *recede* (10, 11), *ominous* (10), *leeward* (10), *litany* (10), *consternation* (10), *raucous* (11), *capricious* (11), *obsessed* (12), *pious* (12, 18, 19), *relegated* (12), *disembodied* (12), *placid* (12), *adamant* (13),

propriety (13), *scrutiny* (13), *repentant* (13, 15), *deprivation* (14), *exuberant* (14), *destitute* (14), *perfunctorily* (14), *conniving* (15), *contemptuously* (15), *apparition* (15), *residue* (15), *admonish* (16), *staccato* (16), *inanity* (16), *compensate* (16), *extricate* (16), *saucy* (17), *titter* (17), *contentious* (18), *rancor* (18), *desolate* (19), *subsistence* (19), and *translucent* (20).

INITIATING ACTIVITIES

1. Read about twins in magazines and books. Discuss the subject in class—especially information concerning the difficulties twins may have growing up. Possible sources include "Two's Company: The Pleasures and Perils of Twindom," *Teen,* vol. 25 (March 1981), 95; and *We Are Twins, But Who Am I?* by Betty Jean Case.

2. Read the following sections of William W. Warner's *Beautiful Swimmers: Watermen, Crabs, and the Chesapeake Bay* (which Katherine Paterson mentions in her acknowledgments): chapter 4, "Follow the Water," especially; also chapter 1, "The Bay," and chapter 5, "Beautiful Swimmer."

3. Read the story of Jacob and Esau in Genesis (chapters 25–33) in the Old Testament. With your classmates, discuss the story, especially the relationship of the two brothers in terms of the birthright and their father's blessing.

DISCUSSION QUESTIONS

1. "Rass Island": What feelings does the speaker seem to have for Rass Island? Why is she returning?

2. Chapter 1: As she begins to tell her story, Louise lets the reader know a little about herself and others. What is she like? How does she feel about Call, about her mother, her grandmother, and her twin sister, Caroline? Why does she feel good about the day? What sours the good feeling?

3. Chapter 2: Why did Louise, as a small child, ask so many questions about herself as a baby? Why does she remember them now? How does she depict her father? In what ways does he seem special to her? What are some ways the family has sacrificed for Caroline? Do you think Louise's feelings toward her sister are natural? Why or why not?

4. Chapter 3: What effect does the war have on Louise and Caroline? What does Louise's suggestion to Mr. Rice about Christmas reveal about her? Does she appreciate Caroline's talent at all? What angers her more—Caroline's imitation of Betty Jean or her parents' response? In what ways does Louise value worry? How does she feel about herself?

5. Chapter 4: Describe Grandma and her relationship with Louise. Why do the two seem so often at odds with each other? At the ferry unloading, why does the old man cause such curiosity?

6. Chapter 5: Why do you think Louise is such a romantic? Why does she insist on finding out about the old man? At the end of the chapter she says, "But I was not a generous person." Is she right? Discuss.

7. Chapter 6: Why does Louise hate her sister? Is it possible to love and hate someone at the same time? Discuss. Who else does Louise hate? Why is her religion a source of confusion and despair for her?

8. Chapters 7 and 8: Why does Call laugh at the Captain's jokes and enjoy his company so much? Why does Louise resent the two of them? Louise

refers to February and August as "dream killers." What is her greatest dream killer? What happens that begins to change her attitude toward the Captain? Why does it change?

9. Chapter 9: Why is the experience with Trudy Braxton's cats so unhappy for Louise? What is the final disappointment?

10. Chapter 10: "There she [Caroline] was, trying to make me look bad in front of Call." To what extent does Caroline do this and to what extent does Louise imagine it? What do their father's reactions to Caroline's sleeping through the hurricane and Louise's not wanting to miss it possibly suggest about his attitude toward each of them? Why is Louise horrified at the thought of the Captain's hearing her snore?

11. Chapter 11: "I loved everyone that morning." As she poles the Captain toward his house, why is Louise so happy? Why is he so solemn? Why is Louise so upset over her reaction to the Captain's dismay? Why do you think she is so attracted to him? Is the attraction unhealthy, as she fears? Discuss.

12. Chapter 12: Louise even imagines that George Washington stares at her disapprovingly from the Stuart painting in the schoolroom. Why does she feel so guilty? Why is she so consistently miserable? To what extent is she responsible for her own unhappiness? To what extent are others responsible, especially Caroline and Grandma?

13. Chapter 13: Who is more genuinely concerned about the Captain's well-being—Louise or Caroline? Discuss.

14. Chapter 14: Why does Louise consider herself "so close to being swallowed up by all that eternal darkness"? Throughout the book she has blamed much of her misery on Caroline. Is Caroline vain and silly and insensitive? Or is she somewhat less unbearable than Louise suggests? Does Louise ever have anything good to say about her?

15. Chapter 15: Why is Louise particularly upset over Grandma's quoting Romans 9:13? After the Captain makes his offer, why does Louise's mother seem to watch her? Why is her mother's own offer so strongly refused? What does Louise want from her mother? After she begins to help her father, why does Louise feel sorry for the she-crabs? What does she regret about her new work? What does she like about it? What does she begin to discover? Why does she not accept her mother's concern for her? At this point how does she feel about her mother? About the Captain? About Call?

16. Chapter 16: Why is Louise moved by her parents' response to "Grandma's foolish jealousies" at the supper table? What do Louise's mother and father want for her? What does she want for herself? Given all her perceived slights, her regrets and disappointments, how has she endured?

17. Chapter 17: Why does Louise invite the Captain to Christmas dinner? Does Grandma deserve in any way the sympathy she receives? Explain. The Captain says, "Youth is a mortal wound." What does he mean, with regard to himself? How does it apply to Louise? What does the Captain mean when he tells her, "You were never meant to be a woman on this island"?

18. Chapter 18: As she and her mother wash windows, Louise breaks down, "leaning against the clapboard, shaking with tears of anger, grief—who knew for what or for whom." For whom does she weep? What finally releases her? And from what is she released?

19. Chapter 19: As Louise proceeds with her education, how does she follow the advice the Captain has given her in their last conversation? How has she changed? How has she remained the same? Why does she fall in love with Joseph?

20. Chapter 20: Louise remembers and expresses concern for the baby in the basket, for obvious reasons. At the very end of the book, as she walks home, why does the melody she hears have such meaning for her?

WRITING ACTIVITIES

1. Throughout the novel, Louise sees herself as a victim whom no one understands. Write a letter she might have sent to Dear Abby asking for advice. Then write a thoughtful reply.

2. Despite her unhappiness with her family, Louise holds her father in a special light. Write an epitaph for Truitt Bradshaw, perhaps in verse form, like the ones Louise admires in chapter 4.

3. Pretend that the indignant Louise writes a letter of complaint to Lyrics Unlimited. Write the letter she might have sent.

4. On Louise's application for college there might have been a question like this: "What are your strengths and weaknesses?" Write her response.

5. To most of today's students, life on Rass Island during the war would have been unbearably slow and uneventful. Write a paper explaining the disadvantages of growing up in such a place as well as the advantages.

6. Except through Louise's sister's eyes, we know little about Caroline. Pretending that she kept a diary, write entries for the following occasions:

   a. the day after the school concert,

   b. the day Call left for the navy,

   c. the day Louise graduated from college.

7. Like many young people, Louise is highly critical of her family. But she is not unwilling to comment at times upon their strengths and contributions—her mother's saintliness, her father's singing to the oysters, their sacrifices for Caroline, and even Caroline's buoyancy. Write a paper describing the strengths and contributions of each member of your family.

8. Write a report on one of the following topics of importance in *Jacob Have I Loved*: the blue crab, German submarine activity off the south Atlantic coast during World War II, or the Chesapeake Bay (especially Smith and Tangier Islands, one of which may have been the source of the novel's setting).

9. Write a story that Louise, the hopeless romantic, might have written describing the life she and Call would have had together.

OTHER ACTIVITIES

1. Draw a coat of arms for the Bradshaws as Louise might have drawn it. The design should represent the family's values, strengths, and accomplishments.

2. Susan Bradshaw made "the best she-crab soup on Rass." Find three recipes for she-crab soup. Compare the three and select one. Then make a pot of soup for the class to sample.

3. Although she occasionally lashes out at Caroline, Louise spends most of the novel suffering in relative silence. Role-play a scene in which she succumbs to despair and discusses her feelings of inadequacy with her parents.

4. For those with the talent and inclination, draw the twin sisters as Louise describes them appearing in such contrast in the rare snapshot taken when they were a year and a half old (chapter 2).

5. Create a mobile or a "split screen" collage, with each side representing one of the twins. Emphasize their personalities, values, and interests.

6. The window-washing scene in chapter 18 provides one of the book's most compelling moments. Act out the scene, perhaps briefly extending the conversation between Louise and her mother.

7. The setting of the Chesapeake Bay permeates *Jacob Have I Loved.* Draw a map of the area where the novel takes place. Identify towns referred to in the book (Crisfield, Salisbury, etc.) and speculate on the location of Rass Island. Two possible sources of information are the October 1980 and June 1993 issues of *National Geographic.*

8. Find a recording of John Jacob Niles's "I Wonder as I Wander," the song that becomes so important to Louise. As the recording is played, perform an original dance expressing Louise's growth from despair to self-appreciation as she moves through the book.

SELECTED TEACHING RESOURCES

Media Aids

Cassettes (2)

Jacob Have I Loved. 3 hrs. Harper Audio.

Internet

ParentsPlace. 1995, 1996. *Parenting Twins or Higher Multiples.* Available: http://www.parentsplace.com/readroom/multiples.html (Accessed March 1, 1997).
This website includes dialogue about twins, a twin's mailing list, an annotated bibliography, and FAQs (frequently asked questions) about twins.

Video

Jacob Have I Loved. 57 min., color, Wonderworks Series. Perma-Bound and Sundance, 1989.

Printed Materials

Articles

Liddie, Patricia A. "Vision of Self in Katherine Paterson's *Jacob Have I Loved*." *The ALAN Review* 21 (Spring 1994): 51–52.

Paterson, Katherine. "Newbery Medal Acceptance." *The Horn Book Magazine* 57 (August 1981): 385–393.

Book

Schmidt, Gary D. *Katherine Paterson*. New York: Twayne Publishers, 1994.

Teaching Aids

Jacob Have I Loved. Novel Unit Guide. Perma-Bound.

Jacob Have I Loved. Novel-Ties. Learning Links.

Tests

Jacob Have I Loved. Essay and objective versions. Perfection Learning Corporation.

The Pigman

Paul Zindel

New York: Harper & Row, 1968
Available in paperback from Bantam.

SUMMARY

Lorraine Jensen and John Conlan are two sophomores who are disenchanted with everything—their school, their friends, and especially their parents, with whom they utterly fail to communicate. John is the more cynical of the two, Lorraine the more receptive; but both are sensitive and vulnerable. While participating in a harmless high school prank, they stumble into a relationship with Mr. Pignati, a lonely retired electrician whose wife has recently died. The Pigman (as they fondly come to call him) reciprocates their attention with gifts and affection; but when they violate his trust by holding a wild party at his house while he is hospitalized, he is hurt and disappointed. Genuinely contrite, John and Lorraine try to patch things up by inviting Mr. Pignati to the zoo. He sadly agrees to meet them, but when he learns of the death of his favorite animal, a baboon named Bobo, the old man collapses and dies, leaving his two friends sadder and wiser and far more aware of their need to be responsible.

APPRAISAL

For over two decades *The Pigman* has been one of the most popular young-adult novels among high school English teachers. Since its publication almost thirty years ago, the book has attracted a wide readership among teachers and students alike, who value its literary quality, its convincing depiction of adolescent needs and concerns, and the opportunities it provides for the meaningful discussion of values and matters of consequence. It is most often taught in grades eight through ten.

THEMES

responsibility, communication, values, friendship, death, the importance of human contact

LITERARY CONCEPTS

point of view, dramatic irony, symbol, characterization, theme, structure

RELATED READING

Students who enjoy *The Pigman* will surely wish to read its sequel, *The Pigman's Legacy*, and possibly other books by Zindel, including *My Darling, My Hamburger*; *I Never Loved Your Mind*; and *Confessions of a Teenage Baboon*. Zindel has also written *The Pigman & Me*, an autobiographical piece, and a Pulitzer Prize–winning play, *The Effect of Gamma Rays on Man-in-the-Moon Marigolds*.

READING PROBLEMS AND OPPORTUNITIES

Partly because it is narrated by two teenagers who alternate from chapter to chapter, *The Pigman* is an easy book to read. For the reluctant reader, it also offers the advantages of brevity, relevance, and a clever collage format of clippings, notes, diagrams, bills, and even a self-graded quiz. The few words that could be used for vocabulary study are as follows (chapter numbers are in parentheses):

avocation (1),	*paranoia* (2, 3, 6, 9),	*voluptuous* (7),
subliminal (2, 7),	*philanthropy* (4),	*mundane* (10),
abominable (2),	*prevarication* (4),	*loathe* (11),
compulsive (2),	*schizophrenic* (4),	*incongruous* (14), and
impressionable (2),	*demented* (5),	*disheartened* (14).

INITIATING ACTIVITIES

1. With three other students, role-play a scene involving Brad, Steve, Mr. Young, and Mrs. Young, who meet somewhat unintentionally when Brad brings Steve home to see some art prints. The four sit down around the kitchen table, and the conversation begins when Mr. Young asks Steve whether he, Steve, can make a good living as an artist. Here are the character descriptions:

   a. Brad, a high school student—quiet, sensitive, defensive. You do not communicate well with your parents. Recently you've struck up a friendship with Steve, a young artist you met at the art museum.

   b. Steve—a quiet but friendly young artist, unconventional in dress and appearance. You tend to like people although your values are quite different from those of most adults. You are twenty-seven years old.

   c. Mr. Young, Brad's father—warm, friendly, but very traditional in values, habits, etc. Brad is a mystery to you, but you tend to let him do his own thing.

   d. Mrs. Young, Brad's mother—uptight, suspicious. Like your husband, you love Brad, but you don't appreciate his values, and you don't communicate well with him. You are very concerned about his new friendship with someone ten years older.

   (*Note:* If the interaction drags in this enactment, keep the roles in mind, as they do not encourage communication. Allow at least seven minutes for the scene; then engage the class in a discussion of communication barriers between parents and children.)

2. Ask your parents the following questions: How do you feel about friendships between high school students and older people (say, people age fifty or over)? Should such friendships be discouraged? Should friendships among the young be restricted to their own age groups? Why or why not? If your parents have no objections, discuss their responses in class with your teacher and other students who have conducted the same informal survey.

DISCUSSION QUESTIONS

1. The Oath: What attitude toward school does the oath reveal about John Conlan and Lorraine Jensen?

2. Chapter 1: From his account in chapter 1, what kind of person does John seem to be? What might be some reasons why he hates school? What does he like? Cite one sign of sensitivity on his part.

3. Chapter 2: What is Lorraine like? How does she feel about John? About herself? About her mother? Do you think she understands John? Why or why not? Up to this point in her narration, do you sense anything about John that you feel Lorraine is unaware of? If so, what?

4. Chapter 3: What does John dislike the most about adults? About his parents in particular? What might the incident about the television symbolize? How does he feel about Lorraine? Why are the two of them writing this "memorial epic"? So far, what is the most intriguing unanswered question?

5. Chapter 4: When it's her turn to call someone, why does Lorraine peek? How does she react to her conversation with Mr. Pignati? Why does he upset her? Why does John's reaction to the conversation upset her? In what ways do John and Lorraine seem different? Why do you think they are such good friends?

6. Chapter 5: Why does John lie? Is his lying understandable? Justifiable? Discuss. Is John immoral? Why do he and Lorraine disagree about visiting Mr. Pignati? What is Mr. Pignati like? Why are John and Lorraine suspicious of him? Why does he insist on showing them how to memorize ten items and then showing them his pig collection? Why do you think he is lonely? How do John and Lorraine feel about him?

7. Chapter 6: According to Lorraine, what are her mother's problems? Do you agree? Or do you see other problems that Lorraine fails to mention? Discuss. Why does Lorraine decide she needs a day off? Why does she dislike the zoo? Why does she feel that the attendants fail at what they do? How is their failure similar to the shortcomings of others in her life? How is Mr. Pignati different? Why is Bobo his best friend?

8. Chapter 7: Why does John enjoy going to the cemetery? Is he afraid of dying? What is he afraid of becoming? For him, how would this be like dying? Why do he and his father fail to communicate? How are their values different? Does John hate his parents? Discuss. How does the relationship of John and Lorraine to Mr. Pignati begin to change? Do their feelings toward him also change? Discuss. If you could give this chapter a title, what would it be? Why?

9. Chapter 8: "It was easy to feel sorry for her, to see how awful her life was." Why does Lorraine feel her mother's life is awful? From what you know, do you agree? To Lorraine, who is sadder: her mother or Mr. Pignati? Why? How does the trip to Beekman's affect the attitude of John and Lorraine to Mr. Pignati? Why does Lorraine worry about her mother's reaction to her gift of the three pairs of stockings? Why is Lorraine upset by the ships in bottles? Why does she have mixed feelings about Mr. Pignati buying her and John gifts? In what ways are the ends of chapters 6 and 8 similar?

10. Chapter 9: Even though we see him largely through his own awareness of himself, how is the John of chapter 9 different from the John of chapter 1?

11. Chapter 10: Why do John and Lorraine decide to tell Mr. Pignati the truth? Why does he tell them about his wife's recent death? Why do you think the author stages this conversation against the backdrop of a television show? Why do you think Lorraine believes that Mr. Pignati's game is accurate—that both she and John value magic above the other qualities? In what ways do they value magic?

12. Chapter 11: Why do John and Lorraine return to Mr. Pignati's house after they leave the hospital? "She lifted her glass, and she was lovely." In what ways does John think Lorraine is lovely?

13. Chapter 12: Is the communication between Lorraine and her mother better or worse than that between John and his parents? After breakfast at Mr. Pignati's house, why does Lorraine think that John is troubled? Why does she smile? Does Lorraine's nightmare suggest anything other than death? Discuss.

14. Chapter 13: What does the decision to have a party reveal about John and Lorraine? How does John feel about the people he invites? Why does he think they have problems? Do you agree? How would John define *problem*? What is his biggest problem? How is the evening of the party at Mr. Pignati's different from other evenings John and Lorraine have spent there? (Ignore obvious differences.)

15. Chapter 14: "I didn't do anything wrong," Lorraine tells her mother. Did she? Who should share responsibility for what happened at Mr. Pignati's? To what extent are John and Lorraine responsible? Their parents? The other kids? Mr. Pignati? What is it that Lorraine's mother "could never really understand"? Why does Lorraine compare what happened at Mr. Pignati's with the kitten playing with a rubber ball? Why does Mr. Pignati agree to meet John and Lorraine at the zoo? Why does Lorraine feel he won't show up? Why does John believe he will? What causes Mr. Pignati's death? Is it the news of Bobo's death—or something else? Discuss.

16. Chapter 15: In this last chapter, what does John finally reveal about himself? What does he mean when he says that maybe we are all "baffled baboons concentrating on all the wrong things"? What are the wrong things? What are the right things? Why is John so cynical? Do you think his cynicism is justified? Why or why not? "Trespassing—that's what he had done." Is John right? Had Mr. Pignati trespassed? Or is John more perceptive later when he says, "We had trespassed too—been where we didn't belong"? Because of their experience with Mr. Pignati, what have

John and Lorraine learned? How have they changed? Do you think that the novel is generally hopeful? Or something less than that? Discuss.

WRITING ACTIVITIES

1. Pretend that Mr. Pignati kept a diary. Write entries he might have made after the first phone call from John and Lorraine, after their first visit to the zoo, and after the party. Keep in mind the kind of person he was and the way he would have reacted.

2. Considering how they felt about him, write an epitaph that John and Lorraine might have composed for Mr. Pignati.

3. Write an editorial arguing that society should make a greater effort to help the elderly lead productive lives in which their talents and experience can be used for the benefit of others. You may wish to refer to Mr. Pignati as an example.

4. Complete the following imaginary want ad that John and Lorraine might have created: "WANTED. Parents. Must be. . . ."

5. Write a diamante poem with one of the following pairs of contrasting words: *parents* and *youth*, *life* and *death*, *old* and *young*. Although the words *John* and *Lorraine* are not exactly contrasting, you might also want to try a poem with them. (See Appendix A.)

6. Write a paper contending that the depiction of parents in *The Pigman* is distorted and unfair.

7. In the Bantam paperback edition of *The Pigman*, "A Personal Note" by Paul Zindel follows the text of the novel. In his remarks, Zindel includes a letter written to him from a girl in Oklahoma who says, "it [the novel] had a part of almost everyone I know in it, and I can't be sure which one was me." Write a paper in which you explain which one of the characters in the book is the most like you and why.

8. Chapter 9 begins with an advice column. Write one of the following letters that might have been sent to Dear Abby during the course of the novel. Then write a sensible, sensitive reply.

    a. a letter from Mrs. Jensen complaining about young people
    b. a letter from Lorraine complaining about how John's parents treat him
    c. a letter from John about parents in general
    d. a letter from Mr. Pignati about his loneliness

9. Write a comparison between Mrs. Jensen and Mrs. Conlan as mothers.

10. Interview several persons age sixty-five or over whom you know. Ask them some questions suggested by the novel: What do you like about being old? What do you dislike? How do you spend your time? What are your opinions about today's teenagers? And so on. Write up your findings in a report.

OTHER ACTIVITIES

1. With three other students, role-play a scene in which Mr. Pignati has a conversation about John and Lorraine with their parents. The student playing Mr. Pignati should begin by saying, "I've been wanting to tell you how wonderful I think your children are."

2. Pretend that Mr. Pignati does not die at the zoo. Instead, he and John and Lorraine leave the zoo after learning of Bobo's death and make their way to a nearby coffee shop. Act out their conversation, in which they talk about Bobo, the party, and other matters on their minds.

3. "Our life would be what we made of it—nothing more, nothing less." Design a collage that communicates what you would like to make of your own life.

4. Design a poster that either John or Lorraine might create to remind them of Mr. Pignati—and of what their experience with him has taught them.

5. After the disastrous party in which many of Mr. Pignati's treasured pigs are broken, John and Lorraine are saddened and ashamed. From papier-mâché, clay, or soft wood, create a pig that they might make as a symbolic gift for their friend, an overture of respect and renewal.

6. Read Paul Zindel's sequel to this novel, *The Pigman's Legacy*, and present an oral report to the class. Compare the two books in terms of realism, characters, narration, style, and theme.

7. John and Lorraine have some qualities that are different and some that are similar, and each is at times a reflection of the other. Create a mobile that represents the two of them and their intermingling qualities.

SELECTED TEACHING RESOURCES

Printed Material

Articles

Agee, Hugh. "*The Pigman* and 'The Bargain.'" *English Journal* 65 (January 1976): 53.

Angelotti, Mike. "The Effect of Gamma Rays on Man-and-the-Writer Zindel: *The Pigman* Plus Twenty and Counting." *The ALAN Review* 16 (Spring 1989): 21–25, 43.

Clarke, Loretta. "*The Pigman*: A Novel of Adolescence." *English Journal* 61 (November 1972): 163–169.

Russick, Larry. "Death and Drama of *The Pigman*." *The ALAN Review* 22 (Spring 1995): 34–38.

Book

Forman, Jack Jacob. *Presenting Paul Zindel*. Boston: Twayne Publishers, 1988.

Teaching Aids

The Pigman. Contemporary Classics series and Portals to Literature series. Perfection Learning Corporation.

The Pigman. Lift series and Novel Ideas series. Sundance.

The Pigman. Literature Unit Plans. Teacher's Pet Publications.

The Pigman. Novel Unit Guide, Perma-Guide, and Student Packet. Perma-Bound.

The Pigman. Novel/Drama Curriculum Units. The Center for Learning.

The Pigman. Novel-Ties series. Learning Links.

Tests

The Pigman. Essay and objective versions. Perfection Learning Corporation.

The Red Pony

John Steinbeck

New York: The Viking Press, 1945
Available in paperback from Penguin.

SUMMARY

At ten, Jody Tiflin is a boy living on a small ranch near Salinas, California, in the early years of the twentieth century. He is still a child, but the harsh realities of life on a ranch have already begun to push him toward maturity. As he matures, he is given a pony only to have it die of consumption; he observes his father deny an old man's wish to live out what's left of his life on their ranch, where he was born; he witnesses the brutal killing of a mare in order to save the foal he was promised; and he experiences the sadness of his grandfather, who lives in a past that has long since disappeared. Through all these sobering events, Jody is dominated by a father who can be cruel and unyielding, and nurtured by the capable Billy Buck, the ranch hand who helps Jody come to terms with a world he is only beginning to understand.

APPRAISAL

The Red Pony is an episodic novel about a boy on the near edge of adolescence. Four separate stories are held together by the thread of Jody's growing up in a world of terrible wonder—especially of violence and death—as well as alienation and confusion in the relationship he has with his parents. Perhaps because of Jody's age, the book is most often taught in middle school, although early high school may be more appropriate.

THEMES

initiation, life and death, family, tradition, duty and responsibility, frontiers

LITERARY CONCEPTS

setting, symbol, characterization, irony, figurative language, coming-of-age novel, episodic novel

RELATED READING

Some of Steinbeck's other novels set in central California would be appropriate for students to read, especially *Of Mice and Men*. Two other highly appropriate novels of initiation, both of which also depict a boy's learning to accommodate the demands of life and death in a rural setting, are *A Day No Pigs Would Die* by Robert Newton Peck and *The Yearling* by Marjorie Kinnan Rawlings.

READING PROBLEMS AND OPPORTUNITIES

Told by a third-person omniscient narrator, this collection of four stories is simple in its narration but demanding in some of its themes and its overall vocabulary. Most of the following words will be challenging to middle school readers (numbers in parentheses refer to the stories):

contemplative (1),
protruded (1),
disciplinarian, discipline, disciplinary (1–three examples),
jovial (1),
frenzied (1),
carrion (1),
sauntered (1, 2, 3),
cartridges (1),
reservations (1),
hampered (1),
routine (1),
irritably (1, 4),
disparagingly (1),
self-consciously (1),
incipient (1),
self-induced (1),
hasp (1),
coaxed (1),
pivoted (1),
rambunctiousness (1),
rejoiced (1),
writhed (1),
contemplate (1),
reproachfully (1),
fallible (1),
contempt (1),
coddled (1),
constricted (1),
listlessly (1, 2, 4),

moped (1),
dispirited (1),
unkempt (1),
calloused (1),
provocatively (1),
incensed (1),
taut (1),
perverse (1),
absently (1),
gravely (1),
convulsively (1),
impersonal (1, 2),
detached (1, 4),
impulse (2),
intent (2),
sidled (2, 3, 4),
disemboweled (2),
perspective (2),
aloof (2),
imperturbability (2),
trudged (2),
repose (2),
probed (2),
fester (2),
diffident (2),
rebuke (2),
rapier (2),
smoldered (2),
profound (2),
pondered (2),
martially (3),

languorous (3),
restively (3),
construed (3),
conscientiously (3),
aimlessly (3),
nonchalance (3)
unprecedented (3),
paternally (3),
hovered (3),
stridently (3),
restrained (3)
coquettishly (3),
docilely (3),
peonage (3),
complacent (3),
fatuous (3),
infallible (3)
prestige (3),
repulsive (3),
counteract (3),
axis (3),
desolation (3),
diagnosis (3),
entrails (3),
arrogant (4),
ominously (4),
earnestness (4),
belied (4),
contemptuously (4),
judiciously (4),

rancor (4),	*staunchness* (4),	*retract* (4),
convened (4),	*piteously* (4),	*disconsolately* (4), and
reverence (4),	*apprehension* (4),	*coaxed* (4).
dirge (4),	*philosophically* (4),	

The book also refers to numerous horse and riding terms, including *curry, hackamore, halter, cayuse, corral, double half-hitch, riata, hames, tugs, saddle horn, pommel, cinch, bridle, stirrup, withers,* and *gelding.*

INITIATING ACTIVITIES

1. When we think of becoming an adult, many of us yearn to be taken seriously and wait to be given some responsibilities that accompany the passage from childhood to adulthood. For many, one of these is learning to drive a car. Make a list of four or five other activities or responsibilities that signify this important transition for you. Rate each responsibility on a scale of 1 (low) to 10 (high) according to each of the following criteria: degree of difficulty, degree of potential risk or danger involved, degree to which parents would approve, degree of educational value. Later, compare your list with the experiences of Jody in the novel.

2. As we grow up, many of us are assisted by people outside our family—like godparents, religious leaders, teachers, and coaches. Write a paragraph about a person like this who has helped you become a stronger, better person.

DISCUSSION QUESTIONS

1. Part 1: The Gift: Just on the basis of the opening paragraph, how do you think Billy Buck sees himself? Is he proud? Humble? Both? How does Jody feel about the way the day begins? The first two paragraphs on pages 12–13 make four references to the same general topic. What is it? Why do you think Steinbeck is so interested in conveying these examples of death? When Jody comes home from school, what are his mother's concerns? What do you think Jody's father has in mind for him the next morning? At the breakfast table, why do Jody's parents seem cross? When he shows Jody the pony, why is Carl Tiflin embarrassed? When Jody shows the boys the pony, what does his speech reveal? Why does Jody torture himself with unpleasant thoughts about Gabilan? How does Jody feel about Billy Buck? Where do you think Billy Buck learned so much about horses? Do you agree that horses—or animals in general—like to be talked to? Why is it important for a horse to be high-spirited? Is his experience with the pony changing Jody? If so, how? Why do you think Billy Buck wants to make a hair rope instead of just buying a rope? What does Jody's father mean by wanting a horse to have dignity? "[Jody] knew that only a mean-souled horse does not resent training." What does this mean? (Looking at it another way, why would a good horse resent training?) As he prepares for the Thanksgiving ride, what concerns Jody the most? When Gabilan gets soaked, how does Jody feel toward Billy Buck? Why do you think Jody's father has such resentment toward

weakness and helplessness? Do you think Jody now sees Billy as weak? Do Jody's mother and Billy Buck differ in their reasons for thinking (or saying) the pony will get well? Does Jody believe them? To whom does Jody seem closer—his father or Billy Buck? Why? How would you describe Billy's efforts to save the horse? Do you think he is telling Jody the truth about Gabilan? Why does he seem so protective? After supper Friday night, why do you think Jody's father builds a fire and tells stories? What does his reaction to Jody's not listening tell us about him? When Billy decides to open a hole in the horse's windpipe, is Jody's decision to stay a sign of courage—or something else? Is Carl Tiflin's wanting Jody to "come on, out of this" surprising to you? Why or why not? Why does Billy angrily say he should be allowed to stay? To Jody, why is the place now "familiar, but curiously changed"? What kinds of things have changed? At the end of the story, why does Jody feel compelled to kill the vulture—especially if Billy Buck is right about his knowing the bird is not responsible? Why do you think the author describes the bird as "impersonal and unafraid and detached"? At the end of this long and difficult experience, what has Jody learned?

2. Part 2: The Great Mountains: The narrator tells us that Jody's behavior toward Doubletree Mutt is caused by boredom rather than cruelty. Does the same thing motivate his killing of the bird? Might the paragraph of description after Jody disposes of the bird be symbolic in any way? Discuss. Why does Jody wonder about the mountains? The great conservationist Aldo Leopold once asked the question, "Of what avail are forty freedoms without a blank spot on the map?" Do you agree that there is something wonderful and mysterious about not knowing what is in a place? Do you agree that something can be both dear to a person and terrible? Discuss. To Jody, how are the mountains to the east different? Is the approaching old man described as safe or threatening? Neither? How does Jody react initially? Why couldn't he "take all this responsibility"? Why does Gitano want to stay at the ranch? Describe his feelings. Why does he seem to feel the Tiflins have an obligation? How would you respond to him? "Carl Tiflin didn't like to be cruel." Do you think he is cruel? Why or why not? As Jody talks to Gitano in the bunkhouse, how do the questions affect the old man? Why do you think he has never returned to the mountains before now? Later Carl Tiflin is described as hating his own brutality toward Gitano "and so he became brutal again." Why do you think he behaves this way? Why does he feel compelled to make the humorous remark about ham and eggs growing on the sidehills? It is easy to call Jody's father cruel and insensitive. Is there anything in the story that suggests he does have feelings? In the bunkhouse that night, why does Gitano not want Jody to see the rapier? Why does he change his mind? Why is the rapier so important to Gitano? Why does Jody feel so strongly that he must honor its secrecy? Why does Gitano ride the old horse up into the mountains? Why do you think Jody feels "a nameless sorrow"? Do you think Jody has changed in any way in the time between this story and "The Gift"? Explain. How do you think he feels about his father?

3. Part 3: The Promise: What time of year is it? As Jody moves down the road, what do his thoughts and actions reveal about him? Do you think his uneasiness about going to see his father is natural? Why or why not? What is the promise? (What is not promised?) What effect does it have on Jody? Do you think you would feel the same way? Does giving a child responsibility increase the likelihood of his or her being responsible? Discuss. When the two horses size each other up, how does Jody's behavior suggest both maturity and immaturity? Later, what are other signs of both as he talks with Billy Buck? Do you think Billy Buck behaves immaturely in his responses to Jody's concerns about the yet-to-be-born colt? Jody thinks of the pig killings, which to him are both fascinating and horrible. Can you think of other events that cause us to experience both fascination and horror? What is Jody counting on that the horse will provide for him? On the basis of this story and the two that preceded it, what would you say is the attitude of the adults toward children? Would you have wanted to be Jody? Why or why not? Is Billy Buck's decision to kill Nelly the best decision? Did he make the decision for Jody—or for himself? Discuss. How do you think Jody's father will react? The outcome of this story is different from that of "The Gift": Jody has a horse. Do you think he is happier than before? What has he learned?

4. Part 4: The Leader of the People: In the first few pages, what more do we learn about Carl Tiflin? About his relationship with Jody's mother? What kind of person apparently is the father of Jody's mother? Why does she tell Jody that he would "probably like to be met"? How does Jody appear to feel about his grandfather? Before the two of them actually meet on the road, what do we learn about the old man? How does he feel about "the new people"? Who are the new people? What does he mean when he tells Jody, "Wait until you head out, and then we'll see"? When Grandfather says that Billy Buck "was one of the few men of the new generation who had not gone soft," do you think he includes Carl Tiflin in that group? As Jody sits with the group after supper, "he arose to heroism." What does this mean? As Billy prepares for his mouse hunt, why does Billy Buck's comment about not knowing what's going to happen surprise him? Do we as readers react to the comment differently? Discuss. Why is Carl Tiflin so impatient with the old man? When he apologizes to Grandfather for his cruel remark, which does he regret more—having made the remark or having to apologize? Why does Grandfather feel the need to tell his stories? Why does everything remind him of the westward journeys? What does "westering" mean to him? Why does he say it "has died out of the people"? What has been lost? To what extent do you think Jody understands this?

   Overall: At the end of the book, how is Jody different from how he was at the beginning? What has he learned? Do you think there has been one incident that has contributed the most to the changes, or have they resulted from everything that has happened? Discuss.

WRITING ACTIVITIES

1. In "The Promise," Jody is described as having a "center-point," which is where the water spills out of a tub to create a perpetually green place out behind the house. It is a soothing place where Jody goes when he is troubled. Write a one-page description of a similar place for you. It might be outside or inside.

2. It might be said that *The Red Pony* is partly about frontiers—and the absence of them. In "The Leader of the People," Grandfather clearly feels they no longer exist, but some people would disagree. Write a one- to two-page paper entitled "The Frontiers of Today and Tomorrow."

3. For Billy Buck as a character, place a mark on each of the following lines to indicate where you think he falls. Then, write a one-page character sketch of Billy Buck. For each of the characteristics (and perhaps others), support your views by referring to specific details and experiences in the novel.

	1	2	3	4	5	
strong	/........../........../........../........../					weak
competent	/........../........../........../........../					incompetent
brave	/........../........../........../........../					cowardly
caring	/........../........../........../........../					uncaring
honest	/........../........../........../........../					dishonest

4. Read the poem "The Death of the Hired Man" by Robert Frost, which is about an old laborer who, after an absence, returns to the place where he spent most of his time working. Then write a paragraph in which you compare Silas in the poem to Gitano in "The Promise." How are the two men the same? Different? Do you agree with the comment in the poem that "home is the place where, when you have to go there, they have to take you in"?

5. Carl Tiflin is described as a "stern father . . . a disciplinarian . . . [whom] Jody obeyed in everything without questions of any kind." In the early years of the twentieth century, such parents were perhaps more typical than they are today, but many people argue that parents have become too lax and permissive. Write a paper in which you express your opinion about the kind of father Carl Tiflin is. Be sure to cite specific incidents in the novel for support.

6. Both Jody's grandfather and Gitano are old men whose most productive days are long behind them. In our present society, we are increasingly faced with the problem of how to best care for the physical, social, and emotional needs of the elderly. After perhaps doing some research on the topic, write a two- to three-page paper on ways of providing for the senior citizens in our communities.

7. In "The Promise," the rapier is described as being almost sacred. Gitano has it wrapped in deerskin, and he is initially reluctant to allow Jody to see it. Even Jody recognizes its value. Do you or your family have any object that you treasure so much that you perhaps keep it hidden or safely stored away? Write a paragraph or two about this item. Describe it in detail and explain its importance.

8. Imagine yourself as Jody. You are assigned by your teacher to write a composition on "The Important People in My Life." Write Jody's paper. What would he have to say about his father, his mother, and Billy Buck?

9. Many "horse words" are used throughout the novel, words like *curry*, *hackamore*, *halter*, *riata*, *pommel*, and *withers*. Compile a glossary of definitions of fifteen to twenty of these words that future readers of the book could refer to as they read.

10. Jody is often quite imaginative in his thoughts about the great adventures in store for him and his yet-to-be-born Black Demon in "The Promise." He dreams of schoolboys begging rides, rodeo contests, even a letter from the president. All of us have such dreams. Write about one of yours.

11. Write about a promise or a gift that was as important to you as the colts were to Jody.

OTHER ACTIVITIES

1. Aaron Copland's musical score *The Red Pony: Suite* was written for the 1949 Lewis Milestone film of the book and recorded by the Mexico City Philharmonic Orchestra on the His Master's Voice label. If the recording is available in your public library, prepare a reading of certain passages from the book with appropriate excerpts from the music as background.

2. Draw a Venn diagram (two large adjacent circles that overlap horizontally). In the left circle, list some characteristics of Carl Tiflin (e.g., stern). In the right circle, list some for Billy Buck (e.g., helpful). In the middle where the two circles overlap, list a few characteristics shared by both men. Compare your diagram with those drawn by other students.

3. The surroundings of the Tiflin ranch are described in some detail throughout the book, especially in the early parts of each chapter. Using these descriptions as sources, draw a pictogram map of the book's setting, including not only the ranch (house, bunkhouse, barn, cypress tree, wooden tub, etc.), but also places like Salinas and the Salinas Valley, the Gabilan Mountains, and Monterey. Obviously it will be helpful to consult a map of California.

4. With other students, role-play a scene that involves Carl Tiflin and his wife, Jody's grandfather, and Gitano—before Gitano makes his decision to ride into the mountains. They are trying to resolve the question of how to best respond to Gitano's wishes.

5. Using pictures from magazines, printed words, even real objects, create a three-part collage that depicts the following: Billy Buck as he is seen by Jody, Billy Buck as he is seen by Jody's mother, and Billy Buck as he sees himself.

SELECTED TEACHING RESOURCES

Media Aids

Cassettes (2)

The Red Pony. Eli Wallach version. Harper Audio.

CD-ROM

The Pearl and The Red Pony CD-ROM. Windows and Macintosh versions. Penguin Electronics, 1996.

Internet

Smith, Jennifer. *Steinbeck Research Center.* January 1997. Available: http://www.sjsu.edu/depts/steinbec/srchome.html (Accessed March 1, 1997). This homepage features a Steinbeck chronology, "Steinbeck Country" (a map, color photograph of a typical setting in rural California, details on settings), and a photograph of the author.

Video

John Steinbeck, The Leader of the People. 24 min., color. Britannica, n.d.

The Red Pony. 89 min., Clearvue/eav, Perma-Bound, and Perfection Learning Corporation, 1949.

Printed Materials

Teaching Aids

The Red Pony. Contemporary Classics series and Portals to Reading series. Perfection Learning Corporation.

The Red Pony. Literature Unit Plans. Teacher's Pet Publications.

The Red Pony. Novel Unit Guide, Perma-Guide, and Student Packet. Perma-Bound.

The Red Pony. Novel/Drama Curriculum Units. The Center for Learning.

The Red Pony. Novel-Ties. Learning Links.

Tests

The Red Pony. Objective and essay versions. Perfection Learning Corporation.

The Call of the Wild

Jack London

New York: Macmillan, 1903
Available in paperback from several publishing companies.

SUMMARY

Buck, a large part–St. Bernard dog, is kidnapped from his pastoral home in California to work as a sled dog in the goldfields of the Yukon in 1897. Over a period of several months he adjusts to the arduous and primitive life of the trail and assumes the leadership of the team after killing a malicious husky named Spitz. Throughout this experience, he senses a return to the primordial roots of his past. After toiling for two demanding but benevolent owners, Buck is rescued from a cruel and foolish trio of amateurs by a veteran miner named John Thornton, to whom he becomes devoted. When Thornton is ambushed and killed by a band of Indians, Buck gains revenge before setting out to join a pack of wolves in response to the "call of the wild."

APPRAISAL

Jack London's masterpiece, *The Call of the Wild,* is at one level a compelling adventure story about a dog; at another level, it has been interpreted by critics as a human allegory and a fictional reflection of Darwinian thought. After over ninety years in print, the novel still enjoys a wide readership. In the schools, it is taught most often in grades eight through ten, where it is appreciated especially by boys.

THEMES

survival, the primitive versus the civilized, courage, heroism, adventure

LITERARY CONCEPTS

myth, naturalism, theme, setting, plot, characterization, point of view, symbol

RELATED READING

For students who like animal stories, related titles abound. A few of the more appropriate ones are Sheila Burnford's *The Incredible Journey,* Eric Knight's *Lassie Come Home*, and Jim Kjelgaard's *Big Red*. A comparable survival story—about an Eskimo girl's adventure with a pack of wolves on the Alaskan tundra—is *Julie of the Wolves* by Jean Craighead George. Also, several novels by Gary Paulsen would be appropriate for parallel reading, especially *Woodsong* and *Dogsong*.

READING PROBLEMS AND OPPORTUNITIES

Because of its brevity (the book is actually a novella), most students find *The Call of the Wild* quite approachable. Still, it contains many words they will not know, words that are therefore useful for vocabulary study. Most of the following occur more than once in the book (chapter numbers are in parentheses):

imperious (1, 6, 7),
wonted, unwonted (1, 3, 7),
impending (1, 3, 5),
latent (1, 7),
morose (1, 4),
primordial (1, 3, 6, 7),
antagonist (2, 3, 6, 7),
writhe, writhing (2, 3, 6, 7)
discomfiture, discomfit (2, 7),
gaunt (2, 3, 7),

arduous (2),
ignominious (2),
malinger, malingerer (2, 3, 5),
callous (2, 5),
resolute, irresolute (3, 5),
articulate, inarticulate (3, 5),
covert (3),
insidious (3),
inexorable (3, 5),
flounder (4),
lugubrious (4),

salient (5, 7),
affirm (5, 7),
superfluous (5, 6),
formidable (5, 7),
insensible (5),
quibble (6),
virility (6, 7),
vigilant (7),
carnivorous (7),
paroxysm (7),
stealthy (7), and
incarnate (7).

INITIATING ACTIVITIES

1. In encyclopedias and other sources (e.g., *Man's Best Friend: The National Geographic Book of Dogs*, rev. ed., Washington, D.C.: National Geographic Society, 1974), read about the St. Bernard, the Scottish shepherd dog (Shetland sheepdog), and the husky. Report to the class on their size, appearance, and qualities.

2. Locate the setting of the novel in an atlas of the Pacific Coast, especially the Yukon Territory. Try to find the Santa Clara Valley (in California), Seattle, Queen Charlotte Sound, Dyea and Skagway, Chilkoot Divide, Lake Bennett, Lake La Barge, the Thirty Mile River, the Yukon River, the White River, the Stewart River, and Dawson. Trace the course of an overland trip from Skagway to Dawson, figure the mileage, and estimate how long it would take by dogsled.

DISCUSSION QUESTIONS

1. Chapter 1: Why is Buck kidnapped? In the next few days, how does he change? What is the *primitive law* to which he is introduced? How does he meet it halfway? For him, what does the man in the red sweater represent?

2. Chapter 2: How is Buck's new life different from the old? What are some of the ways he adjusts? In what ways has there been "a decay . . . of his moral nature"? Why has he become less "civilized"? What is meant by "the ancient song surged through him and he came into his own again"? Cite indications of Buck's intelligence. How are the personalities of the other dogs different? How and why are they suddenly transformed?

3. Chapter 3: How are Buck and Spitz different? In the course of the chapter, how does Buck change? In his attitude toward leadership, why does he gradually move from being patient and deliberate to being assertive and cunning? Why is Buck stirred by the "song of the huskies"? "He was sounding the deeps of his nature, and of the parts of his nature that were deeper than he, going back into the womb of Time." What does this mean? To what has Buck returned? As the chapter ends, what is Buck like? At this point, is it possible that the book has become something more than a dog story? Discuss.

4. Chapter 4: What makes Buck a good leader? As he looks into the fire, what does he remember? Why does he recall the hairy man from the distant past? For Buck, why is the past important? What is important for Dave?

5. Chapter 5: At this time, why were men rushing to the Yukon? Why were strong but weary dogs hurried back out onto the trail? What kind of people were the three new owners? What do they value? Why do you think the author included them in the book? What is Buck's response to them? Why do he and the other dogs continue to pull the sled? Why does Buck finally refuse? Has he lost courage? Discuss.

6. Chapter 6: Why does Buck prefer to love John Thornton from a distance? What effect does this new relationship have upon the dog? Are there limits to his devotion? Why does John Thornton feel that Buck's devotion is both splendid and terrible? After Buck pulls the thousand-pound sled, why does John Thornton curse the Skookum Bench King? Why do the onlookers draw "back to a respectful distance" from Buck and his master?

7. Chapter 7: Why does John Thornton's small party strike off to the east? For what are they searching? For what does Buck seem to be searching? How does he react to the "level country . . . of forest and many streams"? Why does he return to camp? What is Buck's dilemma? Is he merciless when he pursues the moose? To what extent are his actions justifiable? Discuss. How do the Indians respond to Buck's attack—and to subsequent rumors? Discuss how Buck has changed since his kidnapping. Have the changes been inevitable? For the better or the worse? What comment about life and experience, if any, do you think Jack London is making through the book?

WRITING ACTIVITIES

1. Write a ballad about Buck that might have circulated through the Klondike territory years after he joined the wolf pack. Include references to some of his legendary exploits.

2. Write a diamante poem contrasting the words *wild* and *civilized.* (See Appendix A.)

3. Conduct research on the gold rush in the Klondike section of the Yukon Territory during the last years of the nineteenth century. Report to the class on your findings.

4. Write another ending for the novel. Assume that when Buck returns to the camp after the Indian attack, he finds John Thornton severely wounded but alive. What would Buck do? How would he resolve the dilemma of remaining with his beloved master or returning to the wilderness that beckoned so strongly?

5. Write a paper comparing and contrasting Buck between the beginning of the novel and the end. Include at least two of the following areas and any others you wish: attitude toward man, attitude toward self (assuming such a thing is possible among dogs), and sense of responsibility.

6. Buck often dreams about the hairy man. Considering what this figure from the distant past is like, write an adventure that Buck has with him.

7. "There is an ecstasy that marks the summit of life, and beyond which life cannot rise. And such is the paradox of living, this ecstasy comes when one is most alive, and it comes as a complete forgetfulness that one is alive." Write about an experience in your life when you—like Buck in pursuit of the snowshoe hare—felt similarly exhilarated at the mere fact of being alive.

8. Write the legend of the Ghost Dog as told by the Yeehat Indians.

9. Write several diary entries that John Thornton might have kept during the stay in the "broad valley where the gold showed like yellow butter across the bottom of the washing-pan." Include especially his thoughts and observations regarding Buck's occasional disappearances into the wilderness.

10. Write a brief three- to five-sentence description of Buck from the point of view of each of the following characters in the novel: Judge Miller, Francois, and John Thornton. Each description should be different, reflecting the changes in Buck throughout the novel.

OTHER ACTIVITIES

1. Design a poster offering a reward from Judge Miller to anyone having information about the whereabouts of Buck. Include a drawing of the dog that reflects descriptions of him provided in the book, especially in chapter 7.

2. Draw a large map of the Yukon Territory detailing important locales mentioned in the book (see Initiating Activity #2). Include places that depict important events, such as John Thornton's rescuing of Buck and Buck's revenge upon the Indians.

   "Each day mankind and the claims of mankind slipped farther from him. Deep in the forest a call was sounding, and often as he heard this call, mysteriously thrilling and luring, he felt compelled to turn his back upon the fire and the beaten earth around it to plunge into the forest. . . . But as often as he gained the soft, unbroken earth and the green shade, the love of John Thornton drew him back to the fire again."

3. Construct a "split-screen" collage that depicts Buck's divided loyalties between the one world and the other.

4. Read some of Robert Service's poems about the Yukon and the gold rush in his *The Best of Robert Service* or *Yukon Poems*. With several other

students, prepare a choral reading of two or three poems about subjects similar to those in *The Call of the Wild.*

SELECTED TEACHING RESOURCES

Media Aids

Cassette

The Call of the Wild. Abridged. Perfection Learning Corporation.

Cassettes (3)

The Call of the Wild. 4.5 hours. Recorded Books.

Internet

UC Regents. 1996. *The Jack London Collection.* 1996. Available: http://sunsite.berkeley.edu/London/(Accessed March 1, 1997).
   This homepage includes a brief biography, documents, bibliographies, a "slide show" of more than eighty photographs, and complete texts of most of Jack London's works.

Video

The Call of the Wild. 100 min., Charlton Heston version, color. Perma-Bound and Perfection Learning Corporation, 1972.

Printed Materials

Books

Dyer, Daniel. *"The Call of the Wild" by Jack London with an Illustrated Reader's Companion.* Norman, OK: University of Oklahoma Press, 1995.

Tavernier-Courbin, Jacqueline. *"The Call of the Wild": A Naturalistic Romance.* New York: Twayne Publishers, 1994.

Teaching Aids

The Call of the Wild. Contemporary Classics series. Perfection Learning Corporation.

The Call of the Wild. Literature Unit Plans. Teacher's Pet Publications.

The Call of the Wild. Novel Unit Guide, Perma-Guide, and Student Packet. Perma-Bound.

The Call of the Wild. Novel/Drama Curriculum Units. The Center for Learning.

The Call of the Wild. Novel-Ties. Learning Links.

The Call of the Wild. React series. Sundance.

Tests

The Call of the Wild. Essay and objective versions. Perfection Learning Corporation.

My Brother Sam Is Dead

James Lincoln Collier and Christopher Collier

New York: Four Winds Press, 1974
Available in paperback from Scholastic.*

SUMMARY

When Tim Meeker's older brother, Sam, enlists in the Continental Army to fight for the Patriot cause against the British, he embroils his family in a bitter conflict. Tim's father, Life Meeker, leans toward the side of the Tories but far more strongly opposes war in general because of its brutality and senselessness. Tim, who dearly respects his father and admires his brother (and loves them both), is caught in the middle. He envies Sam for his opportunities for adventure and heroism, and he entertains the arguments of both sides. As the conflict drags through months and years, however, his attitude changes. His father is dragged off by so-called Patriots and left to die on a British prison ship; a ten-year-old boy is taken captive; neighbors are brutally killed. Even before Sam is falsely accused by two fellow soldiers of stealing his own cattle, Tim agrees with his mother that "war turns men into beasts," a conclusion confirmed by Sam's subsequent court-martial and execution.

APPRAISAL

A fast-moving plot (made all the more intriguing by the title), compelling characterizations of strong individuals in conflict with each other, the authentic depiction of a time and place important in American history—these factors and others make *My Brother Sam Is Dead* one of the best and most popular historical novels for young adults ever written. A Newbery Honor Book for 1975, the novel presents a balanced view of the American Revolution and a critical view of war in general. It is appropriate for students in grades eight to eleven.

THEMES

growing up, initiation, family conflict and loyalty, the futility of war, justice

LITERARY CONCEPTS

plot, characterization, theme, conflict, point of view, historical fiction, irony, foreshadowing

---

*NOTE: This response guide was prepared by Walt Cottingham, who teaches American history at Hendersonville High School in Hendersonville, NC.

RELATED READING

The most obvious novel for comparison is Esther Forbes's *Johnny Tremain*. Winner of the 1944 Newbery Medal, this depiction of the Revolutionary War presents the more traditional pro-American viewpoint of the conflict. Other books set in the same period include Howard Fast's *April Morning*, which describes the Battle of Lexington, *The Fighting Ground* by Avi, and *A Ride into Morning: The Story of Tempe Wick* by Ann Rinaldi.

READING PROBLEMS AND OPPORTUNITIES

My Brother Sam Is Dead is briskly narrated by an intelligent but uneducated adolescent boy. For this reason the book is easy to read. The few opportunities it offers for vocabulary study are found in the following words (chapter numbers are in parentheses):

prevail (1),
sloth (1),
lasciviousness (1),
subversion (1, 3),
clambering (4),
skirmish (5),
speculating (5),
recalcitrance (7),

headstrong (7, 8, 12, epilogue),
plundering (7),
grimaced (7),
sedition (8),
depreciation (10),
swaggering (10),
fusillade (10),

unscrupulous (12),
compunction (12),
floundering (13),
foreboding (13),
defection (13),
clemency (13, 14), and
commemorate (14).

INITIATING ACTIVITIES

1. Imagine that you are a college-age student and are facing a possible war. Your country is occupied with soldiers from another nation. You are paying taxes to this other country, yet you have no representatives in the government. Soldiers from this country have shot down some of your fellow citizens in the streets. A battle has even occurred between soldiers of the foreign country and ordinary citizens. Given only this knowledge, would you enlist? Consider this question for a moment. Now consider the following three conditions: Would you enlist if you thought your enlistment would bring hardship to your family? If you thought your enlistment would cause the death of someone in your family? If you thought you would die? Given these conditions, would your opinion change? With your classmates, discuss what, if anything, makes war worth fighting and whether people would fight if they understood the personal consequences.

2. With five other students, act out a tavern scene during the American Revolutionary period in which three of you represent Patriots and three represent Tories. Beforehand, individually spend some time researching your different positions in American history texts and library books. In the enactment, begin your conversation cordially, but gradually let politics creep into the talk. Each person should present his or her particular viewpoint as convincingly and realistically as possible.

DISCUSSION QUESTIONS

1. Chapter 1: What is Sam like? What does Tim admire about him? What does Tim regret? Does Tim worship Sam or merely admire him? What are Sam's reasons for running off from school to fight? Describe the boys' father. In what ways do Sam's opinions differ from his father's? Which one of the two argues more convincingly? Why does Tim lean toward his father's viewpoint? When Sam's father describes the horror of war as he has seen it, how does Sam react? Is his reaction based on reason? Why does he leave? How would you have reacted in Sam's place? At the end of the chapter, why does Life Meeker cry? For whom or what is he crying?

2. Chapter 2: At the beginning of chapter 2, the authors provide background information. Why didn't they do this in chapter 1? Why is Tim so confused by the issue between the Tories and the Patriots? When Tim talks to Sam at Tom Warrup's, why doesn't he say which side he'll be on in the war? How does he feel about Sam's having taken the Brown Bess? Have you had to take sides with one member of your family against another? If so, how did you feel?

3. Chapter 3: List at least five chores that Tim performs around the tavern. Is his life hard? How could life in a tavern be considered interesting? Do we have places in America today that compare with the Meeker's tavern? As the months pass, why is Tim so anxious for Sam to come back? At this part in the book, Tim still doesn't know where his allegiance lies. Where does yours? Why?

4. Chapter 4: What purpose in the novel does the Rebel invasion of the tavern serve? After Sam takes the gun away from Tim, what does he reveal about himself in their conversation? About the army? Has he changed? If so, how? What new reason does he give for having enlisted? When Sam sees his father in the tavern, they stare at each other and then Sam runs. What do you think is in the minds of Sam, Tim, and their father during those few seconds? Why does Life Meeker yell? And why does Sam wave?

5. Chapter 5: Does Tim's attitude toward the war change as the book progresses? If so, how? How does the war begin to affect the Meekers for the first time? In describing these effects, what point do the authors seem to be making about war? Why does Tim want so badly to carry the letters for Mr. Heron? What does this reveal about Tim?

6. Chapter 6: What purpose do the events in chapter 6 serve? What does the character of Mr. Heron add to the novel? What similarities of character do Tim and Sam have, as shown in the disobeying of their father's wishes?

7. Chapter 7: What do Sam's letters reveal, especially about him? Why does his mother insist on writing to him? How does Tim feel about his opportunity to accompany his father on the trip to Verplancks Point?

8. Chapters 8 and 9: Why are Mr. Platt's comments about the war so troubling? How do the authors build up the tension as Tim and his father make their way back from Verplancks Point? How does Tim change as a result of the trip? In what ways is he more of a man when he returns than when he left?

9. Chapter 10: Has Tim's attitude toward the war changed? Discuss. How has he changed otherwise? Mrs. Meeker tells Tim that "war turns men into beasts." Describe one action he witnesses that shows the British to be "beasts," and one that shows the Patriots to be.

10. Chapter 11: When the British decide to keep Jerry Sanford as a prisoner, what does Captain Betts's remark ("Don't ask me why they kept a boy") suggest about war? How does Tim react to the Continental troops? When Sam tells of his plans to reenlist, what does Tim discover about his brother? Robert E. Lee once said, "It is well that war is so terrible—we would grow too fond of it." Do you think Sam could learn anything from this statement? Why or why not? Is it immature for a person to want to be a part of something important? Discuss.

11. Chapter 12: This chapter is full of ironies—differences between what could be expected to happen and what happens. Cite some of them. Overall, what comment do they make about war? What attitude do most of the people in Reading begin to have toward the war? Has Sam's attitude toward the war changed? If so, how?

12. Chapter 13: In what ways does the war affect Tim's mother? Why does she give up hope? What is ironic about Sam's arrest? How does he bear up when Tim visits him in the stockade?

13. Chapter 14: Why is Sam court-martialed and found guilty? Why does General Putnam want to make examples of criminals? Why does Tim try to rescue his brother despite such little chance of success? Why does he attend the execution? How do you feel about the authors' description of Sam's death? Why do you think they made it so graphic?

14. Epilogue: What purpose does the epilogue serve in this novel? In his concluding remark, made fifty years later, Tim wonders if "there might have been another way, besides war, to achieve the same end." Discuss what some of these ways might have been.

WRITING ACTIVITIES

1. Write a diamante poem contrasting the words *war* and *peace*. (See Appendix A.)

2. Read *The Spy* by James Fenimore Cooper, a novel in which a family is split between Tory and Patriot sympathies. Write a short paper comparing the Whartons to the Meekers. Tell if you think Sam's fate would have been different if he had faced George Washington (as Henry Wharton did) instead of General Putnam.

3. Read about the execution of Nathan Hale. Write a paper comparing it to Sam's execution. Consider these questions: Which was more significant? Was either execution fair? Which of the two men deserved his sentence—or did neither? Why does Sam leave us with no famous words?

4. Write several diary entries for Sam during the first months of his service before his unit saw any fighting.

5. Choose and do two of the following:

   a. Write a letter Mrs. Meeker might have sent to Sam (chapter 7).

   b. Write a letter Mr. Meeker might have sent from the prison ship.

   c. Assume that Tim delivered the first letter safely. Write the second letter Mr. Heron would have sent by him, too.

   d. Write a letter from Betsy Read to Sam.

6. Read the account of a real Connecticut private, Joseph Plumb Martin, describing his experiences at Valley Forge (*Private Yankee Doodle,* ed. by George P. Scheer, New York: Little, Brown, 1962). Write a brief summary of the private's experiences. Then tell how you think you would have fared under those conditions.

7. Write a newspaper report for the *Rivington Loyal Gazette* describing the British raid on Reading by General Tyron's troops. Write a corresponding article that might have appeared in a Patriot journal.

8. Write brief eulogies for Life Meeker as they might have been composed by the following people: Susannah Meeker, Sam, and Tim.

9. "In war the dead pay the debts of the living." Write a paper supporting Life Meeker's statement using examples from the novel.

10. Perhaps the primary reason Sam joins the army is, as Tim discovers, to become "part of something big." Write about an experience in your life when you were part (or wanted to be part) of something important. Or, write about whether you think you would ever get emotionally involved in an issue or event like this. What kinds of things would motivate you to act so decisively?

Other Activities

1. Throughout American history there has been much discussion about war and peace. Listen to some music from the late 1960s and early 1970s that concerns war. Make a medley of antiwar songs on a tape and play them for the class. Some songs you might include are: "Wooden Ships" by Crosby, Stills, and Nash; "Last Night I Had the Strangest Dream" by Ed McCurdy; "I-Feel-Like-I'm-Fixin'-to-Die Rag" by Country Joe and the Fish; "Give Peace a Chance" by the Beatles, and "Talking World War III Blues" by Bob Dylan.

2. You are a television reporter. Conduct an on-the-spot interview with Sam Meeker after his father has run him out of the house. Then conduct a parallel interview with Sam's father. (This will involve one or two other students.)

3. With several of your classmates, act out the court-martial of Sam Meeker. Roles would include Sam, General Putnam, the two soldiers who accuse Sam, and perhaps a person assigned by the army to defend Sam, as well as a prosecutor.

4. Draw a poster that Sam might have created to motivate local boys his age to join the Continental Army.

5. Consider again, very carefully, Life Meeker's attitude toward the conflict that his son was caught up in. Then draw an editorial cartoon for the local newspaper that expresses this attitude.

6. Find a print of *Guernica* by Pablo Picasso. Examine the painting carefully and then write a brief paper describing your reaction, partly in terms of the theme of war in *My Brother Sam Is Dead.*

SELECTED TEACHING RESOURCES

Media Aids

Cassette

My Brother Sam Is Dead. Learning Links.

Internet

Institute for Learning Technologies. *American Revolution Navigation Tools.* 1993-1995. Available: http://www.ilt.columbia.edu/k12/history/aha/arnav.html (Accessed March 1, 1997.)

This site offers a treasure trove of information on the American Revolution, including sections on dates, music, battles, weapons and uniforms, women, African Americans, documents, and events. Much of the material was developed by public school students working on a project associated with Columbia University.

Printed Materials

Poster

My Brother Sam Is Dead. 17" x 22", color. Perfection Learning Corporation.

Teaching Aids

My Brother Sam Is Dead. Contemporary Classics series and Latitudes series. Perfection Learning Corporation.

My Brother Sam Is Dead. Lift series. Sundance.

My Brother Sam Is Dead. Novel Unit Guide and Perma-Guide. Perma-Bound.

My Brother Sam Is Dead. Novel/Drama Curriculum Units. The Center for Learning.

My Brother Sam Is Dead. Novel-Ties. Learning Links.

Tests

My Brother Sam Is Dead. Essay and objective versions. Perfection Learning Corporation.

Animal Farm

George Orwell

New York: Harcourt, Brace & World, 1946
Available in paperback from Signet.

SUMMARY

When the animals on Manor Farm become disgusted with their drunken master, Mr. Jones, they revolt, run all humans off, and set up an ideal community based on the dreams of the pig, old Major. At first, the Animal Farm is run by two pigs, Napoleon and Snowball, and all animals are equal. The farm is successful for a time, and the animals, led by the clever pigs and the hardworking horse, Boxer, even manage to fend off an attack by humans. When the two leaders begin to quarrel, however, Napoleon ousts Snowball, accusing him of having been a traitor. With the help of the dogs, the pigs continue to gain power, but eventually the animals find themselves worse off than before the revolution. Even poor Boxer is shipped off to be slaughtered. Finally the pigs begin to associate again with humans, eliminate all pretense of equality among the animals, and come to be indistinguishable from the very humans they had earlier overthrown.

APPRAISAL

When Orwell's book was published in 1946, it became an immediate best-seller, was translated into other languages, and established the author's reputation as a writer. In his essay "Why I Write," Orwell declares, "*Animal Farm* was the first book in which I tried, with full consciousness of what I was doing, to fuse political purpose and artistic purpose into one whole." Critics felt that he succeeded, calling his work a "masterpiece" and a "triumph." For years, students of all ages have enjoyed reading and discussing the fable, partly because of its clever structure but mainly because of the wealth of ideas and interpretations it affords. The book is particularly appropriate for grades nine and ten.

THEMES

totalitarianism and democracy, power and its ability to corrupt, revolution, propaganda, equality, exploitation, pursuit of happiness

LITERARY CONCEPTS

fable, fairy tale, allegory, symbol, stereotype, irony, propaganda, euphemism, connotation, satire, anthropomorphism

RELATED READING

Older students interested in the theme of power and its tendency to corrupt, especially in the arena of politics, might wish to read *All the King's Men* by Robert Penn Warren. Other students may want to compare *Animal Farm* with *Lord of the Flies*, seeing both books as examples of efforts to govern gone awry because of the nature of the beast. Students interested in reading other animal fables written for adults might consider *Watership Down* by Richard Adams and *The Book of the Dun Cow* by Walter Wangerin, Jr.

READING PROBLEMS AND OPPORTUNITIES

Because the sentence structure and vocabulary of the book are fairly simple, *Animal Farm* is a good choice for students who are not proficient readers of literature. The book offers a multiplicity of interpretations and thus works well with heterogeneous groups. This is not to say, however, that there are no opportunities for vocabulary study here. Many words in the book may be unfamiliar because they deal with farm life or because they are uniquely British. Others are more general and therefore warrant more concentrated study. The following problem words are listed according to the chapter in which they occur:

scullery, ensconced, paddock, knacker, enmity (1), *vivacious, apathy, capered* (2), *parasitical, obstinate, indefatigable, maxim* (3),

ignominious (4), *blithely, restive* (5), *capitulated, stupefied, categorically, cowered, retribution* (7), *machinations, gambolled, beatifically, unscathed* (8),

superannuated (9), and *taciturn, inebriates* (10).

INITIATING ACTIVITIES

1. American government is based on the premise that "all men are created equal." Discuss with your classmates the meaning of equality. In what ways are people created equal? In what ways are they unequal? What problems does inequality cause?

2. Throughout history there have been many revolutions. Review history textbooks, both American and world, and skim the sections that describe revolutions. You are already familiar with the American Revolution, but check the French Revolution, the Spanish Revolution, and the Russian Revolution. With your classmates, prepare a chart listing the causes and effects (both immediate and long-range) of these revolutions. Review this chart and attempt to draw generalizations about what causes a revolution and what immediate and long-range effects a revolution may have.

3. Using the *Readers' Guide to Periodical Literature* in your library, locate several articles on communal living. After reading these articles, discuss

with your classmates the advantages and disadvantages of this type of economic and social structure.

DISCUSSION QUESTIONS

1. Chapter 1: Why does old Major call a meeting? Why are the animals willing to come to listen to what he has to say? Throughout the book, the author gives the animals human characteristics (e.g., the power of speech). In addition, however, he maintains their unique animal characteristics. Point out examples of Orwell's careful attention to these animal qualities, particularly as the animals gather to hear the speech and as they sing "Beasts of England." What effect does the singing of this song have upon the animals? Can you recall times when you have seen humans respond in the same way to an emotional song? Discuss such occasions.

2. Chapter 2: Compare and contrast Napoleon and Snowball. What are the strengths and weaknesses of each? What is Squealer's greatest skill? Identify current well-known figures in our society who have this same skill. Why are people like this so dangerous? Clover and Boxer are symbols of a large group of people in every society. What kinds of behavior are typical of these people? Why are they dangerous? In the book, what causes the revolt of the animals? What factors make the revolution possible at this particular time?

3. Chapter 3: What motivates the animals to work so hard? What role do the pigs assume on Animal Farm? Why is Mollie's behavior tolerated? Do you feel this is the way vain, selfish people are usually treated? Why or why not? Why is the Sunday ceremony important? What counterparts to this ceremony do you find in our society? In what ways are the pigs gaining more and more control? What role does literacy play in this new society?

4. Chapter 4: In what ways do the names *Foxwood* and *Pinchfield* reflect the qualities of their owners? What is the reaction of the humans to the establishment of Animal Farm? Are these reactions typical of those expressed by groups of people when something new threatens their established way of life? Why or why not? How are the animals able to defeat the humans? Examined from a strictly realistic viewpoint, the battle obviously could not have ended as it did. Why then is the author able to present it in this way? Snowball and Boxer present two conflicting views of war. With which of these characters are you sympathetic? Why? Which human war customs do the animals adopt?

5. Chapter 5: What causes Mollie to be a traitor to Animal Farm? When Snowball and Napoleon begin a power struggle to determine the leader of Animal Farm, what does each use as a means of gaining support? How do leaders today use similar means to gain power? Why is Napoleon finally able to oust Snowball? What then, according to this tale, is the most effective way of gaining and maintaining control? Do you agree or disagree? What is the significance of Napoleon's eliminating the Sunday meetings? Why is it necessary for the pigs to revise the history of Animal Farm? When the animals question decisions, they are presented with the unanswerable argument, "Surely, comrades, you do not want Jones back." Identify

similar unanswerable arguments that are used by authorities today (one example: "It says so in the dictionary"). What difficulties do these types of arguments pose? In what ways might such arguments be refuted?

6. Chapter 6: What ironies begin to appear on Animal Farm, for example, in the voluntary Sunday work? Why do the animals continue to slave away to make Animal Farm succeed? Why are the animals unable to continue a self-sufficient existence? Compare their problems with those of other groups that have tried to be self-sufficient. Are they similar? Why or why not? How is Squealer always able to allay the fears of the other animals and convince them that the decisions being made are for the best? Are human beings in general as gullible as these animals? Why or why not? Refer to specific incidents to support your position. How are the pigs able to fulfill their own desires without violating the original commandments? Do you believe this trick is often used in human society? Discuss. Although Snowball has left Animal Farm, how is he still valuable to Napoleon and the other pigs?

7. Chapter 7: When hard times fall on Animal Farm, Napoleon sets out to deceive the outside world. What contrasts exist between the appearances he arranges and the reality of life for the animals? In the present-day world, which is more important—appearance or reality? What techniques do government officials sometimes use to camouflage reality? How does the incident with the hens illustrate that Napoleon's power is not absolute? Yet how is Napoleon ultimately able to win? Can you find parallels to this situation in current economic activity? Do all of the work stoppages conclude in the same way that the hens' revolt ended? Why or why not? Why do the other animals continue to accept Snowball as a scapegoat in spite of evidence to the contrary? Why do the animals confess to the crimes when they are questioned by Napoleon? Why does Napoleon have all these animals killed? Throughout history, the killing of dissenters has been a means of maintaining control. Do you believe that this is a generally effective means of retaining power? Why or why not? In what ways is Clover able to recognize the difference between the ideal society proposed by old Major and the current society under Napoleon's rule? Why is she unable to voice her insights? Why is "Beasts of England" banned? Why are the animals so distraught about this?

8. Chapter 8: In what ways is Napoleon becoming a monarch? What kinds of diplomatic relations is he carrying on with the humans? How does he manipulate the other animals to support his decisions regarding the humans? How is Napoleon tricked by the humans? Compare the first battle with the humans to the second. What role does Napoleon play in this battle? What irony exists in the animals' celebration of victory? What grave illness is Napoleon suffering from?

9. Chapter 9: What continues to motivate Boxer to work so hard? What is really meant by the term *readjustment*? Cite examples of similar euphemisms used by politicians in recent history. What means are used to secure the position of the pigs as the "ruling class"? What is the irony to be found in the Spontaneous Demonstrations? What type of election is held on Animal Farm? What are the advantages of this type of election?

Why do the pigs tolerate Moses's stories about Sugarcandy Mountain? How do they stand to benefit from these tales? What types of stories in our society are similar to these? What finally causes Benjamin to break down and use his ability to read? How is Boxer memorialized? Where do the pigs get the money to buy another case of whiskey?

10. Chapter 10: Of all the animals, which remained nearly the same as the years passed? Why was this? How do Napoleon and the pigs continue to use the principles of Animalism for their own benefit? Despite all the hardships, why are the animals still proud and hopeful? What does old Major's skull represent? Why is it removed? List the many ways the pigs have come to resemble the despised humans they once overthrew.

WRITING ACTIVITIES

1. In encyclopedias or other sources, read an account of the Russian Revolution of 1917 and the subsequent establishment of communism in that country. Compare the characters of Major, Napoleon, and Snowball to actual historical figures. Write an essay in which you show the parallels between the events in *Animal Farm* and those in the revolution. In the conclusion of your essay, explain what you think Orwell was predicting concerning Russia's future.

2. The subtitle of *Animal Farm* indicates that it is a fairy tale or folktale. Write a brief paper in which you try to explain why Orwell called his book a fairy tale. It will be helpful to review a number of such tales to determine their main characteristics.

3. The film version of the book has a happy ending. Other animals join the hardworking group on the farm in a second revolution in which Napoleon is overthrown and equality and freedom are established. Write an argument in which you support or refute the use of such an ending. How does this type of ending change the author's message? On what grounds is such a change justified? Unjustified?

4. At the end of chapter 7, the animals are forbidden to sing "Beasts of England" any longer, and a new song written by Minimus is introduced. The first two lines of this song are given in the book. Finish the song, keeping in mind that it never seems equal to "Beasts of England" in the hearts of the animals.

5. Write two eulogies for Boxer. One should be a speech that Napoleon might have given to honor the horse; the other, a speech that Clover, Benjamin, or some other animal who worked closely with Boxer might have presented if he or she had been given the chance.

6. Slogans play an important part in *Animal Farm* because they help to simplify issues, to motivate workers, and to maintain power and control. Try your hand at writing some slogans that might have been used by these animals or groups of animals in the book:

   a. the dogs who guarded Napoleon,

   b. the chickens who revolted,

   c. Mollie,

   d. the young pigs who were being groomed for leadership,

   e. Moses, the raven.

7. Write a character sketch of Benjamin, the donkey. In this sketch explore the ways in which Benjamin is a stereotyped character, and also look carefully at those incidents that serve to make him more well-rounded and sympathetic.

8. *Animal Farm* is an allegory, a story in which the characters and events stand for some larger, more universal ideas. Attempt to write an allegory of your own. You may want to deal with some of the current problems of society, such as pollution, hunger, or the risk of nuclear war. As you develop your story, remember that the characters and events must clearly represent ideas in the situation you are presenting.

OTHER ACTIVITIES

1. In chapter 7, Clover recognizes the disparity between the ideals of old Major and the reality of the regime under Napoleon, yet she is unable to verbalize her concerns. Prepare and present to your classmates the speech Clover might have made at the time.

2. Create a caricature of a current or historical political figure whose characteristics are similar to those of one of the figures in *Animal Farm*. Choose an animal (or animal type) in the book as a means of exaggerating the features of this individual. For example, a representation of Squealer could be used to portray a national press secretary.

3. Throughout the book, numerous propaganda devices are used to control the animals. These include hasty generalizations, the misuse of statistics, cause-and-effect fallacies, and personal attacks. Prepare a poster illustrating one of these propaganda techniques. Use illustrations from both *Animal Farm* and current newspapers and magazines.

4. Two flags are described in the book. Draw these two flags—and then a third to be used in the future as Animal Farm once again becomes Manor Farm. The drawings may be done in any appropriate medium of your choice.

5. Design a logo for Animal Farm in its first year. Make sure the design captures the spirit of the farm at that time.

6. Rewrite a section of the book as a play and present it for your classmates. A good possibility might be the Sunday meeting in which Snowball and Napoleon disagree. It will be necessary to add dialogue and stage directions, both of which must be consistent with the characterizations and the language used in the rest of the book.

7. Choose a scene from the book that would be suitable for a comic strip. The scene should be self-contained; it must make a point in and of itself. Draw the strip with pencil, pen, or felt-tipped markers. You might also try your hand at placing the characters in entirely new situations.

SELECTED TEACHING RESOURCES

Media Aids

Cassettes

Animal Farm. Penguin Highbridge Audio.

Cassettes (3)

Animal Farm. 3.2 hrs. Recorded Books.

Video

Animal Farm. 73 min., animated, color. Clearvue/eav, Perma-Bound, and Sundance, 1955.

Printed Materials

Articles

Gulbin, Suzanne. "Parallels and Contrasts in *Lord of the Flies* and *Animal Farm.*" *English Journal* 55 (January 1966): 86–88, 92.

Yorke, Malcolme. "Two Popular Books with One Unpopular Message: Man Is a Beastie." *Use of English* 25 (Summer 1974): 307–311.

Book

Smyer, Richard I. *"Animal Farm": Pastoralism and Politics.* Boston: Twayne Publishers, 1988.

Poster

Animal Farm. 17" x 22", color. Perfection Learning Corporation.

Teaching Aids

Animal Farm. Contemporary Classics series and Portals to Literature series. Perfection Learning Corporation.

Animal Farm. Literature Unit Plans. Teacher's Pet Publications.

Animal Farm. Novel Ideas series and React series. Sundance.

Animal Farm. Novel Unit Guide, Perma-Guide, and Student Packet. Perma-Bound.

Animal Farm. Novel/Drama Curriculum Units. The Center for Learning.

Animal Farm. Novel-Ties. Learning Links.

Tests

Animal Farm. Essay, objective, and alternative assessment versions. Perfection Learning Corporation.

The House on Mango Street

Sandra Cisneros

New York: Knopf, 1994
Available in paperback from Vintage.

SUMMARY

Esperanza is a young Latino girl growing up in a poor part of Chicago. At the book's beginning, she and her family have just moved into a house on Mango Street. It is the newest of many houses over the years and an improvement, but for Esperanza the house is inadequate. "Still, we take what we can get and make the most of it." In Esperanza's world, this includes friends, relatives, eccentric neighbors, boys and men—and especially the mysteries, joys, and pain of growing from a girl into a woman.

APPRAISAL

The House on Mango Street, which won the 1985 Before Columbus American Book Award, is a classic coming-of-age novel written in a style that is simple, authentic, and poetic. The book is very brief—forty-four chapters, vignettes that are often less than a full page in length. It is an excellent choice for ninth- and tenth-grade classes. *The House on Mango Street* speaks especially to the need that adolescent girls—Hispanic girls in particular—have for a sense of authenticity and self-worth. The book could be paired with an initiation novel for boys like *A Day No Pigs Would Die* by Robert Newton Peck or, perhaps more appropriately, *Jesse* by Gary Soto.

THEMES

coming of age, identity (womanhood), belonging, home, family

LITERARY CONCEPTS

voice and narration, figurative language (especially metaphor and simile), characterization, setting and mood, imagery, synesthesia, irony, symbol

RELATED READING

There are countless coming-of-age novels a teacher could recommend. Among the best, especially for girls, are *How the Garcia Girls Lost Their Accents* by Julia Alvarez, *Annie John* by Jamaica Kincaid, *The Member of the Wedding* by Carson McCullers, and *Summer of My German Soldier* by Bette Green. Many girls would also like *Where Angels Glide at Dawn: New Stories from Latin America* by Lori M. Carlson and *Woman Hollering Creek and Other Stories*, also by Cisneros. Boys might prefer *Jesse* and *Baseball in April: And Other Stories*, both by Gary Soto.

READING PROBLEMS AND OPPORTUNITIES

One of the novel's great strengths is its simplicity. Told in the first person by a young adolescent girl, the book has very few words that will be unfamiliar to readers. Among them, perhaps, are (page numbers are in parentheses):

rosettes (7),	*canteen* (51, 54),	*goblet* (77),
cumulus (42),	*anemic* (52),	*babushka* (83),
nimbus (43),	*authority* (59),	*braille* (86), and
salamander (47, 89),	*voodoo* (77),	*hysterical* (97).

Aside from these, a teacher may wish to familiarize students, as necessary, with a few words of Hispanic origin, like

marimbas (23),	*merengue* (60),	*mamacita* (95),
tortillas (37),	*tembleque* (60),	*cuándo* (97), and
frijoles (45),	*abuelito* (68),	*comadres* (112, 126).
tamales (46, 56),	*los espíritus* (78),	
chanclas (55),	*brazer* (81),	

INITIATING ACTIVITIES

1. Have the class brainstorm words and phrases they associate with, first, the word *house* and, second, the word *home*. Write the related words on the blackboard and have the students put them on one or two pages of a notebook or journal. After the novel has been read and discussed, let the students add words or phrases that the book has generated since the earlier activity.

2. Cut words, phrases, and perhaps even pictures from old newspapers and magazines provided by your teacher or parents. Using the clippings, create a poem called "Growing Up." Make the poem an expression of what concerns you the most about becoming an adult. Do not sign the poem, but mount it, and be prepared to turn it in. (*Note:* On the day the poems are due, assign a student to collect and shuffle them so that anonymity is preserved. After you have looked them over, make transparencies of a few to show and discuss before you begin reading the novel.)

DISCUSSION QUESTIONS

1. The House on Mango Street: What do we learn about the family in this first chapter? What do they value? What does the narrator value? What qualities of the speaker do we sense early on?

2. Hairs: What is the speaker trying to convey in this chapter? Expressing her views through the speaker, how does the *author* convey these impressions?

3. Boys & Girls: How does the speaker, Esperanza, view her siblings? She briefly defines a best friend as someone "I can tell my secrets to . . . who will understand my jokes without my having to explain them." How do you define "best friend"? What does the speaker mean by the last sentence in the chapter?

4. My Name: How does Esperanza feel about her name? How does she feel about her great-grandmother? What is there to like about *Esperanza* as a name? Do you think names can be harmful? Helpful? Explain. Why do you think Esperanza would like to change her name? And why to *Zeze the X?* How do you feel about your name?

5. Cathy Queen of Cats: Who is Cathy? What is she like? Is she about the same age as Esperanza? Younger? Older? How does she seem to feel about herself? If she were to remain in the neighborhood, would she likely become the kind of best friend that Esperanza wants? Why or why not?

6. Our Good Day: Why does Esperanza like Lucy and Rachel? How would you describe them? Why did Esperanza know that Cathy would be gone? Why is it a "good day"?

7. Laughter: How is the comparison between the two houses similar to the comparison Esperanza sees between herself and her sister? Does she like the fact that she and Nenny are so alike—or not?

8. Gil's Furniture Bought & Sold: What is the effect of beginning this chapter with "There is a junk store" (as compared with, say, "On Packard Avenue an old man named Gil ran a junk store")? What is the effect of an expression like "Me. I never said nothing"? Why does Esperanza feel she must pretend not to like the music box? Why does she think Nenny is stupider? Is Nenny stupid—or ignorant? What is the difference? What do we learn about Gil at the end of the chapter?

9. Meme Ortiz: This chapter has numerous details—the boy with two names who breaks both arms, the clumsy sheepdog (also with two names), the ramshackle house, the balls in the gutters. What do they suggest about Meme and about the neighborhood?

10. Louie, His Cousin & His Other Cousin: Again, the details in this chapter are revealing. What do we learn about Marin? About the cousin with the Cadillac? Why does Esperanza call the incident with Louie's cousin "important"?

11. Marin: Marin has dreams. Are they realistic or unrealistic? Explain. Why does Esperanza like her? What does Marin know? What does she not know? Does Esperanza know anything that Marin does not? Explain. At this stage in the book, why is Marin important?

12. Those Who Don't: What does the title of this chapter refer to? What does the last sentence mean?

13. There Was an Old Woman She Had So Many Children She Didn't Know What to Do: If you had to change the long title of this chapter to a single word that expresses the gist of it, what would the word be?

14. Alicia Who Sees Mice: This chapter tells us about Alicia—her hopes and fears—but what does it also tell us about her father? Are the mice just mice—or are they possibly meant to represent something else?

15. Darius & the Clouds: Why do you think Esperanza considers Darius's remark about the cloud to be wise? How did he make God "simple"? Why might it be important to make God simple? Why do you think the author includes this incident right after having Esperanza talk about the beauty of the sky and the absence of beauty? What might the observation by Darius suggest about people in general?

16. And Some More: In this chapter, what different kinds of wordplay do the girls engage in? How would you describe the tone of the play during the chapter? Does it remain light and teasing throughout, or does it ever become serious? Even though the play never becomes ugly, it does turn slightly upon a single word. What is that word and how is it perhaps playfully misunderstood? What does this chapter say about friends?

17. The Family of Little Feet: What does Esperanza mean when she says, "It is scary to look down at your foot that is no longer yours and see attached a long long leg"? Why is this both a wonderful chapter and a scary chapter? Do the girls see the events as such? Explain.

18. A Rice Sandwich: Explain the different points of view expressed for allowing or not allowing Esperanza to eat in the canteen. Does the chapter show her to be still more like a child or like a young adult?

19. Chanclas: How is this a chapter about baptism? How would you describe Esperanza's feelings at the end of the evening?

20. Hips: What does the girls' conversation suggest that they know about hips? What does Esperanza mean when she says that Nenny is "in a world we don't belong to anymore"? How does Esperanza feel about no longer belonging to that world?

21. The First Job: At this point in the novel, in what ways have we seen Esperanza beginning to grow up? What other signs of this change does this chapter reveal? In what ways is the change exciting? What else is it?

22. Papa Who Wakes Up Tired in the Dark: Throughout the book, in what ways have we seen Esperanza's parents sacrificing for her and her siblings?

23. Born Bad: Who is this chapter more about—Aunt Lupe or Esperanza? Explain. What do phrases like "I was born on an evil day" and "I don't know who decides who deserves to go bad" suggest about Esperanza? What does her poem tell us about her? Do you believe that Esperanza is bad? Why or why not? At the end of the chapter, what are the dreams they began to dream?

24. Elenita, Cards, Palm, Water/Geraldo No Last Name/Edna's Ruthie: Does Esperanza believe in Elenita's ability to tell fortunes? Why does Esperanza want to believe? Why was Geraldo important to Marin? If you lived on Mango Street, would you like Ruthie? Why or why not? What seems to be her problem?

25. The Earl of Tennessee: The last several chapters have described people that Esperanza knows or knows about in her community. Do these people (or most of them) have anything in common? Is there anything about Mango Street that might attract such people?

26. Sire: How would you describe Esperanza's feelings about Sire? In what way are both she and Lois (especially Lois) typical of young people at this age? To Esperanza, why is everything "holding its breath inside me?"

27. Four Skinny Trees: Obviously Esperanza compares herself with the trees. In what ways are they alike? What do the trees want her to keep? What do the trees teach? What might be the meaning of the last sentence?

28. No Speak English: Why does Rachel say *Mamacita*'s name should be *Mamasota*? What do you think was Cisneros's purpose for including this chapter?

29. Rafaela Who Drinks Coconut & Papaya Juice on Tuesdays: What does this chapter say about women and men like Rafaela and her husband? Why is Rafaela "getting old from leaning out the window so much"? What do you think Esperanza learns from watching her?

30. Sally: Why does Sally's father believe that being beautiful is trouble? What does Sally want? Does she want "to love" or "to be loved"—or both (or something else)? What does Esperanza want? Who is this chapter about?

31. Minerva Writes Poems/Bums in the Attic: Why do women like Miranda who are abused keep letting their husbands or boyfriends return? Why is an older child like Esperanza more likely to be ashamed of her surroundings than a younger child like Nenny?

32. Beautiful and Cruel: How does Esperanza see herself? What does she mean by growing up tame? In what way does she think men have an advantage? Do you agree with her? Why or why not?

33. A Smart Cookie: Do you think Esperanza's mother really could have been "somebody," or is she dreaming? How does shame keep a person down? Why do you think the author includes this chapter at this time?

34. What Sally Said: Is Sally's father—"whose eyes were little from crying" and who "broke into his hands"—deserving of sympathy? Why or why not?

35. The Monkey Garden: How does Esperanza describe the monkey garden? What might it represent for her—and for us as readers? For her, is the garden promising? Threatening? How does Sally's game differ from the game that Esperanza plays in the garden? Why does her behavior make Esperanza want to throw a stick? Why does Sally's mother seem indifferent? How would you describe Esperanza's feelings at the end of the chapter?

36. Red Clowns: In what way does Esperanza believe that Sally lied? How are Sally and Esperanza different? What might the red clowns symbolize?

37. Linoleum Roses: Why doesn't Sally's husband let her talk on the telephone or look out the window? Why do you think Cisneros made him a marshmallow salesman?

38. The Three Sisters: What kind of mood is set in the first two paragraphs of the chapter? Who are the sisters? Why do they come to the house? Does Esperanza like them? How does she feel about the remarks of the one with marble hands? What do you think Esperanza's "selfish wish" was?

39. Alicia & I Talking on Edna's Steps/A House of My Own/Mango Says Goodbye Sometimes: As the book comes to a close, what is the nature of Esperanza's feelings, especially toward her house? Why does she want to leave? Why does she think she will come back? Why does she describe herself as "a girl who didn't want to belong"? How has she changed since the beginning of the book a year ago? Why are books and paper so important to her? How do you think she will help "the ones who cannot out."

WRITING ACTIVITIES

1. In the second chapter ("Hairs"), Esperanza describes the uniqueness of each member of her family in terms of his or her hair. For your own family, however small or large, choose a feature (face, hands, eyes, mouth, etc.). Write a sentence or two about this feature that will distinguish each person from the other.

2. Early in the book Esperanza says that "the boys and the girls live in separate worlds." Do you agree with this comment about adolescents? Write an essay in which you support or refute the statement.

3. Esperanza is not exactly pleased with her name. Write an acrostic poem that uses her name—consisting of nine lines, each beginning with a successive letter in *Esperanza* written vertically down the page—and that conveys in some way her qualities. Or, write an acrostic poem using the letters of your name.

4. In the chapter about Louie and his cousins, the author describes active movement in terms of colors: "Then he took off flooring the car into a yellow blur" and "the cop car's siren spun a dizzy blue." Write five or ten sentences in which you compare different kinds of movement to colors (avoid the words *blur* and *dizzy*). Another example: "The spinning silver bike wheels looked like a dime."

5. In the chapter on clouds ("And Some More"), the girls exchange an assortment of semiserious insults: "foot fleas," "chicken lips," "cockroach jelly," etc. Make a list of insults you and your friends might exchange if you were teasing each other (nothing obscene, please).

6. In the chapter about "Edna's Ruthie," Ruthie is described as seeing "lovely things everywhere"—the moon that looks like a balloon, a cloud like "a sphinx winking," books. Write a list poem entitled "Lovely Things Everywhere" in which you make a list of images you consider beautiful. Try to be very specific—for example, "yellow daffodils decorating green lawns" instead of "pretty flowers."

7. Sandra Cisneros often uses striking comparisons. For example, on p. 88, she describes Earl's dogs that "leap and somersault like an apostrophe and comma." Try writing similar comparisons that refer to other punctuation marks, such as exclamation points, question marks, colons, semicolons, ellipses, parentheses, quotation marks, and slashes. You might even write a poem about one of these marks.

8. In the chapter entitled "Sire," Esperanza imagines a kiss. Read the poem "First Kiss" by Jonathan Holden (in Paul Janeczko's collection of poems *Going Over to Your Place*). Then write a paragraph in which you compare the experiences as described in the two works.

9. Knowing what we do about Minerva ("Minerva Writes Poems"), write a short poem that she might write. You might try a cinquain that begins with the word *Minerva* and ends with the word *misery*. Or try a diamante that begins with *Minerva* and ends with *Esperanza* (see Appendix A).

10. In the chapter called "The Monkey Garden," Esperanza describes the garden with vivid images and figurative language, especially in the third and fourth paragraphs. Write a similar descriptive paragraph or two about an outdoor scene you're familiar with. Try to emulate Cisneros's use of rich, colorful images that appeal to all of the senses.

11. Thomas Wolfe wrote a well-known novel called *You Can't Go Home Again*, in which he comments on the difficulties of reconnecting as an adult with the community one grew up in and left. Write a paragraph in which you express why you agree or disagree with Wolfe's view. Refer to Esperanza and her plans.

OTHER ACTIVITIES

1. Most of us have lived in more than one house or apartment during our lives. Using found objects, print from magazines and newspapers, and especially family photographs, create a collage or perhaps a mobile called *Home* that expresses your feelings about the various places you have lived. If you've lived in only one place, make a collage about it.

2. In the fourth chapter ("My Name"), Esperanza comments on the attitudes she thinks Chinese and Mexicans have toward women: They "don't like their women strong." Using references in the library on women (possibly including the Internet), conduct some research on how different cultures and historical periods have viewed the role of women. Report what you discover to the class.

3. In the chapter entitled "And Some More," Esperanza and the other girls have fun describing and naming different kinds of clouds. Spend a week or more taking particular note of clouds and how they differ. Keep a log in which you record the days, times of day, and conditions when you see them. Try to spot not only the two types mentioned by Esperanza, but others as well. A book like *Clouds and Storms* (National Audubon Society Pocket Guides) will be useful.

4. Marin is described as loving to dance—"cumbias and salsas and rancheras even." Using encyclopedias or other reference books in the library,

conduct research on these and other Hispanic dances. Try to find diagrams of the steps. Write a report on several of these dances and demonstrate some of them for your classmates.

5. During jump rope, Esperanza tells Nenny, "You gotta use your own song. Make it up, you know?" Taking her advice, create your own jump-rope jingle. Try for at least eight lines that rhyme and have a strong beat. Demonstrate it for the class.

6. Pretend that it is five or ten years later and Esperanza, her mother, Marin, Sire, and Sally and her husband are all appearing on an *Oprah* program with the theme "Old and New Worlds for Hispanic Women." Assign different students to role-play the characters and Oprah, whose responsibility will be to ask questions and moderate. Among the questions: How did you feel about the roles that were considered for Hispanic women when you were growing up? How do you feel now? What has changed? What do Hispanic women and other women want? Which is more difficult—being Hispanic (or any other minority) in a basically Anglo culture, or being a woman in a basically male culture?

7. *The House on Mango Street* is, in part, an autobiographical novel. With this as an assumption, find out more about Sandra Cisneros. What kind of life has she led? What kind of writer is she? Has her life affirmed the values and attitudes that Esperanza reveals throughout the novel, especially toward the end? Present a brief talk about her to the class. Reference works like *Chicano Writers, Second Series* in the Dictionary of Literary Biography series, Volume 122, or *Contemporary Literary Criticism*, Volume 69, may be helpful.

SELECTED TEACHING RESOURCES

Media Aids

Cassette

The House on Mango Street; Woman Hollering Creek. Random House Audio, 1992.

Printed Materials

Article

Cisneros, Sandra. "Do You Know Me? I Wrote *The House on Mango Street*." *Americas Review* 15 (Spring 1987): 77–79.

Criticism

"Sandra Cisneros." In *Contemporary Literary Criticism*, Volume 69, edited by Roger Matuz, 143–156. Detroit: Gale Research Inc., 1992.

Teaching Aids

The House on Mango Street. Novel Ideas Plus. Sundance.
The House on Mango Street. Novel Unit Guide and Perma-Guide. Perma-Bound.

Of Mice and Men

John Steinbeck

New York: Triangle Books, 1937
Available in paperback from Penguin.

SUMMARY

George Milton and Lennie Small are two itinerant farm laborers who find work on a ranch in California during the Great Depression. The two are inseparable—George, the leader, small and observant; Lennie, huge and childlike. Their chances of lasting on a job—and of fulfilling their long-held dream of saving enough money to buy a small farm—are jeopardized by Lennie's unpredictable behavior. During a fight provoked by the boss's belligerent son, Curley, Lennie crushes Curley's hand, an event that foreshadows his later panicky killing of Curley's wife in a barn. This unintentional and tragic misdeed requires George to shoot Lennie himself, an act he finds reprehensible but inevitable.

APPRAISAL

Of Mice and Men became an immediate best-seller after its publication in 1937 and has since become an American classic. With its heavy reliance upon dialogue and its spare use of description, the work was adapted by the author as a play in the same year. The book is slim, more of a novella. Its enduring popularity can be traced to the simplicity of its style, the strength of its characterization, and the poignancy of its themes. It is frequently taught in high schools, mostly in grades nine and ten. Despite its strengths, the book may be offensive to some readers because of the use of profanity and the word *nigger* by some of the characters in reference to Crooks. Teachers are encouraged to help students view this usage in the context of the novel as a whole—as language spoken by characters who are uneducated and prejudiced and who fail to see Crooks fully as a vulnerable human being worthy of compassion.

THEMES

the American dream, loneliness, commitment, friendship

LITERARY CONCEPTS

plot, foreshadowing, characterization, setting, irony, dramatic structure, symbol, myth, style

RELATED READING

Much of Steinbeck's other fiction deals with the life of working people in central California during the Great Depression, including his classic *The Grapes of Wrath* and several stories. Other novels about the depression that would reinforce *Of Mice and Men* include *The Wizard's Tide* by Frederick Buechner, *Tracks* by Clayton Bess, and *Dance a Little Longer* by Jane Roberts Wood. Nonfiction accounts include *Children of the Dust Bowl: The True Story of the School at Weedpatch Camp* by Jerry Stanley and *Hard Times: An Oral History of the Great Depression* by Studs Terkel. Another relevant book by Terkel is *American Dreams, Lost and Found*, especially the section on Jessie de la Cruz (pp. 151–161).

READING PROBLEMS AND OPPORTUNITIES

Despite its heavy use of simple dialogue, *Of Mice and Men* is written in third-person omniscient and includes a fair number of words that high school students may be unfamiliar with. Many of the following could be used for vocabulary study (chapter numbers are in parentheses):

debris (1),
mottled (1),
recumbent (1),
morosely (1, 2),
resignedly (1),
lumbered (1),
brusquely (1, 2),
pantomime (1),
contemplated (1),
imperiously (1),
anguished (1),
craftily (1),
scoff (2),
scourges (2),
skeptically (2),
mollified (2),

calculating (2),
pugnacious (2),
gingerly (2),
ominously (2),
derogatory (2),
plaintively (2),
contorted (2, 5),
apprehensive, apprehension (2, 4),
gravity (2),
complacently (2, 5),
derision (3),
subsided (3),
reprehensible (3),
reverently (3),
bemused (3),

wryly (3),
aloof (4),
fawning (4),
disarming (4),
sullenly (4, 5),
contemptuously (4),
indignation (4),
averted (4),
appraised (4),
crestfallen (4),
consoled (5),
earnestly (5),
writhed (5),
sniveled (5),
belligerently (5), and
dutifully (5).

Besides these words, several examples of farm terminology might need to be explained:

bindle—a blanket roll in which a migrant worker often keeps his belongings

jerkline skinner—a worker who drives draft animals like mules and horses; a teamster (note: a *jerkline* is the line used in place of reins to guide the lead horse in a team)

bucker—a ranch or farm laborer who works in the fields, often lifting grain bags *swamper*—a handyman on a ranch whose work may include keeping the bunkhouse clean

stable buck—a ranch worker responsible for the upkeep of the stable and horses

INITIATING ACTIVITIES

1. Discuss the American dream: What do people mean when they talk about it? In what ways has America offered people dreams? Have these opportunities been the same for everyone? Even today, who has the greatest chance of realizing the American dream? Should governments in any way be responsible for helping citizens fulfill their dreams? What is your American dream?

2. Discuss friendship. Think of your best friend. To what extent are you responsible for this person? Would you lend this friend money? Would you give him or her money? Would you sacrifice for your friend in other ways? In what ways do we show that we care for our friends? Can we always be honest with our friends? Does friendship sometimes mean saying "no"? In general, what kinds of commitments does a friendship imply?

DISCUSSION QUESTIONS

1. Chapter 1: What do you first notice about the two men? What are some differences between them? In particular, what is George like? At times he is profane, and he seems impatient and exasperated with Lennie. What are some of his other qualities? Does he care about Lennie? Do you think Lennie in any way serves an important role in George's life? Explain. Does Lennie show any signs of intelligence? What seems to be his main mental shortcoming? Is a person who is mentally deficient as guilty of a crime as one who is able to make fine distinctions between right and wrong? Toward the end of the chapter, why does George tell Lennie the story about the rabbits? What purpose does the story serve for each of the two men? For the reader? Do you think both men believe in the story equally? Comment on Steinbeck's use of setting in this first chapter. Is the setting threatening? Peaceful? Indifferent? Do events in the chapter foreshadow a happy ending or one of disappointment? Explain.

2. Chapter 2: What does the bunkhouse tell you about the men? What do you think is in the western magazines that the men "scoff at and secretly believe"? What do the old man's comments about the blacksmith suggest about the workers? What are the men apparently like? What does the old man's story about the fight between Crooks and Smitty tell us about the men in general? What is your reaction to "the boss"? To Curley? What do you think *handy* means? Later, after Curley's wife leaves, why does George become so angry with Lennie? Do you think his drowning of the puppies is justified? Why or why not? By the end of the chapter, what areas of possible conflict have been established? What questions have been posed for the reader?

3. Chapter 3: What else do we learn about George in his conversation with Slim? Do you think George needs Lennie as much as Lennie needs George? Explain. Do you agree with Slim about "real smart" guys hardly ever being nice? What is the purpose of including the scene with Carlson, Candy, and the old dog? Do you think the situation could have been handled differently? Also, why does Steinbeck include the matter about the letter in the magazine? Is there any significance to the fact that George is so often seen playing solitaire? As we see it here, does Lennie believe the story about living "offa the fatta the lan'"? Does George? What is there about the story that makes it seem unrealistic? Is it in any way realistic? Do you think it is fair for George to accept Candy's offer so quickly? Why or why not? How does the incident with Curley and Lennie affect the story? Are George and Lennie's prospects further jeopardized by it?

4. Chapter 4: From what we know so far, how is Crooks treated? His bunk in the harness room is described in considerable detail. On the basis of these details, what is he like? How important is he to the story? Why is he so taken with the fact that George talks but Lennie doesn't understand? Why does he tease Lennie about George's possibly not returning? Do you think he is justified in being so bitter? Why do you think Steinbeck chose to depict Crooks as an African American? What does Candy's comment about Crooks's room say about people? What does Crooks's reaction to Candy's story say about Crooks? Why does he change his mind at the end of the chapter? What are the implications of the horses' movements in the last few pages of the chapter? What does Crooks mean when he says, "A colored man got to have some rights even if he don't like 'em"? At the end of the chapter, how do you feel about Curley's wife? Is she in any way a sympathetic character? Why is it that we have not been told her name? What event has been clearly foreshadowed in this chapter? At this point in the book, with whom do we sympathize? With whom do we not sympathize?

5. Chapter 5: What does Lennie's reaction to the dead puppy show about his nature? What does his unintentional killing of small animals suggest about his future? What overall theme does this behavior possibly suggest—about the weak and defenseless? When Curley's wife talks to Lennie, what do we realize about her? Why is her particular dream so insubstantial? Do you think that Steinbeck has prepared the reader adequately for Lennie's killing of Curley's wife? Why does Steinbeck include the short paragraph that begins, "As happens sometimes, a moment settled and hovered . . ."? What does George mean when he says, "I should have knew"? Why does George take Carlson's gun? What do the different reactions of Curley and Candy to the killing affirm about them?

6. Chapter 6: Why does Lennie visualize his Aunt Clara and then the giant rabbit? Why do you think Steinbeck includes this passage? What does George mean right before firing when he says, "Sure, right now. I gotta. We gotta"? Who is "we"? Why does George lie about Lennie and the gun? Do you agree with Slim that George had no choice? Why was letting Curley kill Lennie unthinkable? Was this the final measure of responsibility that George felt for Lennie—or was George thinking only of himself? Looking back at the novel as a whole, what do you think Steinbeck was interested

mostly in conveying about the human condition? Do you think he was successful? Explain. On the basis of the book, do you think Steinbeck is an optimist or a pessimist? Explain.

WRITING ACTIVITIES

1. At the time *Of Mice and Men* was written, comparatively few provisions were made for people of limited mental capacity like Lennie. Conduct some research on how your local community (city, county, or state) provides for these people today. You may want to interview the teacher of EMH and TMH students in your school as well as directors and workers in the appropriate local social agencies. Write up your findings in a three- to five-page report.

2. George and Lennie are migrant workers. Do migrant workers still make up a large portion of the agricultural workforce in this country? Use your library to investigate the subject. Find out the parts of the country where migrant labor is still important. What states? What ethnic groups? Have their conditions improved since the 1930s? Write your findings in a two- or three-page report that uses at least three sources.

3. In chapter 3, the young man named Whit reads a letter sent by a former worker named Bill Tenner to a pulp magazine specializing in the kinds of western stories enjoyed by ranch workers, including one involving "the Dark Rider." Try your hand at writing one of these cowboy tales that feature fast-moving plots with strong characters caught up in heroic adventures.

4. George's description of the dream place in chapter 3 is extremely romantic—with fruit trees, chickens and pigs, a windmill, salmon running up a nearby river, a "little fat iron stove," a dog and a couple of cats. Think of what your dream place would look like and write a one-page description of what it would include.

5. Imagine yourself as the owner of the ranch, but one with a strong social conscience. What might you do to make the lives of the men on the ranch more enjoyable and rewarding? Write a list of measures you might take. Or, write a paper in which you argue for or against the following premise: An owner of a farm or ranch is in no way responsible for making the lives of his or her laborers more pleasant and meaningful.

6. Analyze the degree to which George and Lennie's dream was achievable. Find information on the depression-era costs of land, livestock, food, clothing, equipment, etc., as well as the probable output of a ten-acre farm. Write a two-page paper entitled "George and Lennie's Dream: Well Beyond [or Within] Their Reach."

7. *Of Mice and Men* is a poignant story that has a tragic ending. Still, there are occasional moments of humor in the book. In fact, one critic writing about the play version complained that the audience laughed too often, particularly at Lennie, whom they apparently considered a comic figure. Write a paper on humor in the book and on whether you think it depends too heavily on Lennie as a character.

8. Compose a letter that George might have written to the people who own the land inquiring about its availability. Try to write the letter with sensitivity, gently inquiring about the owners' financial situation and the woman's health. You may need to be creative in reminding them of your (i.e., George's) connection to the couple.

9. Imagine what happens after the book ends. Does George give up completely on the idea of buying the farm as the book suggests? Might he still try to combine resources with Candy and perhaps others? Or was his dream tied up with his commitment to Lennie? Examine the situation realistically and write a two- to three-page epilogue in which you project George's decisions over the next several days and weeks.

OTHER ACTIVITIES

1. Find a collection of the paintings of Thomas Hart Benton, a midwestern artist whose work typically features rural people of the first half of the twentieth century. One excellent source is *Thomas Hart Benton: Drawing from Life* by Henry Adams. Identify two or three paintings that are reminiscent of the novel; explain each one in a paragraph.

2. Using pictures, print, found objects, and the like, create a collage or mobile of your American dream. Or, create one that represents George or Lennie.

3. The great troubadour of the Great Depression and the dust bowl was Woody Guthrie. Find a collection or recording of his best-known songs, perhaps at the public library. Play for the class one or two that you think represent people like George, Slim, Carlson, and the other workers on the ranch.

4. John Steinbeck often conveys a great deal by his descriptions of a character's stance and posture, as in the description of the boss early in chapter 2 and of Curley later in the same chapter. Read these passages and then pantomime the postures for the class. See if they can guess your depictions. Also, think of how you would portray Lennie physically without making a buffoon out of him.

5. Several actual geographic locations are mentioned in the novel, all of them in central California: Soledad, the Salinas River, the Gabilan Mountains, Weed, Sacramento, and Auburn. Locate these in an atlas and draw a map of the book's setting. Or, draw a map of George and Lennie's dream place as it is described in chapter 3.

6. Imagine that Lennie survives the end of the novel and is brought to trial. With several other students, conduct his trial. Besides many of the characters in the book, you will need a judge, a prosecutor, and a defense attorney.

SELECTED TEACHING RESOURCES

Media Aids

Cassettes (2)

Of Mice and Men. Unabridged, narrated by Gary Sinise. Recorded Books.

CD-ROM

Of Mice and Men CD-ROM. Perma-Bound, 1995. This includes the complete text of the novel, a biography, criticism, video interviews, video clips from films of the novel, documentary film footage, historical backgrounds, and period photographs.

Internet

Smith, Jennifer. *Steinbeck Research Center.* Updated January 29, 1997. Available: http://www.sjsu.edu/depts/steinbec/srchome.html (Accessed: March 1, 1997).

This homepage features a Steinbeck chronology, "Steinbeck Country" (a map, color photograph of a typical setting in rural California, details on settings), and a photograph of the author.

Videos

Farmworkers Diary. 10 min., color. University of California Ext. Media Center, 1991. Depicts a day in the life of farmworkers in a labor camp in central California. "In the farmworkers' own words, the video captures their dreams and aspirations as well as their anxieties, their longings for their families, and their fear of becoming unemployable."

Of Mice and Men. 110 min., Gary Sinise and John Malkovich version. Perfection Learning Corporation, 1992.

Printed Materials

Article

McCune, Esther. "*Of Mice and Men* by John Steinbeck." *Connecticut English Journal* 15 (Fall 1983): 64–65. A rationale for teaching the novel.

Book

Workman, Brooke. *Writing Seminars in the Content Areas: In Search of Hemingway, Salinger, and Steinbeck.* Champaign-Urbana, IL: National Council of Teachers of English, 1983. Includes thirteen pages on *Of Mice and Men.*

Criticism

"John Steinbeck: *Of Mice and Men.*" In *Contemporary Literary Criticism*, Volume 75, edited by Thomas Votteler, 334–366. Detroit: Gale Research Inc.,

1993. Includes extensive excerpts from criticism of the novel written between 1937 and 1982.

Poster

Of Mice and Men. 17" x 22", color. Perfection Learning Corporation.

Teaching Aids

Of Mice and Men. Contemporary Classics series and Portals to Learning series. Perfection Learning Corporation.

Of Mice and Men. Literature Unit Plans. Teacher's Pet Publications.

Of Mice and Men. Novel Unit Guide, Perma-Guide, and Student Packet. Perma-Bound.

The Pearl/Of Mice and Men. Novel/Drama Curriculum Units. The Center for Learning.

Of Mice and Men. Novel-Ties. Learning Links.

Of Mice and Men. React series. Sundance.

Tests

Of Mice and Men. Essay and objective versions. Perfection Learning Corporation.

To Kill a Mockingbird

Harper Lee

New York: J. B. Lippincott, 1960
Available in paperback from Warner.

SUMMARY

Six-year-old Scout Finch and her older brother, Jem, live with their father Atticus, a lawyer in Maycomb, Alabama, during the Depression. With Dill, a friend who visits during the summer, the children spend much of their time trying to lure the mysterious Boo Radley out of the house he has not left in several years. Their interest in Boo is replaced, however, by concern for Tom Robinson, a black man their father is defending on charges of raping the daughter of a local white "ne'er-do-well." During and after the trial, they learn from Atticus the importance of conscience and courage in fighting prejudice and from Boo Radley the importance of love in fighting ignorance.

APPRAISAL

To Kill a Mockingbird is one of the two or three most popular American novels among teachers. Its nostalgic remembrance of childhood, its affectionate portrayal of Atticus Finch, and its depiction of a town struggling with conflicting values make the book extremely teachable. The novel won the Pulitzer Prize for 1961 and was subsequently made into a memorable motion picture starring Gregory Peck. It is most often taught in the ninth or tenth grade.

THEMES

the importance of conscience, the importance of seeing and dealing with people as individuals, family, courage, prejudice, growing up

LITERARY CONCEPTS

plot, setting, tone, characterization, imagery, theme, figurative language

RELATED READING

Students who want to read more about the efforts of black and whites to live together in racial harmony might consider a number of other books, including *Cry, the Beloved Country* by Alan Paton (which is set in South Africa), *Words by Heart* by Ouida Sebestyen, the young adult novels of Mildred Taylor, and the adult novels of Ernest J. Gaines, especially *A Lesson Before Dying.* John Grisham's *A Time To Kill* could also be recommended.

READING PROBLEMS AND OPPORTUNITIES

Like many first-person accounts, *To Kill a Mockingbird* is told by a narrator recalling a childhood. The language of the novel is rich, precise, and often sophisticated. It includes many words that most high school students will profit from learning and reviewing. Almost all of the words listed here occur more than once in the book, sometimes in other forms (chapter numbers are in parentheses):

detached (1, 11, 18, 20),
eccentric (1, 16, 27),
repertoire (1, 28),
stealthy (1, 18),
meditative (1, 2, 7),
condescend (2, 3),
apprehensive (2, 24, 27, 31),
indigenous (2, 17),
revelation (1, 2),
entailment (2, 15),
speculation (3, 13, 17),
contemptuous (3, 12),
contentious (3, 12),
sever (3, 18),
quell (4, 8, 17),
benign (5, 17),

tacit (5, 21),
placidly (5, 15),
perpetrate (8, 20),
compensation (9, 12),
innate (9, 12),
provocation (9),
tentative (9, 14),
impaired (9, 19),
remorse (9, 12, 26),
vehement (10, 23),
articulate (10, 18),
indignant (12, 21, 23),
dispel (12, 13, 16),
affirmative (13, 17),
induce (13, 19),
discreet (13, 15, 20),
reverent (14, 23),

acquiescence (15, 31),
impassive (15, 22),
amiable (16, 17, 31),
scrutiny (17, 18),
corroborating (17, 20),
ambidextrous (17),
arid (18, 20),
volition (19),
misdemeanor (19),
impudent (19),
temerity (20),
cynical (20, 22),
acquit (21, 23),
credibility (23),
furtive (23, 28),
stolid (23, 30), and
radical (27).

The novel also provides an opportunity for teaching important concepts in language, particularly dialect. Calpurnia's remarks in chapter 12 on why she talks one way at her church and another at the Finch's express a fundamental linguistic principle that all students should learn, namely, that dialects are relative and that there are no absolutes.

INITIATING ACTIVITIES

1. Most people have had experiences during their childhood when they almost enjoyed being afraid of something, something that appeared mysterious and dangerous, perhaps a cemetery or an abandoned house or even a person in the community who seemed strange. Write a two- to three-page paper about such a fear that you had when you were younger.

2. Read the poem "Incident" by Countee Cullen or the short story "After You, My Dear Alphonse" by Shirley Jackson. With one or the other (or both) as a starting point, discuss the nature of prejudice with your teacher and the rest

of the class. Discuss, especially, how prejudice gets started, how it is instilled in children, how it is reinforced, how it can best be fought, and so on.

DISCUSSION QUESTIONS

PART 1

1. Chapter 1: Based on the first several pages, what is the tone of the book, the attitude of the speaker to her subject, especially to Maycomb and its people? How does she seem to feel about her life there? What first intrigues the reader and thus sets the plot in motion? Why are the children so interested in the Radleys?

2. Chapter 2: Why is Miss Caroline upset with Scout's having already learned to read and write? What kind of person is Scout? Is she timid or assertive? Tough or tender-minded? Dependent or self-reliant? Is she perceptive? What is her attitude toward people like the Cunninghams?

3. Chapter 3: Why does Calpurnia get upset with Scout? What is Calpurnia like? Is she unreasonable with Scout? What kinds of mistakes does Miss Caroline make on her first day of teaching? What kind of person is Atticus? Why does he talk to Walter Cunningham about farming? How does he distinguish the Cunninghams from the Ewells? In what ways does Atticus seem wise? In what ways is the family different from most?

4. Chapter 4: Why is Scout so bored with school? The chewing gum and the Indian-head pennies—what might be the source of these? Why do Jem, Dill, and Scout spend so much time playing "Boo Radley"? Why does Atticus discourage it?

5. Chapter 5: Why does Scout consider Miss Maudie "the best lady I know"? Why does Miss Maudie criticize foot-washers? Why are the boys so interested in luring Boo Radley out of the house? Why do you think Dill tells so many lies, at least according to Scout? How does Atticus trick Jem into conceding that they were playing a game about the Radleys?

6. Chapter 6: What does Atticus mean when he says, "they all go through it, Miss Rachel"? What does Scout mean in saying, "It was then, I suppose, that Jem and I first began to part company"?

7. Chapter 7: Why does Jem cry after Atticus tells him that the tree on the corner of the Radley lot isn't dying?

8. Chapter 8: Why does Jem tell Atticus everything? On the basis of the secretive activities attributed to him, what kind of person do you think Boo Radley is? Why do you think he has done these things?

9. Chapter 9: How does Atticus explain to Scout his decision to defend Tom Robinson? What does he mean by saying he could not ask her and Jem to mind him if he did not take the case? How is Uncle Jack different from Atticus? Do you think Atticus is too lenient in dealing with his children? Why or why not? What seems to be his philosophy of child-rearing? Is it a good one? Why or why not? What does Atticus mean by the phrase "Maycomb's usual disease"?

10. Chapters 10 and 11: What does the incident with the mad dog help Jem and Scout learn about their father? Why is it important to them? Why is it unimportant to him? Why does Scout accompany Jem to Mrs. Dubose's? In what way is Mrs. Dubose an example of courage? In what ways is Atticus?

PART 2

11. Chapter 12: In what ways is the experience at Calpurnia's church enlightening for Jem and Scout? Also, what do they learn during their walk home with Calpurnia? Why do they want to visit her? In what ways is she important to them?

12. Chapter 13: Why does Aunt Alexandra come to visit? What kinds of things would she include under "What Is Best for the Family"? Why does Atticus come to talk to Jem and Scout before bedtime? Why does he change his mind about what he wants them to do? Why does Scout say, "It takes a woman to do that kind of work"? Do you agree? Why or why not?

13. Chapter 14: According to Scout, how is Jem changing? How is his relationship with Scout different? In what ways is it still the same? Why has Dill run away from home? What does he find at the Finch's that he does not have at home? Why does he want a baby?

14. Chapter 15: Why does Jem yell to Atticus that the telephone is ringing? What seems to be the reason for the gathering of men outside the Finch house and next morning at church? For the gathering of men in front of the jail? How do the two groups differ? Why does Scout interrupt the confrontation? Why does Jem refuse to leave? What causes Mr. Cunningham to break up the gathering? Is this what Scout intended? Do you think Atticus is proud of his children? Why or why not? What is Atticus's purpose in asking people, "Do you really think so?"

15. Chapter 16: What seems to be the attitude of the townspeople to Atticus Finch? Why hadn't he told Jem and Scout that the court had appointed him to defend Tom Robinson and that, therefore, he had to? What impression do you have of Judge Taylor? Of Mr. Underwood?

16. Chapter 17: Describe the Ewells. Why do so many wretched, unfortunate people like the Ewells try so hard to find others to condemn? Why do you think Atticus asks the sheriff and Mr. Ewell why they had not called a doctor for Mayella?

17. Chapter 18: Why does Mayella feel Atticus is mocking her? Why does he try to construct for the jury a picture of the Ewell's way of life? Why does he ask her if she has any friends? Why does Atticus's tone toward Mayella change? Do you think he becomes too harsh? Why does he say, "He blacked your left eye with his right fist?," when he knows that it was her right eye? How does Atticus feel toward Mayella?

18. Chapter 19: Why is Atticus's job of defending Tom Robinson so difficult and complex, even though there are some, like Mr. Deas, who seem sympathetic? Why does there seem to be disapproval of Tom's statement that he felt sorry for Mayella?

19. Chapter 20: Why does Mr. Raymond say about Dill, "Things haven't caught up with that one's instinct yet. Let him get a little older and he won't get sick and cry"? Why does Atticus loosen his clothing before making his final statement? Do you feel the statement is effective? Why or why not?

20. Chapter 21: Why does the waiting courtroom remind Scout of the day when her father shot the mad dog? Why does she feel she was "watching all the time knowing that the gun was empty"? Were you surprised at the verdict? Why or why not? Does the author provide any hints in the chapter as to what the verdict will be? If so, where?

21. Chapter 22: Aunt Alexandra accuses Atticus of being bitter over the verdict. Is he? Do you think he has a right to be? Why or why not? What is there about him that suggests he isn't bitter? Why does Calpurnia ask, of the blacks who sent Atticus food, "They—they aren't over steppin' themselves, are they?" Miss Maudie believes that the trial represents one small step—toward what? Do you agree? Or should people like her have done more to help Tom Robinson? Discuss.

22. Chapter 23: What does Atticus mean when he says, "There's something in our world that makes men lose their heads—they couldn't be fair if they tried"? Why is Aunt Alexandra so opposed to Walter Cunningham? How would she define the word *trash?* How would Scout? How do Jem and Scout disagree on the importance of a person's background? Why does Jem feel that Boo Radley chooses to stay inside?

23. Chapter 24: At the missionary circle meeting, what do you think Scout concludes about Mrs. Merriweather? About missionary work among the heathen? About hypocrites? Why does Miss Maudie ask, "His food doesn't stick going down, does it?" Why is Aunt Alexandra grateful? Has Aunt Alexandra changed? If so, how? How is Scout changing? How does she modify her definition of *background?*

24. Chapter 25: How does the death of Tom Robinson bring out the worst in the people of Maycomb?

25. Chapter 26: Why have Jem and Scout lost interest in Boo Radley? In what way is Miss Gates's attitude toward prejudice confusing to Scout?

26. Chapter 27: As fall passes, what is mostly on Scout's mind? Do you think her fears are justified? Why or why not? What might be meant by the last sentence in the chapter?

27. Chapters 28 and 29: After she gets home, why does Scout keep asking if Jem is dead? Why is Atticus still unable to "conceive of a man who'd harm children"? How does Scout suddenly realize that the man who had saved their lives was Boo?

28. Chapter 30: Why does Atticus insist that the incident be brought to court? Why does Heck Tate insist that Mr. Ewell stabbed himself? Who is the sheriff protecting? Why? Why does Scout say to her father, "Well, it'd be sort of like shootin' a mockingbird, wouldn't it?"

29. Chapter 31: Why does Boo want to touch Jem? After Boo enters his house, Scout says, "We had given him nothing, and it made me sad." Is she right? Had Scout and Jem given Boo Radley anything? If so, what? What does she realize as she stands on the Radley porch? At the end when Atticus says, "Most people are [real nice], Scout, when you finally see them," to whom does he refer?

30. What are the most important things that Scout and Jem have learned from their father and from the experience with Boo Radley? How much have Scout and Jem changed? How much has Maycomb changed—if any? Do you think that people like Atticus Finch—people whom the majority (or an important minority) "trust . . . to do right"—can be found in large numbers? Discuss.

WRITING ACTIVITIES

1. Write an account of the death of Mr. Ewell as it might have been written by Mr. Underwood for *The Maycomb Tribune*.

2. Write a letter that Scout might have sent to Dill telling him about the events of Halloween night and especially about the involvement of Boo Radley. The letter should explain how Mr. Ewell was killed and also how Scout feels about Boo now that the experience is over.

3. Childhood is often filled with curiosities, superstitions, and folklore, like Jem's explanation of a Hot Steam (chapter 4). Using your own experiences, interviews with parents or other adults, or even books, write a report on at least ten sayings or superstitions that children enjoy and promote.

4. Dill has a creative mind, as his account of running away from home in chapter 14 reveals. Write his story of a bus ride home to Meridian from Maycomb when he found himself sitting beside a man whose suitcase bore the initials *B. R.*

5. Write an argumentative paper supporting or refuting the following point of view: People like the Ewells who do not work to improve their economic status should not be given welfare.

6. You are Atticus. Write a one- or two-page paper explaining your philosophy of rearing children.

7. Write a comparison-contrast paper on one of the following:

   a. the Cunninghams and the Ewells,

   b. Miss Maudie and Aunt Alexandra, or

   c. Scout at the beginning and the end of the book.

8. With references like the ones to the Roosevelts, the WPA, and scrip stamps, *To Kill a Mockingbird* is indelibly set in the Depression. Find out more about what life was like in America during the 1930s, especially in small towns and rural areas. Write up your findings in a report. Two good sources are *Let Us Now Praise Famous Men* by James Agee and Walker Evans and *Hard Times* by Studs Terkel.

9. The narrator frequently includes anecdotes of pranks that the children played at one time or another—tying Eunice Ann Simpson to a chair and putting her in the furnace room of the church, removing the furniture of Misses Tutti and Frutti Barber from their living room to the cellar, and so on. Write about a childhood prank that you once played or heard about.

OTHER ACTIVITIES

1. Whether by design or not, Scout often seems to describe people in very broad strokes, recalling and perhaps exaggerating certain physical features. Referring to her description of Judge Taylor in chapter 16 or Mr. Ewell in chapter 17, draw a caricature of either of the two men.

2. With three other students, act out the Halloween attack as Heck Tate insists that it be reported. Then act it out as it apparently occurred.

3. Make a "split-screen" collage—one side representing Boo Radley as he is perceived by Scout at the beginning of the book; the other, as he is seen by her at the end.

4. In chapter 12, Scout and Jem notice a cartoon captioned "Maycomb's Finch" in the *Montgomery Advertiser.* According to Jem, it compliments Atticus for his diligence in fulfilling important duties. Draw a cartoon that might have appeared in the newspaper after Tom Robinson's trial.

5. In chapter 23, Atticus comments on how long it takes to change a law. Invite an attorney to class to speak on the extent to which civil rights laws in America have changed in the past thirty-five or forty years and on the nature of those changes.

6. To protest what he felt was the gross injustice of the famous Sacco Vanzetti trial in 1920, the artist Ben Shahn produced several highly critical paintings. Examine some of these in books on Shahn in your library. Then paint your own protest against the trial of Tom Robinson. You may choose to make it realistic or abstract.

SELECTED TEACHING RESOURCES

Media Aids

Cassettes (2)

To Kill a Mockingbird. 120 min., interpretation of the novel. Thomas S. Klise Company.

Cassettes (9)

To Kill a Mockingbird. 13.5 hours, Recorded Books.

Video

To Kill a Mockingbird. 129 min., Gregory Peck version, b & w. Perma-Bound and Perfection Learning Corporation, 1962.

Printed Materials

Article

Bruell, Edwin. "Keen Scalpel on Racial Ills." *English Journal* 53 (December 1964): 658–661.

Books

Bloom, Harold, ed. *Harper Lee's "To Kill a Mockingbird."* Broomall, PA: Chelsea House Publishers, 1996.

Johnson, Claudia Durst. *Understanding "To Kill a Mockingbird."* Westport, CT: Greenwood, 1994.

Teaching Aids

To Kill a Mockingbird. Contemporary Classics series. Perfection Learning Corporation.

To Kill a Mockingbird. Novel Unit Guide, Perma-Guide, and Student Packet. Perma-Bound.

To Kill a Mockingbird. Literature Unit Plans. Teacher's Pet Publications.

To Kill a Mockingbird. Novel/Drama Curriculum Units. The Center for Learning.

To Kill a Mockingbird. Novel-Ties series. Learning Links.

To Kill a Mockingbird. React series. Sundance.

Tests

To Kill a Mockingbird. Essay, objective, and alternative assessment versions. Perfection Learning Corporation.

Romeo and Juliet

William Shakespeare

Play: available in paperback from several publishing companies.

SUMMARY

Romeo and Juliet are the son and daughter of the Montagues and Capulets, respectively—two long-feuding families in Verona. As fate would have it, they fall in love and are secretly married by Friar Laurence, who sees an opportunity to unite the families. Immediately afterward, Romeo is banished from the city for killing the ill-tempered Tybalt, the cousin of Juliet who murdered Romeo's friend Mercutio. Juliet's parents then complicate matters by forcing her to prepare to marry Paris, a young nobleman. To avoid this, she feigns death by drinking a sleep-inducing potion prepared by the Friar and is taken to the Capulet burial vault by her mourning family. In distant Mantua, meanwhile, Romeo—who has failed to receive an explanatory letter from the Friar—hears that Juliet is dead. He rushes back in anguish to Verona, breaks open the vault, and drinks some poison when he sees Juliet lying within. She then awakens to a scene of such sorrow that she stabs herself with Romeo's dagger, thus joining him in death. When members of the two families arrive on the scene, the Prince of Verona reproaches them for the mutual hatred that has brought about these needless deaths. Capulet and Montague vow to end the feud by raising statues in the honor of each other's child.

APPRAISAL

The best-known love story ever written, *Romeo and Juliet* is surely the most popular of Shakespeare's plays among high school students. Its appeal is obvious: conflict, intrigue, humor, swordplay, a wonderfully contrived plot, interesting characters, and, of course, romantic love, including some of the most poetic lines ever composed on the subject. The 1977 film version directed by Baz Luhrmann is a contemporary retelling that appeals to students. The play is usually taught in the ninth or tenth grade.

THEMES

fate, love, foolish pride, family, revenge

LITERARY CONCEPTS

tragedy, blank verse, poetic devices (including metaphor, simile, personification, hyperbole, oxymoron), irony, dramatic structure, foreshadowing, imagery, comic relief, soliloquy, sonnet, pun, tone

RELATED READING

Works of literature about love seem limitless. They include titles that range from *Forever* by Judy Blume and *Very Far Away from Anywhere Else* by Ursula LeGuin to *Gone with the Wind* by Margaret Mitchell and *Wuthering Heights* by Emily Brontë. Two works modeled after *Romeo and Juliet* are *West Side Story* by Arthur Laurents and *Fair Annie of Old Mule Hollow* by Beverly Courtney Crook. Girls especially may be interested in *Romeo and Juliet Together (and Alive!) At Last* by Avi.

READING PROBLEMS AND OPPORTUNITIES

Like any of Shakespeare's plays, *Romeo and Juliet* presents its share of reading problems to high school students, largely because of its flowery poetic language. Still, the play is quite approachable. Most of the archaic words or skewed meanings will be explained in marginal notes, but a few of them should perhaps be taught in advance, especially these: *I would thou wert* (I wish you were), *have at thee* (I will attack you; defend yourself), *an she agree* (if she agrees), *go to* (an expression of derision or impatience), *withal* (with; with it), and—most important of all, of course—*wherefore art thou Romeo* (why are you Romeo?). The possibly unfamiliar words that have retained their meanings through the centuries are relatively few. Several of them follow (act and scene numbers are in parentheses):

piteous (Prologue; 3:2; 3:3; 5:3),
pernicious (1:1),
portentous (1:1),
oppression (1:1; 1:4; 5:1),
disparage (1:5),
prodigious (1:5),

enmity (2:2; 5:3),
baleful (2:3),
lamentable (2:4; 4:5; 5:3),
lamentation (3:2; 3:3),
loathsome, loathed (2:6; 3:5; 4:3; 5:1),
amorous (3:2; 5:3),

beguiled (3:2; 4:4),
abhor (3:5; 5:3),
inundation (4:1),
pensive (4:1),
abate (4:1),
inexorable (5:3),
inauspicious (5:3), and
ambiguity (5:3).

INITIATING ACTIVITIES

1. With other students, discuss the idea of destiny or fate. To what extent do you believe that events sometimes occur because of a certain inevitability over which people have no control? Include in your discussion the subject of predestination—the idea that the course of our lives is charted for us by a higher power and that we have little influence over the pattern of events.

2. Based on what you know about the subject from books, movies, television, advertising, or even personal experience, write a brief paper on how people act when they fall in love. Try to consider their feelings, thoughts, concerns, and fears—and how their behavior differs from when they are not in love.

DISCUSSION QUESTIONS

1. Prologue: What is the purpose of the prologue? What kind of play does it prepare the reader for? What kind of tone is established? What does "star-cross'd" mean?

2. Act 1, scene 1: What two families ("houses") are mentioned early in the scene? What kind of relationship do they seem to have? On the basis of their opening lines, how do Benvolio and Tybalt seem different? What is Tybalt anxious to do? How does the fight begin? Do Capulet and Montague serve as peacemakers? Who is the Prince? Why is he so angry? What restrictions does he impose? Do you think they will work? Why or why not? Afterward, what concern does Montague express about his son, Romeo? What do you think is the cause of Romeo's melancholy? As he speaks to Benvolio, what frame of mind does Romeo's use of contradictions, *oxymorons*, suggest that he is in? Why is he so certain that his love will not be returned? Why does he think he will be unable to take Benvolio's advice? Is it good advice? Why or why not? Why, apparently, has Romeo fallen in love? How do you feel about his reactions to his being in love? Are his actions exaggerated? Why or why not?

3. Act 1, scene 2: Why does Capulet want to delay Paris's wooing of his daughter? How is his advice to Paris and Benvolio's to Romeo similar? Whom does Romeo love? Does he really believe "the all-seeing sun / Never saw her match since first the world begun"? What figure of speech is this? What role does the servant play in informing the reader?

4. Act 1, scene 3: What kind of person is the Nurse? What is her attitude toward marriage? What is Lady Capulet's? Why do you think they want Juliet to show an interest in Paris? How does her mother's appeal differ from the Nurse's? How does Juliet respond?

5. Act 1, scene 4: "You have dancing shoes / With nimble soles, I have a soul full of lead / So stakes me to the ground I cannot move." What does Romeo mean? Find other examples of puns in this scene. How do the young men plan to keep from being detected at Capulet's party? When Romeo suggests that he has dreamed of ill omens, how does Mercutio respond? Why does Romeo have misgivings? What does he mean by "my mind misgives / Some consequence yet hanging in the stars"?

6. Act 1, scene 5: Why does Capulet insist that Romeo be allowed to remain at the party? What is Romeo's response on seeing Juliet? How does he describe her? To what does he compare her? Do you believe in love at first sight? Why or why not? What does Tybalt's disagreement with Capulet foreshadow? In what manner does Romeo approach Juliet? Is he brash? Shy? How does she respond to him? Is she indifferent? Why do you think Shakespeare chose to write their words to each other in rhyme? In what poetic form are their

words—in the fourteen lines from "If I profane" to "while my prayer's effect I take"? What concern does each of them express at the end of the scene?

7. Act 2, Prologue: What problem does the Chorus anticipate Romeo and Juliet may have in their courtship? What may enable them to deal with it?

8. Act 2, scenes 1 and 2: How does Romeo react to Mercutio's jesting? With what does Romeo compare Juliet's eyes? In what way? With what part of her face were her eyes, despite their brightness, dim in comparison? Again, upon what does Romeo base his attraction to Juliet? What does Juliet wish for Romeo to do? Why? What does she mean by the famous line "a rose / By any other name would smell as sweet"? As they talk, who is the more assertive? Why does Juliet fear she has been too forward? Why is she suddenly reluctant? Does her reluctance seem natural? Why or why not? Based on what you know of her so far, what is Juliet like? Is she impulsive? Indecisive? Do you think the lovers' strong feelings and their rush to proceed will cause them any problems? If so, what? In what ways for them is parting "such sweet sorrow"?

9. Act 2, scene 3: What is the essence of Friar Laurence's opening remarks? How do they perhaps relate to the play? Are the Friar's words that "young men's love then lies / Not truly in their hearts, but in their eyes" true about Romeo? About most or all young men? About young women? What explanation does the Friar have for Rosaline's not having reciprocated Romeo's love? What hope does Romeo's new love give to the Friar?

10. Act 2, scene 4: What kind of man is Mercutio? Why does he seem to enjoy bantering with Romeo? What is the Nurse like? What kind of role does she seem to have in the play?

11. Act 2, scenes 5 and 6: How does the Nurse irritate Juliet? In his cell, what concerns Friar Laurence as he prepares Romeo and Juliet? Is Romeo concerned with this? Why or why not?

12. Act 3, scene 1: How does Mercutio characterize Benvolio? Which of the two does seem the more likely to start a fight? Is Tybalt alone responsible for the fight with Mercutio? Why is Romeo reluctant? Why does the wounded Mercutio repeat, "A plague o' both your houses"? Why does Romeo say, "This day's black fate on more days doth depend"? Why does he cry, "O, I am fortune's fool"? What does he blame the events on? Does Benvolio give the Prince an accurate account of the events? If he believes Romeo's murder of Tybalt was retaliatory, why does the Prince banish Romeo? Is this fair? Why or why not?

13. Act 3, scene 2: What does Juliet mean by "Lovers can see to do their amorous rites / By their own beauties"? Earlier Romeo had compared Juliet's eyes to stars. In what way does she pay him a similar compliment? How does the Nurse confuse things again? What is Juliet's response? Why does she seem so inconsistent and unsettled?

14. Act 3, scene 3: "Affliction is enamour'd of thy parts / And art wedded to calamity." What does Friar Laurence mean by this? How do he and Romeo disagree as to the significance of banishment? Romeo tells the Friar, "Thou canst not speak of that thou dost not feel." Do you agree with this? Is it possible to understand what we have not experienced? Why or why

not? Why does the Friar become so exasperated with Romeo? Of what does he accuse him? Why does he think Romeo should be more positive?

15. Act 3, scenes 4 and 5: How does Capulet misjudge Juliet? At Juliet's window, why do she and Romeo disagree as to whether it is morning? As he leaves, why does she say, "O, God, I have an ill-divining soul"? Upon what does she call to send Romeo back? What does this suggest about her? For her, what seems to dictate events? How does Juliet deceive her mother regarding her feelings for Romeo and his role in Tybalt's death? (Note especially lines 93–95: "Indeed I never shall . . . a kinsman vexed.") Why does Capulet become so angry with her? Are Juliet's interests uppermost in his mind? Discuss. Toward the end of the act, what does Juliet blame her distressful situation on? How does her view of love and marriage differ from the views of her parents and the Nurse?

16. Act 4, scene 1: Romeo and Juliet often seem resigned to their fate ("What must be shall be"). What effect does the Friar often have on them in this regard? Why does he intercede on their behalf? Do you think he is a meddler? Why or why not? What does he propose as a solution to Juliet's dilemma? What device does his solution depend upon?

17. Act 4, scenes 2, 3, and 4: Why is Capulet so easily deceived by Juliet? In scene 3, cite another example of Juliet's belief in fate. As she prepares to drink the potion, what fears does she express? Which of them do you think is most justified? What is the purpose of scene 4, which consists largely of light-hearted jesting?

18. Act 4, scene 5: How would Juliet react to the cries and lamentations of those who find her "dead"? How is the Friar's chiding of the mourners more accurate than they realize? How does even he suggest that the fates have played a part in this?

19. Act 5, scene 1: "My dreams presage some joyful news at hand." What effect did Shakespeare intend for Romeo's words to have upon the audience? When he receives the inaccurate news of Juliet's death, what does Romeo mean by "Then I defy you, stars!"? How is this in keeping with a theme that appears throughout the play? How does Romeo's mood change with the news? Why does he suddenly seem so resolute? What does he mean by "I sell thee poison; thou has sold me none"?

20. Act 5, scene 2: What stroke of bad luck prevented Friar John from delivering Friar Laurence's important letter to Romeo? With what result?

21. Act 5, scene 3: What is Romeo's mental state as he opens the door of the tomb? How do his words, *maw*, *gorged*, *cram*, reinforce the sense of anguish he conveys? After he kills Paris, why does Romeo bury him with Juliet? How does he see himself and Paris as victims? Why is he attentive to Tybalt? Why does he think Juliet seems "yet so fair"? To the end, to what do Romeo—and in a moment the Friar—attribute the play's sad series of events? Does the Prince's assessment differ? If so, how? Were there other factors besides fate and the hatred of the families toward each other? Were Romeo and Juliet themselves in any way to blame? Discuss. Just before their deaths, how had Romeo and Juliet changed from what they were like at the beginning of the play?

WRITING ACTIVITIES

1. Both Romeo and Juliet felt themselves to be victims of fate. From the perspective of the play's beginning, write astrology charts for each of them that describe what they are like and suggest what is in store for them.

2. Both of the lovers seem rather immature: They fall in love at first sight, and their expressions of love for each other seem substantially based on looks. Compile a thoughtful list of Good Reasons to Fall in Love—Besides Looks. Try to include at least ten.

3. You are Romeo. During your exile in Mantua, write a letter to the Prince of Verona appealing his decision to banish you. Explain that you are married to Juliet and that the two of you offer the best chance for bringing the Montagues and Capulets together. Give other reasons why the Prince should allow you to return.

4. Read (and perhaps listen to) *West Side Story*, the Broadway musical patterned after *Romeo and Juliet*. Write a comparison between this modern version of the Romeo and Juliet story and the version by Shakespeare.

5. Write the letter that was never delivered—the one Friar Laurence wrote to Romeo and sent by Friar John, who was delayed. Keep in mind that the letter was "full of charge / Of dear import . . . ." Or, write the letter Tybalt allegedly sent to Romeo (act 2, scene 4), remembering Tybalt's nature as you compose it.

6. The expression of romantic sentiments has changed very little in four hundred years. The compliment that Romeo pays to Rosaline ("the all-seeing sun / Ne'er saw her match since first the world begun") is not unlike the John Denver song: "Leaves will bow down when you walk by / And morning bells will chime." Try your hand at writing several exaggerated poetic compliments of this sort.

7. Throughout the play Shakespeare uses contrasting images of light and dark to represent and convey the pleasant and unpleasant, especially in scenes with one or the other (or both) of the two lovers. Write a paper in which you cite and explain at least three of these images. (One example, of course, is Romeo's first reference to Juliet in act 1, scene 5: "O, she doth teach the torches to burn bright!")

8. "Death lies on her like an untimely frost / Upon the sweetest flower of all the field." This sad remark by Capulet could serve as Juliet's epitaph. Write a similar epitaph for Romeo—a couplet in blank verse. Try to summarize one or two of his most important traits in the two lines.

9. *Romeo and Juliet* is in many ways a play of contrasts: light and dark, love and hate, life and death, reason and emotion. Write a diamante poem for one of these contrasts. The first and seventh lines should be the contrasting words with the intervening lines consisting, in part, of references to the play. (See Appendix A.)

10. If possible, find a recording of the Andy Griffith version of the Romeo and Juliet story. After listening to it several times, write a paragraph or two explaining how his version differs from the original.

11. You are a news reporter for the *National Enquirer* who arrives at the Capulet burial vault at the same time as the Prince. Write the article that will appear on the front page of the next edition.

OTHER ACTIVITIES

1. Create a valentine that Romeo might have drawn to send to Rosaline at the beginning of the play. Then draw one he would have sent to Juliet from Mantua. Make sure your decorations and sentiments reflect the two different Romeos.

2. Act out a scene in which Friar Laurence, Balthasar, the Apothecary, and Capulet are brought to trial before the Prince for their roles in the tragedy. Each must defend himself, with either the Prince or the audience deciding on their fate.

3. Draw the statues (or mold it from clay or papier-mâché) that Capulet and Montague intend to build in tribute to their children. It may be realistic or abstract, but it should communicate the qualities and values of Romeo and Juliet that you think the two fathers would wish to honor.

4. Keeping in mind Capulet's respect for Friar Laurence ("This reverend holy Friar, / All our whole city is much bound to him."), role-play a scene in which Juliet decides to reveal her love for Romeo to her parents before her marriage to him and to beg their mercy—in the presence of the Friar.

5. Create an artistic representation of the following quotation:

Give me my Romeo; and, when he shall die,
Take him and cut him out in little stars,
And he will make the face of heaven so fine
That all the world will be in love with night
And pay no worship to the garish sun.
(Act 3, scene 2)

SELECTED TEACHING RESOURCES

Media Aids

Cassettes

Romeo and Juliet. 166 min., Claire Bloom and Albert Finney version. Clearvue/eav.

CD-ROM

Romeo and Juliet CD-ROM. Windows. Clearvue/eav.

Filmstrip/cassette

Romeo and Juliet. 12 min. Thomas S. Klise Company.

Internet

Gray, Terry A. 1997. Mr. William Shakespeare and the Internet. 1995-1997. Available: http://www.palomar.edu/Library/shake.html (Accessed March 1, 1997.)

    This site contains numerous links to wonderful homepages devoted to Shakespeare, including several on the teaching of Shakespeare.

Videos

Romeo and Juliet. 138 min., color, Zeffirelli version. Sundance, 1968.

Romeo and Juliet. 167 min., BBC version with Sir John Gielgud. Ambrose Video Publishing, Inc., n.d.

Romeo and Juliet. 81 min., color. Films for the Humanities & Sciences, n.d.

Same Difference. 38 min. A contemporary retelling with a Jewish girl and Catholic boy. Media Guild, 1996.

Printed Materials

Abridged Text

Romeo and Juliet. Shakespeare for Young People series (text shortened, language unchanged). Perfection Learning Corporation.

Articles

Cohen, Lauren W. "*Romeo and Juliet*: Living Is Being Relevant." *English Journal* 59 (December 1970): 1263–1265, 1269.

Hanke, Jeanette J. "*Romeo and Juliet* and the Disadvantaged." *English Journal* 59 (February 1970): 273–276.

Reed, Vic. "The Escalus Report: Shakespeare's Prince of Verona as a Touchstone for Plot Development." *Media & Methods* 16 (February 1980): 31–33.

Scheidler, Katherine P. "*Romeo and Juliet* and *The Glass Menagerie* as Reading Programs." *English Journal* 70 (January 1981): 34–36.

Taylor, Gary J. "*Romeo and Juliet* and *West Side Story*: An Experimental Unit." *English Journal* 51 (October 1962): 484-485.

Books

Elliot, Marian. "*Romeo and Juliet*." In *Teaching Shakespeare*, edited by Arthur Mizener. New York: New American Library, 1969.

Evans, Bertrand. *Teaching Shakespeare in the High School*, New York: Macmillan, 1966.

O'Brien, Peggy, ed. *Shakespeare Set Free: Teaching "Romeo and Juliet," "Macbeth," and "A Midsummer Night's Dream."* Washington, D.C.: The Folger Library, 1993. (Available from Perma-Bound.)

Parallel Text

Romeo and Juliet. Features original text and contemporary paraphrase side-by-side. Perfection Learning Corporation.

Posters

Romeo and Juliet. Set of five, 17" x 22", color. Perfection Learning Corporation.

Teaching Aids

Romeo and Juliet. Insight series and React series. Sundance.

Romeo and Juliet. Literature Unit Plans. Teacher's Pet Publications.

Romeo and Juliet. Masterprose series. Perfection Learning Corporation.

Romeo and Juliet. Novel Unit Guide, Perma-Guide, and Student Packet. Perma-Bound.

Romeo and Juliet. Novel/Drama Curriculum Units. The Center for Learning.

Romeo and Juliet. Novel-Ties. Learning Links.

Tests

Romeo and Juliet. Essay, objective, and alternative assessment versions. Perfection Learning Corporation.

A Raisin in the Sun

Lorraine Hansberry

New York: Random House, 1959
Play: available in paperback from Vintage.

SUMMARY

Walter Younger dreams of using his mother's insurance money to buy part ownership in a liquor store, which will lift him and his family out of the Southside Chicago ghetto where they live. His mother's strong opposition and a partner's escape with the money shatter the dream, but Walter salvages his pride and self-respect by confirming the family's commitment to buying a house in a white neighborhood where they are not wanted.

APPRAISAL

This moving play about the hope, despair, and pride of a black family won the New York Drama Critics Circle Award as the best play of the 1958–1959 season. Its author, Lorraine Hansberry, was the youngest American playwright, the fifth woman and the first black ever to win this award. *A Raisin in the Sun* is most often taught in the ninth and tenth grades.

THEMES

hope and despair, courage, pride and self-respect, family, prejudice, dreams deferred

LITERARY CONCEPTS

atmosphere, characterization, conflict, symbolism, irony, stage directions, dialogue, inference

RELATED READING

The efforts of blacks to overcome the barriers of racism and poverty have been detailed in numerous works of literature. Many of these are shocking and graphic (e.g., *Manchild in the Promised Land* by Claude Brown, *The Autobiography of Malcolm X* by Malcolm X and Alex Haley, and the searing *Soul on Ice* by Eldridge Cleaver). Others are more tempered, but no less persuasive (e.g., *The Autobiography of Miss Jane Pittman* and *A Lesson Before Dying* by Ernest J. Gaines and *Your Blues Ain't Like Mine* by Bebe Moore Campbell). Students may also want to read *To Be Young, Gifted and Black: Lorraine Hansberry in Her Own Words*.

READING PROBLEMS AND OPPORTUNITIES

Like most plays, especially those about people at the edge of poverty with limited education, *A Raisin in the Sun* offers few reading difficulties. The only words in the dialogue that may be unfamiliar to high school students are *neurotic, assimilation, mutilate, eccentric, oppressive,* and *martyr.* Numerous words in the all-important stage directions, however, may be used for vocabulary study. The more important ones are listed here (act and scene numbers are in parentheses):

indictment (1:1),
indifference (1:2; 2:1; 2:2),
exasperate (1:1; 1:2; 2:2; 3),
oppression (1:1),
sullen (1:1; 2:1; 3),
defiance (1:1; 2:1),
anguish (1:1; 3),
defensively (1:1; 1:2),
unobtrusively (1:1),

self-righteously (1:1),
tentatively (1:1; 2:1),
raucous (1:1; 3),
profound (1:1; 3),
indignantly (1:2; 2:3),
forlornly (1:2; 2:3),
quizzical (1:2; 2:3),
beseechingly (1:2),
incredulity (1:2; 2:1),
humiliation (2:1),

plaintively (2:1; 2:3),
resignation (2:1),
revelation (2:1; 2:2),
exuberant (2:1; 2:3),
facetiousness (2:3),
ludicrous (2:3),
ominous (3),
flippancy (3),
reverie (3), and
precariously (3).

Many of the words, especially those in act 1, might be grouped and taught as Words of Despair.

INITIATING ACTIVITIES

1. The title of this play comes from "Montage of a Dream Deferred," a poem by Langston Hughes. A well-known excerpt from the poem appears just before the beginning of act 1. Read the excerpt (or the entire poem) and discuss its implications. What does *deferred* mean? What does the speaker think happens when dreams are delayed? What is meant by "Or does it explode?"

2. On a sheet of paper, write down some dreams that you have for the future—things you would like to have, to be, and so on. Then for each of them, list the "requirements" for the dream, what you would have to do or be for the dream to be fulfilled. Finally, list circumstances that might result in the dream's not being realized.

3. Rank the following items from 1 (of highest value to you) to 6 (of lowest value): a college education, first prize of $100,000 in a sweepstakes, a twenty-acre lot by a lake in the mountains, a successful career, self-respect, a stable marriage. Discuss your list with the rankings compiled by your classmates.

DISCUSSION QUESTIONS

ACT 1, SCENE 1

1. The upholstered couch and the worn carpet are given as evidence that "weariness has, in fact, won in [the Younger living] room." What is some other evidence that this is a sad, defeated place?

2. Describe the early morning talk between Ruth and Walter. What seems to irritate each of them? What are Walter and Travis looking forward to in the next day or so? After nagging him, why does Ruth tease Travis by talking as he would talk?

3. Why does Walter give Travis a dollar? Why does he stare at Ruth as he gives the boy the money?

4. What does Walter want Ruth to help him to do? Why does it seem so important to him? According to Walter, what is the main difference between men and women, especially black men and women?

5. Why does Walter become upset with Beneatha? Why is he afraid that no one in the house is ever going to understand him?

6. What disagreement do Ruth and Mama have over Travis? Do you think it is a serious and bitter disagreement? Why or why not? Why is Mama opposed to Walter's plan to use the money to buy a liquor store? How does Ruth feel about it? Why is her reaction mixed? How would you feel about owning and operating such a business?

7. What is Ruth like? Is she strong? Is she impatient? Indifferent? Devoted?

8. What is Mama's dream for using the money? Why is it just as important to her as Walter's dream is to him? How are Walter and his father alike?

9. What is Beneatha like? What does she seem to want out of life? How well does she seem to know herself? Discuss. Why does Mama slap her? Is this totally justified? Why or why not? In what way(s) is Beneatha "still a little girl"?

10. Mama worries about her children. To what does she compare them? How are Walter and Beneatha different? Alike?

ACT 1, SCENE 2

11. What difference between Mama and Beneatha does the conversation about Africa reveal? What differences do Beneatha and Asagai have? What does Asagai mean by saying Beneatha "mutilates" her hair? Why is he opposed to it? What does he mean by *assimilationism*? Why does she deny this? Why does she thank him for calling her Alaiyo?

12. Why does Mama try to downplay the importance of the check? After she opens it, why does she become sad?

13. What does Walter mean when he says, "I want so many things"? What does he want? Is it money, as he says? Or is it more than that? Discuss.

14. Why is Walter unable to reply to Mama at the end of act 1?

ACT 2, SCENE 1

15. Why does Beneatha dress up in the Nigerian costume and dance? Why does Walter join in? What basic disagreement do Beneatha and George have? Why does Walter lie about having been to New York? Why does he claim to be "a giant surrounded by . . . ants who can't even understand what it is the giant is talking about"? Do you think Walter understands himself? Why or why not?

16. What seems to be at the root of the division between Ruth and Walter? Just when things seem at an impasse, why does she offer him hot milk? What does he mean by "we scared to talk softness to each other"?

17. How does Mama unintentionally make things worse for Walter sometimes? Compare the mother-to-son interactions right after Mama tells about buying the house. Who takes the greater beating—Travis or Walter? How is Mama's dream different from Walter's? How are their dreams alike?

ACT 2, SCENE 2

18. Why has Walter taken Willie Harris's car for long drives? In what ways does this scene present turning points in the play?

ACT 2, SCENE 3

19. Why do you think Walter's mood has changed so dramatically? Do you think he is a foolish person? Why or why not? Is he selfish? Discuss.

20. How does Walter respond to Mr. Lindner? Is it different from how he might have responded earlier in the play? Why or why not? How do Ruth and Beneatha respond to the visitor? Why does Mr. Lindner take so long to make his proposal? How is the proposal ironic? Given his earlier concern for money, why doesn't Walter accept Mr. Lindner's offer? Of what possible significance is Mr. Lindner's leaving his card?

21. Why are the gardening tools such an appropriate gift for Mama?

22. Why does Walter hesitate to answer the bell? Why does Ruth sense something forboding before he does? Compare Walter's sense of loss with Mama's.

ACT 3

23. In this play about dreams, what is Asagai's? How does his dream differ from Walter's? Why is Beneatha confused?

24. What change has come over Walter? What does he seem willing to sacrifice? When Mr. Lindner arrives, why does Mama insist that Travis remain in the room? Why does Walter then reverse himself and commit the family to moving into their new house? Why does the family deliberately "try to ignore the nobility of the . . . moment"?

25. At the end, Mama says, "He finally come into his manhood today, didn't he?" Do you agree with this? If so, describe how Walter has become a man? Has he replaced his earlier dream with another? If so, what is it and how is it different?

*W*RITING ACTIVITIES

1. Write a diamante poem contrasting *hope* and *despair*. (See Appendix A.)

2. Pretend that Willy Harris is apprehended and that you are the prosecuting attorney. In one or two paragraphs, write what you would accuse him of. (Consider "crimes" other than stealing.)

3. Joseph Asagai and George Murchison are two contrasting minor characters in the play. Although they are both friends of Beneatha, the two men never meet. Write a dialogue—at least ten exchanges—that might take place between the two men if they did run into each other at the Younger apartment.

4. Write a paper in which you compare and contrast the dreams and ambitions of one of the following pairs of characters:

   a. Joseph Asagai and George Murchison,

   b. Ruth and Beneatha, or

   c. Walter and Mama.

5. An age-old argument concerns the extent to which poor people are responsible for their own poverty. Write an essay in which you take a position on this issue.

6. Beneatha can be feisty at times. Write a letter of complaint she might have sent to the Chicago Housing Authority concerning Lindner's visit and offer.

7. Referring partly to characters and events in the play, write a list poem on one of the following topics: hope, pride, or prejudice. Your poem should contain at least five lines following the pattern "Hope is. . . ."

8. Read about Prometheus in a book on mythology. Then write a paragraph explaining why George Murchison calls Walter Prometheus in act 1, scene 1.

9. Listen to a recording of Martin Luther King Jr.'s famous "I Have a Dream" speech given at the Lincoln Memorial in 1963. Then write a paper comparing the dreams he expressed in that speech with those Walter seems to have (even though he may not always express them).

OTHER ACTIVITIES

1. In act 1, scene 2, Walter tells Mama, "I want so many things." Create a collage that expresses all of the things you think Walter wants, including his spiritual as well as material desires.

2. Mama and Ruth tease Beneatha about her tendency "to flit so from one thing to another all the time." Beneatha says she is merely trying to express herself. Use some art form (dance, sculpture, abstract design, painting, or other) to express Beneatha's sense of her emerging self.

3. Instead of writing dialogue, act out the scene referred to in Writing Activity #3. Roles should include Joseph and George, Beneatha, Ruth, and perhaps even Walter and Mama.

4. Construct a mobile contrasting Walter's dream with Mama's.

5. Act out the scene that would take place when the Youngers arrive at their new house and find three people waiting for them: Mr. Lindner, a white minister in the Clybourne Park community, and a man who is among those who "can get awful worked up when they feel that their whole way of life and everything they've ever worked for is threatened."

6. In recent years many people have traced their family histories back through the generations and have written up their discoveries in published and unpublished books. Design the cover for such a book that Walter Younger might write. The cover should reflect the family's strengths and values as Walter has come to appreciate them by the end of the play when he proudly and tearfully refuses Mr. Lindner's offer.

SELECTED TEACHING RESOURCES

Media Aids

Cassettes (2)

A Raisin in the Sun. Perfection Learning Corporation.

Internet

Penguin USA. 1994. *A Teacher's Guide to the Signet and Plume Editions of the Screenplay of Lorraine Hansberry's "A Raisin in the Sun".* 1994. Available: http://www/penguin.com/usa/academic/classics/raisin/contents.html (Accessed March 1, 1997).

This online guide to the original screenplay includes a synopsis, brief biography of the playwright, and classroom considerations before, during, and after the reading of the screenplay.

Videos

A Raisin in the Sun. 128 min., b & w. Perma-Bound, Perfection Learning Corporation, and Sundance, 1961.

Lorraine Hansberry: The Black Experience in the Creation of Drama. 35 min., color. Films for the Humanities & Sciences, 1976.

Printed Materials

Article

Gill, Glenda. "Techniques of Teaching Lorraine Hansberry: Liberation from Boredom." *Negro American Literature Forum* 8 (Summer 1974): 226–228.

Criticism

"Lorraine Hansberry." In *Contemporary Literary Criticism*, Volume 62, edited by Roger Matuz, 209–248. Detroit: Gale Research Inc., 1991. Article devoted entirely to *A Raisin in the Sun.*

Teaching Aids

A Raisin in the Sun. Contemporary Classics series. Perfection Learning Corporation.

A Raisin in the Sun. Literature Unit Plans. Teacher's Pet Publications.

A Raisin in the Sun. Novel Unit Guide, Student Packet, and Perma-Guide. Perma-Bound.

A Raisin in the Sun. Novel/Drama Curriculum Units. The Center for Learning.

A Raisin in the Sun. Novel-Ties. Learning Links.

A Raisin in the Sun. Insight series and React series. Sundance.

Test

A Raisin in the Sun. Essay and objective versions. Perfection Learning Corporation.

The Old Man and the Sea

Ernest Hemingway

New York: Charles Scribner's Sons, 1952
Available in paperback from Scribner.

SUMMARY

Santiago, an old Cuban fisherman, has gone eighty-four days without a catch. On the eighty-fifth, he hooks an enormous marlin far out at sea. For the next two days the fish pulls the small skiff further out before the tired old man is finally able to harpoon him. After lashing the fish to the boat, Santiago sets sail for home only to have sharks, attracted by the smell of blood, strip the carcass bare before he arrives. Leaving the marlin's skeleton on the beach, Santiago struggles home to sleep and dream, injured and bitterly exhausted, but undefeated.

APPRAISAL

The publication of *The Old Man and the Sea* led to the awarding of the 1954 Nobel Prize for Literature to Ernest Hemingway for a body of work that includes *A Farewell to Arms*, *The Sun Also Rises*, and *For Whom the Bell Tolls*. Of all these novels, this story of courage and dignity in the face of destruction may be the most teachable to a wide range of students in high school because of its brevity, simplicity, and timeless relevance.

THEMES

courage, heroism, fate, "grace under pressure"

LITERARY CONCEPTS

allegory, symbol, irony, dialogue, style, code hero, characterization, theme, point of view, monologue, plot, flashback, diction

RELATED READING

Students who are interested in reading more fishing and hunting stories involving the Hemingway code hero should explore those about Nick Adams in *In Our Time*. One of the best recent books about adventures at sea is *My Old Man and the Sea: A Father and Son Sail Around Cape Horn* by David Hays and Daniel Hays.

READING PROBLEMS AND OPPORTUNITIES

One of the great virtues of this brief modern classic is its simplicity. On the literal level it is an easy book to read, offering only a few important words that may not be familiar (page numbers are in parentheses):

resolution (23, 101, 102),
iridescent (35, 36),
filament (35, 36),
mysticism (37),

annul (40),
coagulate (52),
undulation (60),
rapier (62),
mechanically (65),

perceptible (73, 117),
sustenance (74),
leprous (78),
interminable (93), and
detached (96).

The Old Man and the Sea provides a close look at fishing, boats, and the world of the Gulf Stream. For students who may be interested in these subjects, some of the terms mentioned or explained are these: *skiff, gaff, block and tackle, thwart, dolphin, mast, fathom, flying fish, tern, albacore, man-of-war bird, plankton, Portuguese man-of-war, marlin, porpoise, bow, stern, gunwale, bonito, Sargasso weed, trade wind, harpoon, bitt, tiller, Mako shark,* and *shovel-nosed shark.*

INITIATING ACTIVITIES

1. With your classmates, discuss the following men in terms of heroic manliness:

   a. a man who might be described as macho—aggressive, strong, dominant, courageous, who hunts big-game animals with infinite skill and success, but often to the point of ignoring game laws in order to accumulate trophies; and

   b. a man who is also strong and courageous, skillful as a hunter, not always successful, but rigidly faithful to the rules.

   On an expedition for lions where the limit is one, the first man uses a bow and arrow, killing one and mortally wounding another, which he elects not to pursue; the second man wounds a lion with a rifle and spends the rest of the day in unsuccessful pursuit of the animal, thus losing his opportunity for a chance at another trophy. Which is more of a man? Which is more honorable? Why? What do we mean when we say, "There is a real man"? (*Note*: Teachers concerned with sexism might substitute *woman* for *man* in this activity, although the latter is certainly more in keeping with the Hemingway hero.)

2. To many people, certain species of animals possess a strength of character or a nobility of spirit that is mysterious and unattainable by humans. One thinks, perhaps, of eagles, lions, porpoises, and wolves, among many others. After reading and reflecting on this subject, write a paper in which you express your opinion. Are some animals more noble and admirable than humans? If so, in what ways?

DISCUSSION QUESTIONS

1. Discuss the relationship between Santiago and the boy. Why is the boy not allowed to help him? Why does he want to so badly? How does Santiago feel about the eighty-four days? Why does he think he has attained humility? How can one have humility and "true pride" at the same time? What is *true pride*?

2. What does the description of the old man's shack reveal about him? Why do he and the boy go through the fictions of the pot of yellow rice and the cast net every day? What does Santiago feel you must have to catch fish? What in addition to faith?

3. What seems to be the feeling of others, like the owner of the Terrace, toward Santiago? Do you think they pity him? Why or why not? Why does he seem so interested in baseball and especially the great DiMaggio? What does he mean when he says, "I have resolution"? Why do you think he dreams only of places and of the lions on the beach? Why does he love the boy? Why does the boy love him?

4. Why does Santiago feel sorry for the terns? How does he feel about the sea? In what way does he excuse the sea? In what ways does he demonstrate care and perception as a fisherman? Why does he prefer precision to luck? Why does he love the turtles? Why does he say he has a heart like theirs?

5. How does the old man react as the marlin nibbles the bait? Why does he remember the earlier incident when the male marlin had stayed with its mate? Why does he pity the fish he has hooked? How does he relate to it? What part does he think choice has played in their coming together? What part has fate or luck played? Why does he keep wishing he had the boy with him? What might the boy represent for him?

6. Why does Santiago wish he could feed the marlin? Why does he talk to the fish? Why does he talk to his cramped hand? Why does he feel that a cramp is humiliating, especially when one is alone? Why does he feel that the marlin is more noble than man? How does he feel about his own ability to battle the fish? Is he confident? Why does he say his prayers? Why does he feel it is unjust to kill the fish? Yet why does he feel he must do it?

7. What does the old man seem to admire—in both men and animals? Which does he admire the most? Why?

8. As the marlin circles the boat and the old man draws him closer, what does Santiago fear the most? How does he combat the fear? Why does he prevail? After he kills the fish, why does he wish to feel him? Why does he wonder who is bringing in whom? Why is the question momentarily important to him?

9. In battling the shark, what is the old man's attitude? Besides the obvious economic loss, what regrets does he have about the attack on his marlin? How does he feel about killing the shark? Is he in any way regretful? Discuss. How does he feel about sin and especially killing? What does he

mean by "Fishing kills me exactly as it keeps me alive"? What seems to be the old man's state of mind as he waits?

10. When Santiago sees the two shovel-nosed sharks, he says, "Ay," and the narrator tells us, "There is no translation for this word." What do you think the old man means by it? Comment on the comparison, "such as . . . feeling the nail go through his hands and into the wood." What does Santiago mean when he says, "I'm sorry about it, fish. It makes everything go wrong"? Why is the comparison of the marlin's color to the silver backing of a mirror appropriate?

11. Why is the old man sorry that he went out too far? How much importance does he attach to luck? Why does he continue to fight the sharks when he knows doing so is useless?

12. As he approaches his home port, how does the old man feel about what has happened? Does he pity himself? Does he feel defeated? Discuss. Do the following passages remind you of anything you have read before—and if so, what? "He tried to get up. But it was too difficult and he sat there with the mast on his shoulder and looked at the road." And—"He pulled the blanket over his shoulders and then over his back and legs and he slept face down on the newspapers with his arms out straight and the palms of his hands up."

13. The boy says, "But we will fish together now for I still have much to learn." What does he have to learn from Santiago? How does the old man respond? Will they go out again in a few days? Why or why not?

14. In what way did the old man fail? In what way, if any, did he succeed? Is the book sad? Depressing? Despairing? Discuss.

Writing Activities

1. Santiago has great respect for the fish he battles: "He is wonderful and strange and who knows how old he is, he thought." Write a report on the blue marlin, paying particular attention to the size, range, and reputation of the species as a game fish.

2. *The Old Man and the Sea* has almost epic overtones. Write the story of Santiago and the great marlin as it might be told a hundred years from now in small Cuban fishing villages. Your version should take on the characteristics of myth or legend.

3. Pretend that you are the director and screenwriter for a film version of the novel. Write the script and a description of the shots you would use for what would be the film's final scene—not necessarily the final scene in the book, but one that is faithful to the novel's style and themes.

4. Unlike most novels, *The Old Man and the Sea* is not divided into chapters. Write a paper of several paragraphs, the first of which explains why you think Hemingway chose to omit chapters. The remaining paragraphs should explain how you might break the novel into chapters and why.

5. Early in the book Santiago calls himself "a strange old man." Later he refers to the marlin as "wonderful and strange." Write a paper in which you compare the old man and the fish as figures of significance in the novel. Illustrate your points with quotations from the book.

6. Hemingway believed that life, for the most part, is a losing battle but that what is important is how a person conducts oneself while he or she is losing. Write about an experience when you (or perhaps another member of your family) displayed courage and dignity in the face of defeat.

7. Write a short critique (a brief analysis of some technical question concerning the writing of a novel or play). Address this question: What might have been Hemingway's purpose for including the book's final scene between the tourists and the waiter? What point might he have been making about the old man's experience and the reaction of others to it? Write at least a paragraph.

8. Write a dialogue that might take place between Santiago and a reporter from a wildlife conservation magazine who is concerned about the endangered status of fish like, perhaps, the blue marlin. Let the reporter's first question be "Why do you fish?", to which Santiago should respond at length. Then write at least five other sets of questions and responses.

9. The relationship between Santiago and Manolin is a special one built on love and respect. Write about a relationship that you have had with an elderly person from which you both benefited.

10. From the descriptions on pages 25 and 81, write an interpretation of Santiago's dreams about the lions on the beach. Why have these dreams replaced his earlier ones? What do these things, "the long golden beaches and the white beaches, so white they hurt your eyes, and the high capes and the great brown mountains . . . and the lions on the beach," represent for him?

OTHER ACTIVITIES

1. Role-play two scenes between Manolin and his parents in which Manolin requests permission to continue going out with Santiago to fish—one before the eighty-fifth day and the other after it.

2. "What a fish it was," the proprietor said. "There has never been such a fish." With blue marlins typically weighing between fifty and four hundred pounds, Santiago's fish was indeed a record catch, one that the local people had a right to be proud of. Design a plaque that might have been created to commemorate the event. As part of the plaque, include a single quotation from the novel that, for you, captures the essence of the struggle between Santiago and the fish.

3. Using encyclopedias or other reference books as sources, draw sketches to scale of the following fish mentioned in the novel: marlin, albacore, bonito, flying fish, dolphin, Mako shark, and shovel-nosed shark. Then draw a picture, also to scale, of Santiago's eighteen-foot marlin.

4. Santiago is not an artist, but he does have a clear sensitivity to beauty, especially the beauty of the sea: "She is kind and very beautiful. But she can be so cruel." Using finger-paint or poster paint, create a picture of the sea as Santiago might have depicted it.

5. Role-play a conversation that takes place at the Terrace the day after Santiago returns. The roles should include the proprietor, Manolin's father, a young fisherman like those described on pages 29–30, and an older fisherman like the ones described on page 11. The participant who plays the young fisherman should begin by saying, "He is an old man. He has no business fishing alone."

SELECTED TEACHING RESOURCES

Media Aids

Cassettes (2)

The Old Man and the Sea. Perfection Learning Corporation.

CD-ROM

The Time, Life, and Works of Hemingway CD-ROM. Macintosh and Windows. Clearvue/eav.

Internet

Gagne, David V. 1997. *Ernest M. Hemingway Home Page.* 1995-1997. Available: http://www.atlantic.net/~gagne/hem/hem.html (Accessed: March 1, 1997). Maintained by the University of Florida English Department, this homepage includes a time line and links to a mailing list, bibliography, and photographs.

Videos

Ernest Hemingway: Grace Under Pressure. 55 min., color. Films for the Humanities and Sciences, n.d.

The Old Man and the Sea. 97 min., Anthony Quinn version. Clearvue/eav, n.d.

The Old Man and the Sea. 86 min., color, Spencer Tracy version. Films Incorporated Video, 1958.

Printed Materials

Articles

Nagle, John M. "A View of Literature Too Often Neglected." *English Journal* 58 (March 1969): 399–407.

Scoville, Samuel. "The *Weltanschauung* of Steinbeck and Hemingway." *English Journal* 56 (January 1967): 60–63, 66.

Books

Brenner, Gerry. *"The Old Man and the Sea": Story of a Common Man*. New York: Twayne Publishers, 1991.

Commission on English, ed. *Twelve Thousand Students and Their English Teachers*. Princeton, NJ: College Entrance Examination Board, 1968.

Workman, Brooke. *Writing Seminars in the Content Areas: In Search of Hemingway, Salinger, and Steinbeck*. Champaign-Urbana, IL: National Council of Teachers of English, 1983.

Teaching Aids

The Old Man and the Sea. Contemporary Classics series. Perfection Learning Corporation.

The Old Man and the Sea. Literature Unit Plans. Teacher's Pet Publications.

The Old Man and the Sea. Novel Unit Guide, Perma-Guide, and Student Packet. Perma-Bound.

The Old Man and the Sea. Novel/Drama Curriculum Units. The Center for Learning.

The Old Man and the Sea. Novel-Ties. Learning Links.

The Old Man and the Sea. React series. Sundance.

Tests

The Old Man and the Sea. Essay and objective versions. Perfection Learning Corporation.

The Glass Menagerie

Tennessee Williams

New York: Random House, 1945
Play: available in paperback from Signet.

SUMMARY

Tom Wingfield, a factory worker who longs for adventure, tries to keep peace in a household consisting of his mother, Amanda, a faded southern belle who lives in the past, and his sister, Laura, a shy, crippled girl who has retreated into her own world of phonograph records and a glass animal collection. To pacify his mother, Tom agrees to invite a gentleman caller to the house for Laura. Jim O'Connor, the visitor, brings a fleeting moment of hope to the family, but since he is already engaged, the chances for Laura to be safely married decrease. Finally, Tom leaves home to become a merchant seaman, but the memory of his sister still haunts him.

APPRAISAL

Although Tennessee Williams had written other plays before *The Glass Menagerie* opened in 1945, this work established his national reputation. In his essay "The Catastrophe of Success," Williams writes, "I was snatched out of virtual oblivion and thrust into sudden prominence." The play won the New York Drama Critics Circle Award and enjoyed great success on Broadway. Since then, it has become a popular work for community theater groups throughout the United States and has often been anthologized for use in high schools, usually in the eleventh grade, where it is among the two or three most widely taught American plays. Its enduring success may be attributed to its almost delicate mood and its strong, vulnerable characters, who arouse the sympathy and pity of its readers and audience.

THEMES

illusion versus reality, selfishness and selflessness, search for adventure, living in the past, conflict between parents and children

LITERARY CONCEPTS

narrator, symbolism, memory play, characterization, theme, use of lighting and setting for symbolic effect (particularly a lighted scrim with legends and images), use of music

RELATED READING

Students who respond favorably to the atmosphere and characterizations in *The Glass Menagerie* may wish to consider other plays by Tennessee Williams, particularly *Cat on a Hot Tin Roof* and *A Streetcar Named Desire*. Another drama of declining moral values in an old southern family is Lillian Hellman's *The Little Foxes*.

READING PROBLEMS AND OPPORTUNITIES

Most of the dialogue in *The Glass Menagerie* is simple and straightforward. As with many modern plays, however, the stage directions contain certain words that may require explanation if the play is to be fully understood. The poet-narrator, Tom, also makes use of unusual vocabulary as he sets the scenes. Words that may require study include the following:

1. Scene 1—*conglomerations, cellular, symptomatic, fluidity, differentiation, interfused, automatism, ineluctably, matriculating,* and *emissary;*

2. Scene 3—*archetype, allusion, sceptre, sublimations, precipitated,* and *gesticulating;*

3. Scene 4—*motley, grotesquely,* and *fiasco*

4. Scene 5—*annunciation* and *emulate*

5. Scene 6—*translucent, unobtrusive, cotillion, ominous, imperiously, vivacity,* and *paragon*

6. Scene 7—*rhapsodic, indolently, perturbation, abates,* and *jauntily*

INITIATING ACTIVITIES

1. Make a list of things from the past that you have collected. Share your list with other members of your class. Discuss the following questions with them: Why have you collected these items? What value do they have? How has their value changed as time passes? What value do you think they may have in the future? Is the collection of items like this a completely harmless (and even beneficial) activity? Or can it have negative effects of any kind?

2. Choose an important goal in your life and write a paragraph in which you imagine what it will be like to achieve that goal. Explain what that all-important day will be like; try to imagine your feelings and reactions on that occasion. Save this paragraph for later use.

DISCUSSION QUESTIONS

SCENE 1

1. In the stage directions, the playwright indicates that this scene is not realistic because it is a memory. He says, "Memory takes a lot of poetic license." What does he mean by this statement?

2. Tom explains his function in his first speech, saying he is the opposite of a magician. What does he mean? Tom also explains the social background of the play. Why? What is the function of music in the play? Why is the gentleman caller a symbol in the play? What events might he stand for in your life?

3. In this scene, the three main characters—Tom, Amanda, and Laura—are introduced. What relationship exists between Tom and Amanda? Between Laura and Amanda? How does Tom play two roles in this scene—as a character and as narrator-director?

SCENE 2

4. What clues in the stage directions and in the opening dialogue of this scene give the audience the idea that Laura already knows what has happened? Why does Laura fail to return to the business college? Why does she go to such lengths to deceive her mother? Do you think she should have done this? Why or why not?

5. Why is Amanda so concerned about Laura's future? What does she feel are Laura's only alternatives? Is this a realistic appraisal? Why or why not? In what ways is Amanda unable to face the truth about her daughter?

SCENE 3

6. Why does Amanda begin selling subscriptions? How successful is she? How do you account for her success or lack of it?

7. Why do Amanda and Tom quarrel? Do you feel more sympathy for Tom or Amanda? Or do both have their own legitimate points to make in the argument? Explain your position. How does Tom seek to further antagonize his mother? How does she react?

SCENE 4

8. What evidence that Tom has been drinking do you find in this scene? In what ways does Laura try to play the role of peacemaker between her mother and brother? Why does Tom give in and apologize to his mother?

9. How does Amanda continue to harass Tom? Why does she do this? What does Tom seek in life that his mother cannot understand? Why does Amanda appeal to Tom only for the sake of his sister? Do you think she is being unselfish or does she believe that this type of appeal will carry more weight? Support your answer with a discussion of the characters in the play.

SCENE 5

10. Contrast the alley scene and the Paradise Dance Hall with the Winfield's apartment. How are the two different? According to Tom, the two also have commonalities. What are they?

11. Amanda meets Tom's announcement that he has invited a gentleman caller with mixed reactions. Why is she delighted? Why is she distressed? Based on your own experiences, are her demands for details about the gentleman caller a common reaction of parents in similar situations? Why or why not? Amanda states, "The last thing I want for my daughter's a boy who drinks!" Why is she adamant on this point?

12. Once again, in her conversation with Tom, Amanda shows that she cannot face the truth about her daughter. What pain does this cause her? What pain does it cause Laura?

SCENE 6

13. Explain the significance of the "Gay Deceivers." Why does Amanda insist on them? Why is Laura opposed to them? How do these powder puffs symbolize the differences of the two women in their attitudes toward themselves and toward relationships between men and women?

14. Why does Laura refuse to answer the door when her brother arrives home? Would you have expected this of her? Why or why not?

15. According to Jim, what are the requirements for success? Compare and contrast Tom and Jim's views of their future prospects. How is Tom able to justify his proposed actions?

16. Despite Amanda's outlandish appearance, she manages to win the day. Which of her characteristics allows her to do this? How does she continue to manipulate Laura to assure the success of her plans? Why is she insensitive to her daughter's needs? Do you find her despicable for her actions? Or do you have sympathy for her attempts on her daughter's behalf? Discuss.

SCENE 7

17. How does Jim attempt to cover for Tom when the lights go out? Do you think this is an admirable quality in a friend? Why or why not? How does Jim try to make Laura feel at ease? What is his analysis of Laura's problem?

18. Jim was a young man who showed great promise in high school, but he has not been as successful in life. What do you believe has kept him from achieving the success that others had envisioned for him?

19. Which of Jim's actions seem to help Laura overcome her shyness and enjoy herself? How does he go too far? What is he forced to do then? How does Laura react to his revelations about his girlfriend?

20. How does Amanda respond to the news about the gentleman caller? On whom does she place the blame? What are her motives for doing this? Is she, in part, trying to cover up for her own shortcomings? Discuss.

21. What is the irony in Amanda's continually calling Tom selfish? What does she finally drive him to do? In what ways is Tom able to pull away and find his dream? In what ways is he still tied to the past?

WRITING ACTIVITIES

1. Look again at your paragraph on achieving a goal in your life (Initiating Activity #2). How does your goal compare to the long-awaited goal of the gentleman caller in the play? Write an essay in which you compare your goal and its projected attainment with the events in the play.

2. Although the character of the father never appears in the play except as a photograph over the mantel, he is discussed at some length, making it

possible for one to draw a fairly accurate picture of the man. Write a character sketch of Mr. Wingfield in which you try to portray him objectively, without the hatred that is expressed in the play by Amanda and Tom. Search the dialogue carefully to find clues about his appearance and behavior as a young man.

3. Several scenes in *The Glass Menagerie* are described and discussed but never actually presented. Write one of the following scenes as it might have occurred. Be sure to keep the dialogue consistent with the characters as they are presented in the play. Decide ahead of time whether your scene will be a realistic one or a memory and write it accordingly.

    a. Amanda's confrontation with the instructor at Rubicam's Business College

    b. Tom's inviting Jim to come to dinner

    c. Laura's encounter with Jim at chorus rehearsal

    d. Tom's leaving home

4. Throughout the play Tennessee Williams uses legends and images flashed on a screen to help present the story. He explains their use as follows:

    > The purpose of this will probably be apparent. It is to give accent to certain values in each scene. Each scene contains a particular point (or several) which is structurally the most important. In an episodic play, such as this, the basic structure or narrative line may be obscured from the audience; the effect may seem fragmentary rather than architectural. The legend or image upon the screen will strengthen the effect of what is merely allusion in the writing and allow the primary point to be made more simply and lightly than if the entire responsibility were on the spoken lines. (Production Notes, p. 8)

    Decide whether you agree with Williams's justification for the use of this technique. In a well-organized essay, support or refute his argument. Refer to specific scenes in the play to show why the technique is or is not useful.

5. Choose two symbols used in the play from the following list. Write an explanation of these symbols, including how they function in the play, how they change, and how members of the audience might identify with them in relation to their own lives.

    a. the fire escape

    b. the glass menagerie

    c. the unicorn

    d. old phonograph records

    e. blue roses

    f. the gentleman caller

    g. the Paradise Dance Hall

6. Examine the arguments between Tom and Amanda. Write about an argument that you have had (or might have had) with your parents that is similar to one of these. Or, write the argument itself in script format.

7. Research some of the events discussed in the play, such as Tom's monologue in scene 5 in which he says, "Suspended in the mist over Berchtesgaden, caught in the folds of Chamberlain's umbrella—in the folds there was Guernica!" Write a report in which you explain these events and the world situation at the time, and relate them to the play.

8. Because he feels trapped in a dead-end job, Tom is often miserable and goes to the movies to escape. Write him a letter in which you offer suggestions for improving his situation.

9. *The Glass Menagerie* opens with Tom's monologue, which sets the scene and introduces the characters. Rewrite the monologue as Laura or Amanda might have introduced the play.

10. In scene 4, Amanda tells Laura to make a wish on the moon, but Laura does not know what to wish for. Imagine that you are Laura and write the wish she might have made for herself.

11. Write a horoscope for Tom, Laura, Amanda, and Jim for the day of Jim's visit to the Wingfield home. Make sure that each horoscope reflects what will happen to each character on that particular day.

OTHER ACTIVITIES

1. If you wrote the scene in Writing Activity #3, prepare a dramatic presentation of it with other members of your class. Choose students who thoroughly understand the characters to play the required roles.

2. Design a model of the set to be used for this play. In order to do this, you will need to reread the stage directions carefully. You may select materials in your home or classroom that are appropriate for the scene.

3. Prepare an artistic representation of Laura's world in a medium of your choice. Because they would allow you to retain the memory qualities of the play, watercolors or pastels would be particularly appropriate.

4. With your classmates, discuss each of the following lines taken from the play. Remember that there are no right or wrong positions in such a discussion; the objective is to explore the possibilities and arrive at new understandings.

    a. "It isn't enough for a girl to be possessed of a pretty face and a graceful figure. . . . She also needs to have a nimble tongue to meet all occasions."

    b. "Only animals have to satisfy instincts."

    c. "The past turns into everlasting regret if you don't plan for it."

    d. "Old maids are better off than wives of drunkards."

    e. "All pretty girls are a trap, a pretty trap, and men expect them to be."

    f. "Some people say that science clears up all the mysteries for us. In my opinion it only creates more!"

    g. "Being different is nothing to be ashamed of."

5. With a classmate, improvise a scene between a parent and child that is similar to the ones between Tom and his mother or Laura and her mother. In this scene, the parent should cling to some dream or notion of theirs regarding the future of the child, who should respond with his or her own point of view.

6. Amanda claims that a little padding is necessary to help a woman catch a man. Present a style show for your class featuring some of the "Gay Deceivers" currently in vogue, such as make-up, wigs, false fingernails, and articles of clothing. Afterward, discuss with the class the advantages and disadvantages of such items.

SELECTED TEACHING RESOURCES

Media Aids

Videos

The Glass Menagerie. 134 min. Perma-Bound, 1987.

Tennessee Williams: Orpheus of the American Stage. 90 min., color. Films for the Humanities & Sciences, n.d.

Printed Materials

Articles

Capasso, Ralph, et al. "Through a Glass Starkly." *English Journal* 57 (February 1968): 209–212, 220.

Scheidler, Katherine P. "*Romeo and Juliet* and *The Glass Menagerie* as Reading Programs." *English Journal* 70 (January 1981): 34–36.

Book

Presley, Delma Eugene. *"The Glass Menagerie": An American Memory.* Boston, Twayne Publishers, 1990.

Teaching Aids

The Glass Menagerie. Contemporary Classics series. Perfection Learning Corporation.

The Glass Menagerie. Literature Unit Plans. Teacher's Pet Publications.

The Glass Menagerie. Novel Unit Guide, Perma-Guide, and Student Packet. Perma-Bound.

The Glass Menagerie. Novel/Drama Curriculum Units. The Center for Learning.

Tests

The Glass Menagerie. Essay and objective versions. Perfection Learning Corporation.

Our Town

Thornton Wilder

New York: Harper & Row, 1938, 1957
Play: available in paperback from HarperCollins.

SUMMARY

As an omniscient observer of events and a sometime participant in the play, the Stage Manager leads the reader (and the audience) through three separate days in the lives of ordinary citizens in Grover's Corners, New Hampshire, in the early 1900s. He dwells especially on two families, the Webbs and the Gibbses. He oversees the courtship of Emily Webb and George Gibbs in act 1, which culminates in their wedding in act 2, as well as Emily's funeral in act 3. Throughout the play, the Stage Manager is interested mostly in everyday occurrences, the daily rituals and conversations, the births and deaths—and in the sad and inevitable inability of people to appreciate life as they live it.

APPRAISAL

Thornton Wilder's *Our Town* has taken its place as one of America's most beloved and respected plays since its debut in 1938, when it won the Pulitzer Prize for drama. Innovative in stagecraft and largely affirmative in theme, it is among the more teachable plays for high school students, who can appreciate its humor, its uniqueness as theater, and its effort (to use Wilder's own words) "to find a value above all price for the smallest events in our daily life." The play is usually taught in the eleventh grade.

THEMES

the universality of experience, the importance of human relationships, and the ability to appreciate the importance of ordinary daily events in our lives

LITERARY CONCEPTS

stagecraft (especially such innovations as the Stage Manager, the lack of scenery and props, and the involvement of the audience), theme, irony, allegory

RELATED READING

Books like *Mama's Bank Account* by Kathryn Forbes and *Life with Father* by Clarence Day offer additional glimpses into the simpler lifestyle near the turn of the century—without *Our Town*'s philosophical musings. Other plays by Wilder, such as *The Skin of Our Teeth* and *The Happy Journey to Trenton and Camden,* further explore the themes of universality and daily life.

READING PROBLEMS AND OPPORTUNITIES

Because it is a drama of simple, ordinary people, *Our Town* is a most approachable play, at least on the literal level. Except for Professor Willard's scholarly monologue, the dialogue contains very few unfamiliar words. The stage directions, however, may pose a few problems—with such words in act 1 as *unobtrusively* (also in act 2), *savant*, and *careening*; in act 2, *meditatively, alacrity, crestfallen, affronted, musingly, tableau,* and *cynicism*; and in act 3, *lugubriousness* and *anguished.* The greatest problem for students who read the play will be in visualizing the stage. In response to this, teachers will need to clarify terms (*proscenium pillar,* for example) and perhaps lead the class in staging parts of the play, like the ladder scene in act 1.

INITIATING ACTIVITIES

1. Imagine that in three days you will be separated from your family, never to see them again. What would you do—and, especially, what would you take with you—that would later help you remember them? List at least five items and keep the list for future reference.

2. For one day (or part of a day) try to keep an extremely detailed account of everything you do: what you eat for breakfast, with whom, conversations you have, how you get to school, what you do in each class, what you do between classes, etc. (*Note:* After the students have done this, have them code the activities in some way, perhaps with an *I* for important, a *B* for boring, an *F* for fun, and an *R* for routine. They should keep these accounts to refer to later as the class gets into the play.)

3. Consider dramas you have seen produced for the stage or for movies and television. What have most of them had in common, particularly the stage plays? Think of things like structure (acts, scenes), scenery, characters, costumes, and so on. Discuss this with the other members of your class.

DISCUSSION QUESTIONS

ACT 1

1. From the outset, what is different about this play, about how it is staged? What seems to be the role of the Stage Manager? What unusual powers does he have? What is his attitude toward scenery?

2. What time of day is it? What time of year? What is Dr. Gibbs coming home from? What might be an implication of all this?

3. "Anything serious goin' on in the world since Wednesday?" How does Joe Crowell answer Dr. Gibbs's question? What does this suggest about Joe and his perception of "the world"? Later, what does the Stage Manager mean when he says, about Joe, "All that education for nothing"?

4. What is Grover's Corners like? What are the main topics of conversation? As the Gibbs and Webb children eat breakfast, what are their mothers concerned about? What mildly upsets them? What is the effect of having the two family scenes enacted simultaneously on stage?

5. Why does Mrs. Gibbs want to go to Paris? Why doesn't Dr. Gibbs want to?

6. Why does the Stage Manager ask Professor Willard to speak? What might have been Thornton Wilder's purpose for including this information? Describe the interaction between the belligerent man and Editor Webb. Do you think Mr. Webb's reply satisfies the man? Why or why not? How does Mr. Webb characterize culture in Grover's Corners? Does there seem to be much sensitivity to beauty and culture in the town? Explain. How would you compare this to your own town today?

7. What does George Gibbs seem mostly interested in? What interests Emily Webb? What concerns her? How does her mother frustrate her momentarily?

8. Why is the Stage Manager so interested in placing artifacts of Grover's Corners in the cornerstone of the new bank? Why does he intend to include a copy of the play?

9. Describe the staging of the scene with George and Emily doing their homework. What does Emily mean when she says, "The moonlight's so terrible"? Later, why does Dr. Gibbs rebuke George and then give him an increase in weekly spending money?

10. What seems to be the source of Simon Stimson's problems?

11. How do Emily and her father's reactions differ to the sights and smells of the evening? Why is Rebecca so impressed with the address on the letter Jane Crofut received from her minister? Why do you think the playwright ended the act with this scene?

ACT 2

12. As act 2 begins, what time of day is it? Compare the beginning of act 2 with that of act 1. What point might Thornton Wilder be making by having the beginnings so similar? Why does the Stage Manager comment that the two hardworking mothers never had a nervous breakdown?

13. Why does Mrs. Gibbs say that "weddings are perfectly awful things"? Why are she and Dr. Gibbs concerned? How does George act on this, the morning of his wedding? Does he seem awestruck or nonchalant—or neither?

14. Why does the Stage Manager ask the audience to try to remember what it was like to be very young and in love?

15. In the flashback scene, what criticism does Emily have of George? Do you think she thinks George is conceited—or something else? Discuss. How does George respond? What happens in the scene that makes the two of them realize, as the Stage Manager says, "they were meant for one another"?

16. Why is the wedding scene staged so that George and Emily enter down the aisle of the theater through the audience? Why are the participants so confused at the wedding? What do George and Emily both seem to want, at least momentarily? What finally seems to comfort them?

17. What might the Stage Manager mean by his last statement: "The cottage, the go-cart, the Sunday-afternoon drives in the Ford . . . —Once in a thousand times it's interesting"?

ACT 3

18. Describe the stage as act 3 opens. What changes have taken place in the nine years that have passed since act 2? What distinctions does the Stage Manager make between the living and the dead? What might he mean when he says, "Everybody knows in their bones that something is eternal, and that something has to do with human beings"?

19. Why does the news that Emily Webb died in childbirth remind Mrs. Soames that life is "awful—and wonderful"?

20. The group by the grave sings "Blessed Be the Tie That Binds." Why do you think Thornton Wilder selected this particular hymn? Why does it seem appropriate?

21. How does Emily differ from those who have been dead for some time? What have the dead forgotten?

22. Why does Emily want to relive a day in her life? Why do the others not want her to? Why does Mrs. Gibbs insist that she "choose the least important day" in her life?

23. What does the beginning of the day Emily chooses remind you of? What does she notice? How does she react? What does she mean by "I can't look at everything hard enough" and "Let's look at one another"? And finally, what does she mean by "Oh, earth, you're too wonderful for anybody to realize you"?

24. Why is Simon Stimson so bitter? What might have been the purpose of including him in the play?

25. What is it that the living "don't understand"?

26. Why does the Stage Manager end by saying, "Scholars haven't settled the matter yet, but they seem to think there are no living beings there [on the stars]. Just chalk . . . or fire"?

27. In retrospect, why do you think Thornton Wilder chose to keep scenery and props in the play to a minimum? How might their absence reinforce one of the play's themes? Also, why did he create the Stage Manager with his ability to move in and out of the play, address the audience, and move backward and forward in time?

WRITING ACTIVITIES

1. Near the play's end Emily takes one last look at the world of the living and bids good-bye to "clocks ticking . . . and Mama's sunflowers and food and coffee. And new ironed dresses and hot baths . . . and sleeping and waking up." For a comparison, read lines twenty-six through fifty-eight of Rupert Brooke's poem "The Great Lover." Then write your own list poem entitled "These I Have Loved."

2. Choose a day in your life you would relive if you were given the opportunity—in the same way Emily did. Write about the day, about what made it memorable. Then write about how you might change the day to make it even more wonderful and meaningful. As you do this, keep in mind what Emily learned.

3. At one point near the beginning of act 3, the Stage Manager says, "Wherever you come near the human race, there's layers and layers of nonsense." Write two paragraphs: one discussing what you think he means by this and the other what you would mean by it.

4. Some might argue that life can never again be as simple as it was in small towns during the early part of this century. Interview a person who grew up sometime between 1920 and 1940, preferably in a small town or in the country. Ask him or her what life was like then and how it differed from life today. Also ask how it was better and worse than today. Write up your findings and report them to the class.

5. Just before the wedding in act 2, the Stage Manager says, "The real hero of this scene isn't on the stage at all, and you know who that is." Who is it? Think about this at length, keeping the whole play in mind. Then write an opinion of at least one page.

6. Mother Gibbs left George and Emily a legacy of $350 when she died. When Emily arrives among the dead, she mentions how they used the money, but Mrs. Gibbs seems neither aware nor interested. Write the will Mrs. Gibbs might have written after she had been dead for a long time. How might she have changed her legacy?

7. When the class has finished the play, redo Initiating Activity #1 or #2. (*Note:* The purpose of this activity, of course, is to see whether or not the reading of *Our Town* affects values and perceptions. Don't expect miracles, but try to help students who work with the activity to approach it seriously and honestly.)

8. More often than not, news in Grover's Corners has a distinctly local flavor—the schoolteacher's getting married to a man from Concord, the rescue of a Polish fellow from almost freezing to death. Write an account of George and Emily's wedding as it might have appeared in the Grover's Corners *Sentinel*.

9. Plays are often transformed into musicals. For example, Thornton Wilder's *The Matchmaker* later became the musical *Hello, Dolly!* Try your hand at writing a song for an appropriate moment in Our Town, perhaps when the Stage Manager introduces the town in act 1 or when Emily returns from trying to relive her day in the past.

10. Some social critics argue that today's children grow up far too fast, that they are pressured too often and too soon into assuming adult habits, roles, and values. Write a paper in which you compare our society with that of Grover's Corners in this regard, keeping in mind that George and Emily were married at eighteen. Or, write a paper in which you argue that today's children are (or are not) hurried too fast.

OTHER ACTIVITIES

1. The Stage Manager tells Emily that only poets and saints, perhaps, realize life as they live it. Find a poem that reflects this quality—the ability of the poet (or at least the speaker in the poem) to find value and beauty in everyday events. (For one example, read "The Blessing" by James Wright in the poetry collection *Some Haystacks Don't Even Have Any Needle*, edited by Stephen Dunning et al.) Copy your poem, perhaps in calligraphy, and illustrate or decorate it appropriately.

2. In act 1, the Stage Manager refers to a time capsule, a collection of items to be placed in the cornerstone of the new bank "for people to dig up . . . a thousand years from now." Using any art medium, create a representation of items and artifacts that would help future generations to understand "this is the way we were: in our growing up and in our marrying and in our living and in our dying"—in the America of the present.

3. Imagine that it is ten years after the play ends. George Gibbs has just died of pneumonia and is arriving among the dead. Act out the scene that might take place as George tries to adjust to his new surroundings. Roles might include George, Emily, Mrs. Gibbs, Simon Stimson, and others.

4. Since props are used so sparingly in *Our Town*, much of the action is pantomimed. With two or three other students, pantomime one of the scenes in the play. One good choice might be the drugstore scene in act 2.

5. A playbill is the program a person receives as he enters the theater. It contains the cast of characters, credits, an outline of acts and scenes, and even advertisements. Design the cover for a playbill that might be produced for *Our Town*. Your design should somehow reflect not only the setting and subject of the play but also its unique flavor and concerns.

SELECTED TEACHING RESOURCES

Media Aids

Videos

Our Town. 120 min., Hal Holbrook version, color. Perfection Learning Corporation and Sundance, 1977.

Our Town. c. 30 min. Clearvue/eav. Analysis/interpretation, n.d.

Printed Materials

Book

Haberman, Donald C. *"Our Town": An American Play*. Boston: Twayne Publishers, 1989.

Teaching Aids

Our Town. Contemporary Classics series. Perfection Learning Corporation.

Our Town. Literature Unit Plans. Teacher's Pet Publications.

Our Town. Novel Unit Guide and Student Packet. Perma-Bound.

Our Town. Novel/Drama Curriculum Units. The Center for Learning.

Our Town. Novel-Ties. Learning Links.

Tests

Our Town. Essay and objective versions. Perfection Learning Corporation.

The Adventures of Huckleberry Finn

Mark Twain

1885
Available in paperback from several publishing companies.

SUMMARY

Upset over the efforts of the Widow Douglas and Miss Watson to "sivilize" him and afraid of his drunken pap, Huckleberry Finn lights out on a raft down the Mississippi River. On Jackson Island he meets up with Miss Watson's Nigger Jim, who is running off to escape being sold. Huck promises not to tell on Jim, and the two of them set off on a series of adventures with an assortment of hypocrites, liars, and cheats they meet along the river, most notably a pair of swindlers posing as a duke and a king. Throughout the journey, Huck wrestles with his conscience over his decision to help Jim, whom he loves and whose goodness he recognizes, before concluding he will "go to hell" if necessary to do what his instinct tells him is right. When Jim is captured on a farm in Arkansas, Huck is able to rescue him with the imaginative help of Tom Sawyer, who is visiting his Aunt Sally. At the end, Huck is off again "for the territory ahead of the rest" to escape Aunt Sally's plans to adopt and civilize him: "I can't stand it. I been there before."

APPRAISAL

In a famous literary remark, Ernest Hemingway once said that American literature began with a book by Mark Twain about a boy named Huckleberry Finn. Few readers and critics will disagree with the claim that this is one of the two or three greatest American novels ever written. Quintessentially American in language, setting, and theme, the book is perhaps the favorite novel among high school English teachers in the United States. Although it is occasionally read by students in middle school, the book is typically taught in the eleventh grade. Because of the racial prejudice that permeates the riverbank societies of the book (highlighted by the frequent use of the word *nigger*), *Huckleberry Finn* has often been a target of well-meaning censors, who fail to appreciate its great literary value and, more important, to see the novel in a broader context—as a plea for racial understanding and human compassion.

THEMES

freedom versus the restraints of civilization, prejudice, hypocrisy, human folly, appearance versus reality

LITERARY CONCEPTS

point of view, structure, satire, symbolism, dialect, irony (especially dramatic irony), characterization, picaresque novel, setting, theme, plot, figurative language

RELATED READING

Some students may wish to read *The Further Adventures of Huckleberry Finn* by Greg Matthews (New York: Crown, 1983), which follows Huck and Jim into the goldfields of California. Other related works by Mark Twain include *The Adventures of Tom Sawyer* and *Life on the Mississippi*. Students interested in a modern-day nonfiction account of one man's journey down the Mississippi River might read Jonathan Raban's *Old Glory: An American Voyage.* Younger or less able readers interested in slavery could consider *The Slave Dancer* by Paula Fox.

READING PROBLEMS AND OPPORTUNITIES

Because it is narrated by an ill-educated boy along the Mississippi River frontier of the mid-1800s, *The Adventures of Huckleberry Finn* would seem to offer few reading difficulties to most eleventh graders. Their greatest problem may be with dialects, which, as Mark Twain notes in his explanatory section at the beginning of the book, are used to great effect. The dialects provide the novel with much of its realism, flavor, and humor, but for some students, they will be as difficult to navigate as the river that serves as their setting. For teachers and students interested in the historical varieties of American English, however, the language of Huck and Jim and the riverbank characters they encounter offers a fascinating look at colorful words and phrases of another time and place. The following are only a few examples:

dog my cats—the equivalent of "bless my soul"

fat up—to put on weight

bullyrag—to threaten or intimidate someone

give me the fantods—to make me nervous

truck—"stuff," trash

answer up square—to tell the truth

infernal mean—extremely mean

I'm nation sorry for you—I'm extremely sorry for you

in a sweat—worried, nervous, hurried

here's the ticket—this is what we're going to do, this is what we need

dad fetch it—an exclamation similar to "darn it"

to have someone's kiss-the-Bible—to have someone's solemn promise

beats and bummers—rascals, frauds, good-for-nothings

she had the grit to pray for Judas—she had courage

there warn't no time to swap knives—there was no time to waste

leather-headed—stupid

to smooch—to steal

that would be a pretty howdy-do—that would be nice; that would be appropriate (said sarcastically)

INITIATING ACTIVITIES

1. Using the encyclopedia and other reference works, read about the status of slavery in America around 1850, particularly along the Mississippi River frontier. Take particular note of which states along the river allowed slavery and which did not. Report to the class.

2. With other students, prepare and conduct a debate (or simply hold a discussion) on the following question: In a civilized democracy like our own, where does one strike the balance between allowing the individual to live a totally free and unencumbered life on the one hand and submitting the individual to restrictions and laws and even morality required by the society on the other? To what extent can a democracy allow its citizens complete freedom to do as they please, to live where they please, to avoid the draft, to vote, to not pay taxes, and so on?

DISCUSSION QUESTIONS

1. Chapter 1: Who is the narrator of the book? Why is life with the Widow Douglas so frustrating for Huck? Why is he opposed to being "sivilized"? Why does he say he won't try for "the good place"? Based on just these few pages, what is Huckleberry Finn like?

2. Chapter 2: How are Huck and Tom Sawyer different? What is ironic about Huck's comments about Jim's superstitions? Why does Tom insist on doing things by the book? He and the other boys seem almost obsessed with violence. What keeps their fascination with it in humorous perspective?

3. Chapter 3: Why is Huck disappointed and confused by praying? How does he distinguish between the Widow Douglas and Miss Watson? Why do he and the other boys become disenchanted with Tom Sawyer? Throughout the chapter Huck expresses unhappiness about several things. What do the sources of his complaints have in common? Cite examples of the difference between the apparent and the real things that bother him.

4. Chapter 4: Why does Huck try to get Judge Thatcher to take his money? Does the judge really buy the money from him? How do you think Huck will respond to Jim's fortune-telling? Why might Huck feel satisfied with it? Disappointed with it?

5. Chapter 5: How do Huck and his pap feel toward each other? Who is the more resentful? Why? What kind of people does Mark Twain make fun of in the last part of the chapter?

6. Chapter 6: What is so ironic about Pap's criticism of the government and the "free nigger"?

7. Chapter 7: What does Huck's elaborate procedure for making people think he was murdered reveal about him? Why does he decide to head down the river? What are his feelings about the river?

8. Chapters 8 and 9: Why has Jim run away from Miss Watson? How does Huck feel about his promise not to turn Jim in? What do the two chapters reveal about Jim? About Huck's feelings toward Jim? How do Jim and Huck feel about their situation on the island? What do they like about it?

9. Chapter 10: Why had Jim not wanted Huck to see the dead man? In what ways is Jim smart? How is it possible to be intelligent without being educated?

10. Chapter 11: Why does Huck go ashore? What does his story about being a runaway apprentice reveal about him? Why does he build a fire at the head of Jackson Island?

11. Chapters 12 and 13: How do Huck and Jim rationalize their stealing fruits and vegetables? On the wrecked steamboat, why does Jake Packard say that killing Jim Turner "ain't good morals"? Besides involving a murder, why is the latter example of "immorality" more significant than the former? What is Huck's response to the conversation he overhears? What does this—and his concern for the men left behind on the *Walter Scott*—suggest about him? In describing the watchman, what kind of people is Mark Twain satirizing?

12. Chapter 14: "He had an uncommon level head for a nigger." How does Huck perceive Jim? If he likes and respects him, why does he refer to him as a nigger? Later Huck says, "You can't learn a nigger to argue." Are Jim's arguments illogical? Is he illogical or uneducated? Discuss. Is Huck prejudiced? Discuss.

13. Chapter 15: How does the revelation of Huck's lie affect Jim? Do you think Jim overreacts? Explain? How does Jim's response affect Huck? Why is Huck's apology so significant?

14. Chapter 16: Why does Huck's conscience bother him? "Here was this nigger, which I had as good as helped run away, coming right out flat-footed and saying he would steal his children—children that belonged to a man I didn't even know." What is Huck blind to that the reader understands? What does he finally decide to do? Why does he think he is weak and wrong? How does he resolve the question of when "to do right"?

15. Chapter 17: What are the Grangerfords like? Buck in particular? Does Huck like him? Why or why not? Why do you think Emmeline Grangerford dwelled on sadness and death? How does Huck feel about her painting and poetry? How do you think Mark Twain meant for the reader to feel about Emmeline's artistic efforts?

16. Chapter 18: "I wished I hadn't ever come ashore that night to see such things." Why is Huck so upset? Besides the killings, what is so senseless about the Grangerford-Shepherdson feud—to the reader if not to Huck? What distinction is Huck beginning to make between life on land and life on the river?

17. Chapter 19: For Huck and Jim, why is it so "lovely to live on a raft" and the river? What does their discussion about the stars and the moon reveal about Huck and Jim? Their next encounter with inhabitants of the shore involves the king and the duke. What are they like? Why does Huck agree to pamper them?

18. Chapters 20 through 22: In his accounts of the events that occur off the river in both Pokeville and the town where Boggs is killed, what might Mark Twain be saying about human nature? Is his tone one of amusement or scorn? Is he more critical of Colonel Sherburn or of the townspeople who intend to Lynch him? Do you agree with Sherburn's criticism of men in general? Why or why not? At the circus—to what extent has Huck's association with the king and the duke made him less naive? Why do you think he remains relatively innocent?

19. Chapter 23: Do you think Huck's views toward Jim have changed since the beginning of their journey down the river? Why or why not?

20. Chapters 24 through 29: "It was enough to make a body ashamed of the human race." Have Huck's feelings toward his two companions begun to change as they begin their scheme against the Wilks family? If so, in what way? What disgusts Huck about the reactions of the people to the Wilks? Why does he decide to turn against the two impostors? What is there about Mary Jane that Huck admires but recognizes as a weakness in dealing with frauds? In his actions on behalf of Mary Jane, is Huck dishonest? Is he immoral? Discuss.

21. Chapters 30 and 31: What does the heated conversation between the king and the duke on the raft reveal about them? As Huck wrestles with his conscience on the raft, what is at the heart of the conflict within him? Why does he think he has sinned? What does he try to do to absolve it? Why doesn't it work? "All right, then, I'll go to hell." What kind of person does this show Huck to be? What kind of choice has he made? Why does he decide to go to the Phelps farm?

22. Chapters 32 and 33: Despite his decision, what does Huck's response to Aunt Sally—"No'm. Killed a nigger"—reveal about him? When he learns of the king and duke's predicament, why does he set out with Tom to help them? In what way is he still confused about conscience?

23. Chapters 34 through 36: Why is Tom Sawyer always so insistent about doing things the right way? How is it a matter of honor with him? Why does he sometimes violate the rules himself? How does he justify doing so? Why does Huck often fail to see the point of Tom's going by the "authorities"? Huck says that Tom is "full of principle." Are there ways in which Huck is more principled? Discuss. Are Tom's reasons for wanting to help Jim escape any different from Huck's? If so, how?

24. Chapters 37 through 41: Tom's calculated plans for Jim's escape and the resulting escapades are filled with irony, like freeing Jim to help roll the grindstone. Cite some others. Discuss Tom's expectations of Jim as a participant in his elaborate schemes. Is Tom just overly adventuresome? Is he insensitive?

25. Chapters 42 and 43: When Tom wakes up in the sickroom, why does he tell Aunt Sally the truth? Why does his revelation about Jim's having been set free in Miss Watson's will make Huck feel better about Tom? During the journey down the river, to what extent, if any, has Huck changed? What has he learned? What does he plan to do? What is his major weakness? What is his primary strength? At the end, is he less or more afraid than ever of being "sivilized"? Why?

WRITING ACTIVITIES

1. In his simple, untutored way, Huckleberry Finn often describes the beauty of the river and the land with great skill and feeling, as he does near the beginning of chapter 9 when the storm strikes. Using sensory images, as Huck does, describe in a long paragraph a scene you consider beautiful.

2. Pretend that Huck, Tom, and Jim do "go for howling adventures amongst the Injuns, over in the territory" after the book ends. Write the oath that Tom Sawyer might create to bond the band together and define its purpose and activities.

3. Read about one of the following topics and write a three- to four-page report, using at least three sources of information:

    a. Mississippi River steamboats in the mid-1800s,

    b. common American superstitions,

    c. Mark Twain's boyhood.

4. You are Tom Sawyer. Write a plan for rescuing the duke and king from their captors—before they are to be tarred and feathered. Keep in mind Tom's insistence upon elaborate adventures.

5. Pretend that Emmeline Grangerford had not died. Write a poem she might have composed to commemorate the battle by the river in which her brother was killed. Remember her tendency to sentimentalize, as evident in her "Ode to Stephen Dowling Bots, Dec'd."

6. In chapter 8, Huck and Jim discuss a number of signs (e.g., shaking a tablecloth after sundown will bring bad luck). By interviewing several adults (especially the elderly), compile a list of signs of good or bad luck that people still seem to believe.

7. Huck is a master at improvising elaborate lies to explain his way out of ticklish situations, as he does at the beginning of chapter 20. At times, of course, he feels pressured to tell the truth, especially when he is "up a stump," as he is with Aunt Sally just before her husband arrives home in chapter 32. Pretend that Uncle Silas does not arrive and that Huck improvises his way out of trouble. Write what he might say to Aunt Sally, using his dialect.

8. In his confusion over morality and religion and society's expectations, Huck resigns himself to hell and damnation in chapter 31. Write a defense for Huck that, at the proper time, would gain him admission to "the good place."

9. At the end of chapter 33, Huck sadly concludes that "human beings can be awfully cruel to one another." Write a list of at least five instances in the novel that might have caused him to reach this conclusion.

10. Like *The Adventures of Tom Sawyer*, this novel has often been referred to as a children's book. Write a paper in which you argue that *The Adventures of Huckleberry Finn* is *not* a children's book.

11. Huck resolves his great moral dilemma by doing what he fears is wrong, but what he feels is right by going against the grain of society's respectable morality. Write a paper about a current social issue on which you believe the prevailing majority opinion is wrong.

12. One critic, Lionel Trilling, has written that Jim serves as a "true father" to Huck in the novel. Write a paper contrasting Pap and Jim as father figures to Huck.

OTHER ACTIVITIES

1. In chapter 38, Tom Sawyer insists that Jim leave his coat of arms inscribed upon the stolen grindstone. Draw a coat of arms for the Finns based on Huck's values, achievements, and goals.

2. Huck's description of the river at the beginning of chapter 19 is one of the most famous in literature. Using an appropriate medium (oils, colored pencils, watercolor), draw or paint the scene as Huck describes it.

3. Role-play a scene in which several people who encounter Huck during the novel—the Widow Douglas, Miss Watson, Judith Loftus, the king, Mary Jane Wilks, Dr. Robinson, Silas Phelps—come together to discuss the following assertion: Huckleberry Finn is, in effect, a hopeless sinner, a "bad boy" who lies, cheats, and cares little for the personal property of others.

4. Draw an editorial cartoon against slavery that features Huck and Jim and alludes to an incident or incidents in the book.

5. In chapter 21, the duke prints up a batch of fake "wanted" posters or handbills for Jim. Using Huck's description of them, draw the poster, or draw one that someone might have printed and posted on the king and the duke.

6. Huck's lingering confusion over morality—"I knowed very well I had done wrong, and I see it warn't no use for me to try to learn to do right"—derives from a conflict between what he thinks adult society expects of people concerning morality and what he himself feels is right. Make a "split-screen" collage that reflects this conflict: one side conveying what Huck feels society's ideas are about "doing right"; the other, what his own ideas are.

SELECTED TEACHING RESOURCES

Media Aids

Cassettes (8)

The Adventures of Huckleberry Finn. 11.75 hours. Recorded Books.

CD-ROM

Huckleberry Finn. Macintosh. Perfection Learning Corporation.

Twain's World CD-ROM. Windows version. Clearvue/eav.

Internet

Zwick, Jim. January 12, 1995. *Mark Twain Resources on the World Wide Web.* 1995-1997. Available: http://web.syr.edu/~fjzwick/twainwww.html (Accessed: March 1, 1997).

   This is an extensive homepage with links to others. It includes sections on Exhibits, Complete Texts, Maxims and Quotations, Popular Culture, Biography and Criticism, and Teaching Resources.

Cope, Virginia. 1995. *Mark Twain's Huckleberry Finn.* 1995. Available: http://etext.lib.virginia.edu/twain/huckfinn.html (Accessed: March 1, 1997).

   This homepage includes the complete text of the novel, 174 illustrations from the first edition, and several early reviews.

Videos

The Adventures of Huckleberry Finn. 103 min., color. Lucerne Media, 1979.

The Art of "Huckleberry Finn," II. 25 min., color. (Also available on videodisc.) Britannica, n.d.

Huckleberry Finn. 50 min., color, analysis and critique. Films for the Humanities & Sciences, n.d.

"Huckleberry Finn" and the American Experience, III. 27 min., color. (Also available on videodisc.) Britannica, n.d.

Mark Twain, Huckleberry Finn and the Mississippi. 25 min., interpretation. Clearvue/eav, n.d.

What Does "Huckleberry Finn" Say, I. 28 min., color. (Also available on videodisc.) Britannica, n.d.

Printed Materials

Articles

Brooks, Cleanth. "The Teaching of the Novel: *Huckleberry Finn.*" In *Essays on the Teaching of English: Reports on the Yale Conference on the Teaching of English,* edited by Edward J. Gordon and Edward S. Noyes, 203–215. New York: Appleton-Century-Crofts, 1968.

Gibson, Donald B. "Mark Twain's Jim in the Classroom." *English Journal* 57 (February 1968): 196–199, 202.

Lynn, Kenneth S. "Welcome Back from the Raft, Huck Honey!" *American Scholar* 46 (Summer 1977): 338–347.

Books

Howes, Alan B. "The Many Worlds of Huckleberry Finn." Part 4 of *Teaching Literature to Adolescents: Novels*. Glenview, IL: Scott, Foresman, 1972.

Johnson, Claudia Durst. *Understanding "The Adventures of Huckleberry Finn."* Westport, CT: Greenwood, 1996.

Lettis, Richard et al., eds. *Huck Finn and His Critics*. New York: Macmillan, 1962. (criticism)

Matthews, Greg. *The Further Adventures of Huckleberry Finn*. New York: Crown, 1983. (novel)

Miller, Bruce E. *Teaching the Art of Literature*. Champaign-Urbana, IL: National Council of Teachers of English, 1980. (Suggestions for teaching the novel, pp. 93–108.)

Sloan, David. E. E. *"The Adventures of Huckleberry Finn": American Comic Vision*. Boston: Twayne Publishers, 1988.

Map

Huck Finn Map. Set of two, two-color 17" x 22" posters. Perfection Learning Corporation.

Poster

The Adventures of Huckleberry Finn. 17" x 22", color. Perfection Learning Corporation.

Teaching Aids

The Adventures of Huckleberry Finn. Literature Unit Plans. Teacher's Pet Publications.

The Adventures of Huckleberry Finn. Masterprose series and Portals to Literature series. Perfection Learning Corporation.

The Adventures of Huckleberry Finn. Novel Ideas Plus series and React series. Sundance.

The Adventures of Huckleberry Finn. Novel Unit Guide, Perma-Guide, and Student Packet. Perma-Bound.

The Adventures of Huckleberry Finn. Novel/Drama Curriculum Units. The Center for Learning.

The Adventures of Huckleberry Finn. Novel-Ties series. Learning Links.

Tests

The Adventures of Huckleberry Finn. Essay, objective, and alternative assessment versions. Perfection Learning Corporation.

The Scarlet Letter

Nathaniel Hawthorne

1850
Available in paperback from several publishing companies.

SUMMARY

In the mid-1600s in Boston, Massachusetts, Hester Prynne is found guilty of adultery and sentenced to wear forever a scarlet letter *A* upon her dress. She refuses to identify the father of her child, Pearl, whom she is allowed to keep only through the intercession of the Reverend Mr. Dimmesdale, the town's eminent young minister. As the years pass, Hester lives in silence and shame, her only companion the capricious Pearl, who is a source of joy and unceasing anxiety. Meanwhile, the health of the exalted Mr. Dimmesdale worsens mysteriously despite the solicitous care of his doctor, Roger Chillingworth, who is (as only Hester knows and has sworn not to reveal) Hester's vengeful former husband. Racked with an agony that only he can remove, Mr. Dimmesdale—with Hester's help—finally rejects the sinister physician and the guilt of seven tortuous years by confessing before the assembled townspeople that he is the father of Pearl.

APPRAISAL

The Scarlet Letter is considered by critics one of the three or four most important American novels. It is Hawthorne's greatest work, a grim but fascinating view of a dark epoch in American history, the guilt-ridden early years of Puritan New England. So foreign to the values and mores of contemporary society, the novel will not be readily embraced by most students without a teacher's help and enthusiasm. Still, it can win them over with its compelling plot, its hint of the supernatural, and its reflection upon guilt, sin, and the forces of good against evil—all themes of enduring relevance. The book is most often taught in the eleventh grade.

THEMES

guilt and repentance, sin, pride, good versus evil, intuition versus reason, the importance of honesty and truth

LITERARY CONCEPTS

theme, symbol, irony, atmosphere, plot, foreshadowing, characterization, understatement, figurative language, setting

RELATED READING

Students intrigued by the atmosphere of sin and guilt in Puritan New England may wish to read *The Devil's Shadow: The Story of Witchcraft in Massachusetts* by Clifford Lindsey Alderman and *The Witchcraft of Salem Village* by Shirley Jackson. A contemporary play that treats the subject is *The Crucible* by Arthur Miller. Other works by Hawthorne with similar themes are *The House of the Seven Gables* and the short stories "Young Goodman Brown" and "The Minister's Black Veil."

READING PROBLEMS AND OPPORTUNITIES

The Scarlet Letter is not an easy book. Written in the extended sentences and multisyllabic words of nineteenth-century prose, the novel may require orientation to Hawthorne's style (with its abundance of commas, among other features) and to such archaic words as *marry* (truly), *wherefore* (why), and *wot* (know). For teachers who wish to teach vocabulary within the context of literature, the novel is a rich source of numerous words that occur again and again, among which are the following (in parentheses, CH refers to Custom House, numbers to chapters):

revelation (CH, 5, 11, 12, 16, 23, 24),

decorum, decorous (CH, 10, 12, 20),

edifice (CH, 1, 2, 7, 20, 22),

infirm, infirmity (CH, 9, 11, 12, 17, 21, 22),

discern, discerning (CH, 3, 5, 6, 9, 11, 12, 13, 14, 17, 24),

venerable (CH, 2, 5, 8, 9, 12, 20, 22, 23),

retribution (CH, 4, 5, 8, 10, 14, 15),

tempestuous (CH, 4, 21, 22),

talisman (CH, 5, 15, 19),

pious (CH, 8, 9, 10, 11, 12, 20, 22),

tremulous (CH, 3, 8, 9, 11, 12, 17, 23),

sensibility (CH, 3, 9, 10, 15, 22, 23, 24),

countenance (CH, 2, 13, 21, 22, 23),

repose (CH, 10, 13, 22, 23),

demeanor (CH, 2, 4, 22, 24),

ponderous (CH, 1, 2, 7, 9, 22),

affirm (CH, 21, 22, 24),

ignominy, ignominious (CH, 2, 3, 4, 5, 7, 8, 9, 12, 13, 17, 18, 22, 23, 24),

scourge (2, 6, 11, 12),

transgress (2, 3, 8, 12, 18, 21),

infamy (2, 3, 4, 5, 9, 13, 18, 23),

grievous (2, 3, 5, 10, 17),

iniquity (2, 3, 10, 11),

visage (2, 3, 9, 12, 14, 21, 22),

deportment (2, 6, 9, 13, 19, 21),

pillory (2, 3, 9, 18, 21, 22, 23),

mien (2, 3, 21, 23),

preternatural (2, 6, 11, 19, 21, 22),

attribute (3, 9, 11, 13, 16),

remorse, remorseful (3, 10, 11, 12, 13, 14, 18, 23, 24),

lurid (3, 5, 12, 14, 23, 24),

efficacy (4, 6, 12,13),

impel (4, 7, 8, 9, 12, 13, 19, 20, 23),

delude, delusive, delusion (4, 5, 6, 11, 17, 22),

penance (5, 6, 11, 13, 17, 21, 24),

diffused, diffusion (5, 19, 20, 22),

irreverent (5, 10, 15, 22, 23),

piety (5, 9, 10, 21),

despondency (6, 9, 12, 16, 17),

caprice, capricious (6, 7, 15, 19),

requite, requital (8, 13, 15, 20, 22),

emaciated (8, 9, 10, 20),

renown (9, 17, 22, 23),

eminent (9, 11, 13, 21, 22, 23),

intrude, intrusive (9, 10, 20, 21, 22),   *celestial* (11, 12, 20, 23, 24), and
ethereal, etherealized (11, 13, 23, 24),   *stigma, stigmatize* (13, 18, 22, 23, 24).

INITIATING ACTIVITIES

1. Using encyclopedias and other sources (e.g., *Puritanism in America* by Larzer Ziff), read about Puritanism in New England in the seventeenth century. Report to the class on the definition of Puritanism, its origin, the beliefs and values it promoted, and its effects upon the people whose lives it permeated.

2. Write a two- or three-page composition about a time in your life when you did something that caused you to feel guilty. It need not have been something necessarily serious. Describe the incident briefly, but explain in detail why you felt guilty, how you responded to your feelings, and what the consequences were.

3. Rank the following actions (using your own opinion) in terms of their degree of wrongfulness or sinfulness (assigning 1 to the worst, 2 to the next worst, etc.). Keep your responses for discussion after you have read the novel.

   a. committing adultery
   b. allowing another person to accept blame for a crime you committed
   c. obsessively seeking revenge for wrongs committed against you
   d. condemning among others the wrongs that you yourself have committed

DISCUSSION QUESTIONS

1. The Custom House: What kind of relationship does the narrator wish to have with the reader? What is his expressed purpose for including the Custom House sketch? What are his feelings toward Salem? Why does he view the city with conditional affection? How are his views toward his ancestors similar? Why are they mixed? What is his attitude toward his fellow workers at the Custom House? Does he like them? Respect them? Why has he come to work at the Custom House? Why, ultimately, does he leave? Why is the narrator so intrigued by the letter of scarlet cloth? What is suggested by his involuntary shudder? What are the implications of the letter's having survived for two hundred years?

2. Chapter 1: What kind of mood is established in the first chapter? List details that contribute to the mood. What is the single contrasting element?

3. Chapter 2: What are the people like who are gathered about the prison? What is meant by "a people amongst whom religion and law were almost identical"? How do they react to Hester Prynne? Why is their reaction so severe? Why is Hester made to stand on the scaffold? How does she respond? Is she proud? Defiant? Submissive? Indifferent? Troubled?

4. Chapter 3: What is Hester's response to the stranger in the crowd? Why does she react this way? Why does the stranger insist that the father "will be known"? Why do the older occupants of the balcony insist that Mr.

Dimmesdale address Hester? How does he respond? In your opinion, why does Hester refuse to name the father? As the chapter ends, what are some questions that remain in the reader's mind?

5. Chapter 4: How is Hester persuaded to drink the medicine? Why does Roger Chillingworth feel he is partly to blame for her predicament? Do you feel that he is? Why or why not? Why do you think he is obsessed with learning the name of Hester's paramour? What is his purpose? What are her fears?

6. Chapter 5: Why does Hester remain in Boston? Into what kind of life does she settle? Why do the townspeople dwell upon her past transgression? Is she in any way accepted? Why does she feel guilty about her needlework? What new insights does her shame provide and how does she feel about them? Is Hester totally without hope? Discuss.

7. Chapter 6: Describe Pearl. What is appealing about her? What is there about her that disturbs her mother? Why does Hester hesitate to discipline Pearl? For Hester, what fears does the child represent?

8. Chapter 7: Does Hester's decision to visit Governor Bellingham seem surprising? Why or why not? Why does she dress Pearl in scarlet? In the governor's house, how do the reflections in the armor symbolize Hester's anguish regarding herself and Pearl?

9. Chapter 8: Why does Hester turn to Mr. Dimmesdale for help? How does he argue in her favor? Is his argument logical? Is his attitude toward Hester and her child different from that of the other men? If so, how? How does Roger Chillingworth respond? How does Pearl?

10. Chapter 9: Why are Roger Chillingworth and Mr. Dimmesdale attracted to each other? Why do you think the latter's health is failing? What is the narrator's attitude toward the former? What is the attitude of the "uninstructed multitude" toward Roger Chillingworth? Why? How does the narrator feel about this suspicion held by the people? What larger point might the author be making—about the value of intuition as opposed to reason?

11. Chapter 10: What motivates Roger Chillingworth? What does he seek? How do he and Mr. Dimmesdale disagree over the importance of revealing one's sins? When Pearl decorates her mother's scarlet letter with sticky burrs, what larger meaning might the author intend? And what might be meant by her taunt, "But he cannot catch little Pearl"? Why does Mr. Dimmesdale refuse to reveal his troubled soul to his physician? Yet, why does he apologize later? In the last scene, what do you think Roger Chillingworth sees? Why does he respond with such ecstasy?

12. Chapter 11: At this point in the novel, what seems to be the narrator's attitude toward Mr. Dimmesdale? Toward Roger Chillingworth? How has the former changed? The latter? How has Mr. Dimmesdale's anguish affected his relationship with the people in his church?

13. Chapter 12: Why does Mr. Dimmesdale visit the scaffold? Why does he ask for Pearl's hand? Why does she ask him to "stand here with mother and me, tomorrow noontide?" How is this scaffold scene different from the first one?

14. Chapter 13: In the years since her trial, how has Hester changed? Why has she chosen to help the weak and downtrodden? Why have the "men of rank" been less willing to acknowledge her goodness than the people? "The scarlet letter had not done its office." What might this mean? How do you think Hester feels about herself? Is she proud? Defiant? Discuss.

15. Chapter 14: Why does Hester appeal to Roger Chillingworth? Is he unwilling to respond—or unable? Discuss. How does he feel about himself? Why does he feel that Mr. Dimmesdale has "increased the debt"? What is the "dismal maze" that Hester refers to? What does Roger Chillingworth mean when he says, "Let the black flower blossom as it may"?

16. Chapter 15: Why does Hester hate Roger Chillingworth? Is her hate in any way justified? Why or why not? How are Pearl and her mother different? What hopes does Hester have for Pearl? Why is Hester unable to answer her daughter's questions? What is ironic about her last remark to Pearl?

17. Chapter 16: What might be the larger meaning of the conversation that Hester and Pearl have about the sunshine? What might the brook foreshadow? Why does Mr. Dimmesdale so often hold his hand over his heart?

18. Chapter 17: "And thou, Arthur Dimmesdale, dost thou yet live?" What does Hester mean? Why does she tell Mr. Dimmesdale the truth? What does the latter mean when he says that Roger Chillingworth "has violated, in cold blood, the sanctity of a human heart"? What does Hester mean by her response, "What we did had a consecration of its own"? Is Mr. Dimmesdale weak? Are there ways in which he is strong? Discuss. What is meant by the last line in the chapter?

19. Chapter 18: Why does the narrator now refer to "Arthur Dimmesdale"? To what extent has the minister suddenly changed? What has caused this change—the strength of Hester's character or something else? How is Pearl depicted near the end of the chapter? How do you think she will respond to her mother and to Arthur Dimmesdale? Why?

20. Chapter 19: At the brookside, why is Pearl upset with her mother? Why does she insist that her mother "come and take" the scarlet letter up? Why does the restoration of the letter to its proper place satisfy Pearl? Is her negative reaction to Arthur Dimmesdale's kiss an act of jealousy—or something else? Discuss.

21. Chapter 20: How does Mr. Dimmesdale perceive himself to be different from the man who had left the town? How is he different? Why does he have improper impulses? What is the "deadly sin" to which he has yielded?

22. Chapter 21: Why might Hester have possibly regretted the change that was about to take place in her life? Why does Pearl consider Mr. Dimmesdale strange? "Be quiet, Pearl!" says her mother. "Thou understandest not these things." Does Pearl understand? Discuss. How and why is the mood in the marketplace different from usual? Why are the sailors treated differently? What is the narrator's attitude toward all this? What do you think is Roger Chillingworth's intent?

23. Chapter 22: As she watches him pass in the procession, why does Hester Prynne fear there can be no bond between herself and Mr. Dimmesdale? Why does Roger Chillingworth plan to bring the young minister with him on the voyage?

24. Chapter 23: For Arthur Dimmesdale, what does his revelation at the scaffold signify? For Hester Prynne? For Pearl? Why was it the only place where he was safe from Roger Chillingworth?

25. Chapter 24: What is the meaning of the moral, "Be true! Be true! Be true!"? Why does Hester return to New England after many years? Why does she resume wearing the scarlet letter? For what does she hope? Upon the tombstone that serves both Hester Prynne and Arthur Dimmesdale, what is the larger meaning of the motto? In their lives what was the "ever-glowing point of light gloomier than the shadow"? Of the main characters in the novel, who committed the greatest sin and what was it? Justify your answer.

WRITING ACTIVITIES

1. In chapter 21, the narrator explains that the immediate descendants of the emigrants described in the novel "wore the blackest shade of Puritanism, and so darkened the national visage with it, that all the subsequent years have not sufficed to clear it up." Write a report about the New England Puritans of the late 1600s, especially about the witch trials. Use at least three sources.

2. You are Hester Prynne living in your small cottage some twenty years after the death of Arthur Dimmesdale. Among the distraught women who come to you for advice is none other than the granddaughter of former Governor Bellingham—a young, unmarried girl whose spurned affections for a young Salem minister have led her to believe she is a witch. Write the advice you would give her.

3. Through much of the novel, Roger Chillingworth is suspected of being in league with the devil. Write a conversation that he might have had with Satan after the conclusion of chapter 10.

4. Write a diamante poem with one of the following pairs of contrasting words: *Chillingworth* and *Dimmesdale* or *Hester* and *Pearl*. (See Appendix A.)

5. Write an account of Election Day from beginning to end (including the scaffold scene) as it might have appeared in the Boston newspaper of the time. Be objective.

6. Throughout most of the novel, we know very little of Hester's feelings toward Mr. Dimmesdale. Write diary entries that she might have made after each of the following incidents:

   a. the initial scene at the scaffold when Mr. Dimmesdale asks that she reveal the identity of Pearl's father,

   b. the scene where Mr. Dimmesdale successfully argues that she be allowed to keep Pearl, and

   c. the scene in the forest between her and the minister.

7. Write an account of the events of the initial scaffold scene in chapters 2 and 3 from the point of view of Roger Chillingworth.

8. Write a fantasy that Mistress Hibbins might have created about the meeting in the forest of Hester, Pearl, and Mr. Dimmesdale.

9. "The story of the scarlet letter grew into a legend." Write not a legend, but a ballad—"The Ballad of Hester Prynne"—in which you tell in song her sad and tragic story. In preparation, examine some books about ballads and the ballads themselves, such as "Barbara Allen."

10. Although the reader is told of the passion and impact of the Reverend Mr. Dimmesdale's Election Sermon, the reader does not hear it. Keeping in mind its general content and the awesome event that follows at the scaffold, write the final paragraph or two of the sermon—at least three hundred words. How does the minister conclude? Is his confession planned? Does he allude to it in any way?

OTHER ACTIVITIES

1. Each of the four main characters in the novel is physically described in some detail: Hester Prynne in chapter 2, Roger Chillingworth and Mr. Dimmesdale in chapter 3, and Pearl in chapter 6, among other places. With descriptions as guides, draw pictures—or perhaps in keeping with the Puritan mind, construct silhouettes—of each of these characters.

2. "The scarlet letter ceased to be a stigma which attracted the world's scorn and bitterness, and became a type of something to be sorrowed over, and looked upon with awe, yet with reverence, too." Draw or carve the image of the letter as you think it appeared etched on Hester Prynne's headstone.

3. Hester Prynne was forced to wear the scarlet letter *A* as a symbol of sin and shame. Design a needlepoint letter that she might have created for Roger Chillingworth, representing his greatest sin and suggesting, perhaps through color and shape, his undesirable qualities.

4. Invite a local religious leader to class to discuss sin and guilt as issues in contemporary life. If the minister or rabbi is familiar with *The Scarlet Letter*, ask him or her to comment on the novel.

5. Create a collage around the subject of guilt.

6. Imagine that Mr. Dimmesdale had survived his confession. With four other classmates, act out a trial in which three students representing characters from the novel (Reverend Wilson, Governor Bellingham, and the young wife standing at the jail in chapter 2) and two other students playing themselves determine his fate.

7. Read Richard Armour's humorous commentary on *The Scarlet Letter* in *The Classics Reclassified* (New York: McGraw-Hill, 1960).

SELECTED TEACHING RESOURCES

Media Aids

CD-ROM

The Time, Life, and Works of Hawthorne CD-ROM. Macintosh and Windows. Clearvue/eav.

Internet

Edred, Eric. 1997. *Nathaniel Hawthorne.* 1996, 1997. Available: http://www.ti-ac.net/users/eldred/nh/hawthorne.html (Accessed: March 1, 1997).

This extensive site includes information on the author as well as sections on Notes, a Glossary, Names of Characters, numerous examples of Art, Lesson Plans, a Video Bibliography, and the complete text of *The Scarlet Letter*, among other works.

Video

Nathaniel Hawthorne: The Scarlet Letter. 4 hrs., color, the WGBH/Jodie Foster version. Films for the Humanities & Sciences, n.d.

Printed Materials

Articles

Lasser, Michael L. "Mirror Imagery in *The Scarlet Letter*." *English Journal* 56 (February 1967): 274–277.

McWalters, John B. and Louise DeSalvo. "Hester Prynne as a Role Model: Pro and Con." *Media & Methods* 16 (April 1980): 36–37.

Tanner, Bernard R. "Tone as an Approach to *The Scarlet Letter*." *English Journal* 53 (October 1964): 528–530.

Book

Johnson, Claudia Durst. *Understanding "The Scarlet Letter."* Westport, CT: Greenwood, 1995.

Teaching Aids

The Scarlet Letter. Insight series and React series. Sundance.

The Scarlet Letter. Literature Unit Plans. Teacher's Pet Publications.

The Scarlet Letter. Masterprose series. Perfection Learning Corporation.

The Scarlet Letter. Novel Unit Guide, Perma-Guide, and Student Packet. Perma-Bound.

The Scarlet Letter. Novel/Drama Curriculum Units. The Center for Learning.

The Scarlet Letter. Novel-Ties. Learning Links.

Tests

The Scarlet Letter. Essay, objective, and alternative assessment versions. Perfection Learning Corporation.

A Separate Peace

John Knowles

New York: Macmillan, 1959
Available in paperback from Bantam.

SUMMARY

Gene Forrester narrates this story of a year spent at a New England prep school during World War II. Like all the other boys, Gene lives in bemused awe of his roommate, the joyous and fearless Phineas, who constantly challenges everyone in sports and in the exhilarant breaking of school rules. In an impulsive moment of envy and hatred, Gene causes Finny to fall from a tree and break his leg. Despite Finny's unwillingness to lay blame or to succumb to self-pity, Gene feels guilty, fearful, and broken. Only after they discuss and come to terms with the experience, just before Finny's death following a second fall, does Gene achieve the harmony and wholeness of character he had so fitfully but genuinely appreciated in the beloved Phineas.

APPRAISAL

This poignant story of initiation has been one of the most widely taught novels in American high schools, particularly in the upper grades, since its publication in 1959. For many students, Phineas is a person they would like to be—or at least to know: an appealing, irrepressible, uncompromising individual whose appreciation of self and love of life in a world gone haywire is intoxicating. And Gene is the person who many students are: vulnerable, afraid, uncertain, but sensitive and capable of growth and a certain wounded wholeness.

THEMES

initiation, loss of innocence, identity, friendship, fear, envy, the importance of love, (especially love of self), the importance of inner peace, the importance of being a participant in life

LITERARY CONCEPTS

plot, flashback, dramatic irony, symbol, setting, foreshadowing, imagery, point of view, tone, theme, characterization, archetype

RELATED READING

Initiation is a dominant theme in literature, especially American literature. Readers who respond to Gene's loss of innocence might also appreciate Hemingway's Nick Adams stories in *In Our Time*, William Faulkner's *Intruder in the Dust*, Gordon Parks's *The Learning Tree*, J. D. Salinger's *The Catcher in the Rye*, John Steinbeck's *The Red Pony*, Paul Zindel's *The Pigman*, Herman Raucher's *Summer of '42*, and Robert Cormier's *The Chocolate War*. Knowles wrote a sequel of sorts to *A Separate Peace* entitled *Peace Breaks Out* in 1981.

READING PROBLEMS AND OPPORTUNITIES

Although *A Separate Peace* was written for adults, like many other initiation novels about adolescents, this book has been read in recent years almost entirely by high school students. For most of them, it is quite readable, but it does contain many words with which students will be only passingly familiar. The book, therefore, offers much potential for vocabulary study. Words that occur more than once—and a few that appear singly—are as follows (chapter numbers are in parentheses):

tacit (1, 11),
salient (1, 7),
prodigious (1),
inveigle (1, 11),
rhetorically (1, 8),
indignation, indignant (1, 2, 6, 8, 11),
formidable (1, 3),
grave, gravely (2, 11),
resonant (2, 3, 11),
insidious (3),
tentative (4, 6, 7),
spectral (4),

discern (4, 7, 8),
detonation (4, 5),
enmity (4),
indiscriminate (4, 11),
nondescript (1, 4),
absently (4, 8),
undulation (4, 12),
visionary (5, 9),
erratic (5, 12, 13),
exhort (6, 8),
vindicate (6),
idiosyncratic (6, 7),
invoke (6, 7, 9),

sinecure (6),
egotism (6, 9),
maimed (6),
stealthily (6, 11),
insinuate (7, 8),
contemptuous (7, 11),
whim, whimsical (8, 9),
poignance (8, 13),
austerity (10, 11),
deranged (11),
impervious (12),
bellicose (13), and
parry (13).

INITIATING ACTIVITIES

1. Write a two- or three-page paper about your best friend. At some length, discuss what there is about your friend that you especially like. Also consider what you admire about him or her. Finally, and here you must try to be especially honest, discuss any qualities your friend has that are so admirable you have sometimes felt a tinge of envy or jealousy.

2. Do a little research to get a feeling for what life in the United States was like during World War II. Visit the public library and browse through old issues of *Life* magazine or *The Life Picture History of World War II*. Interview people who were your age during the war. In your reading and talking, focus on how ordinary citizens on the home front were affected by the experience, especially students who were faced with service overseas.

DISCUSSION QUESTIONS

1. Chapter 1: What feelings does the speaker have as he returns to Devon School? How many years has it been since he left? What kind of day is it? Why does he want to return to the First Academy Building and then to the river? What might he mean by "how far my convalescence had gone"? What kind of difficulty does he have reaching the river? What does he find there? How does the tree differ from his memories of it? What do you think he might mean by "Changed, I headed back through the mud"? What kind of person does Phineas seem to be? How is he described as different from the others? What does he expect from the others?

2. Chapter 2: How does Finny explain his and Gene's infraction to Mr. Prud'homme? Why does Mr. Prud'homme relent? Why does Finny get away with so much? Why is Gene disappointed that he gets away with wearing the Devon tie as a belt? Do you agree with Gene's subsequent remark that sarcasm is "the protest of people who are weak"? Why or why not? To Gene, why do the Devon Woods seem like "the beginning of the great northern forests . . . the tame fringe of the last and greatest wilderness"? What larger meaning might this have? In what way did the students "spend that summer in complete selfishness"? How does Finny's control over Gene increase?

3. Chapter 3: To what extent, if any, does Gene's affection and respect for Finny have limits? Discuss. Why is Gene so unwilling to lose face or break rank with Finny? Why do sports seem so important to Finny? Why does he reject badminton? How does blitzball typify his relationship with the boys, especially with Gene? Why does Finny insist that Gene not mention the record-breaking swim? To what extent, if any, does Gene see himself as Finny's rival? Why is he unable to reciprocate Finny's remark about being his best friend?

4. Chapter 4: What happens to change Gene's feelings for Finny? At this point, do you think Gene is right? Why or why not? How does Gene's newfound concern for academics differ from Finny's concern for sports? Gene says, "I didn't want Finny to understand me as I understood him." Does Gene understand Finny? Does he understand himself? Discuss. At the end of the chapter, why does he shake the limb and cause Finny to fall? What new fear has Gene discovered?

5. Chapter 5: Why does Gene put on Finny's clothes? Why does it give him relief? Why does he feel he must tell Finny the truth? When he finally does, why does Finny react the way he does? Why does Gene feel he has injured him worse? Do you feel he has? Why or why not? Is it better sometimes not to tell people the truth? Discuss. What does Gene mean by the last sentence?

6. Chapter 6: Why does Gene feel that the emphasis on continuity and tradition at Devon is now false? In what ways have traditions been broken and what has been the result? Why is Gene unable to go into Brinker's room? What larger meaning do the two rivers—one pure, the other unpleasant, with the Devon School astride them both—possibly have?

Why does Gene hit Quackenbush? In particular, why does the word *maimed* infuriate him? Does he strike the blow for Finny—or for someone else? Discuss. Why does Gene say: "If only I had . . . seized and held and prized the multitude of advantages the summer offered me; if only I had"? What were those advantages? Why does Finny finally call Gene? Why does he get upset over Gene's trying out for assistant crew manager? Why has Gene given up on sports? Why does he feel the need "to become a part of Phineas"?

7. Chapter 7: Why is the incident in the Butt Room so uncomfortable to Gene? Why do he and the other boys agree to pick apples and shovel snow? (How might Finny have reacted differently?) Why is Leper opposed to downhill skiing? How does Gene's attitude toward him begin to change? How is Leper like Finny? Why does Gene decide to enlist? Is the reason perhaps more complicated than he realizes? Discuss.

8. Chapter 8: Why does Gene change his mind about enlisting? Why does he think Finny needs him? Do you agree that Finny needs him? Why or why not? What is the significance of Finny's passing up the Trophy Room for the locker room? How does Finny's view of the war—and his relationship to it—differ from Gene's? Why does Finny want to deny it? What does having suffered allow him to understand? Why does he insist that Gene train for the Olympics?

9. Chapter 9: How does Leper's enlistment affect the boys? Why do they jokingly project him into every campaign and battle? Why does Finny create the Winter Carnival? For Gene, especially, what does it become?

10. Chapter 10: Gene says that he would spend a good part of his life "traveling through an unknown countryside from one unknown settlement to another." What might he have meant? What are examples of this in this chapter? How is Leper now unknown to him? What has happened to Leper? What has he learned? How has he changed? How is Gene's comment about the snow-covered fields possibly symbolic? What about Leper's comment pertaining to "Snow White with Brinker's face on her"? Why does Gene run off?

11. Chapter 11: How is Finny's participation in the snowball fight so typical of him? How does his statement "Sure. There isn't any war" represent a change, at least from Gene's point of view? How do Finny's attitude and ability regarding music symbolize his situation in general? Why are Finny and Gene taken to the Assembly Room? How do their responses to the inquiry differ? Why does Gene keep commenting on the acoustics? Why does Finny tell Brinker that Leper is on campus? Why does Leper refuse to answer the last question? Why does Finny flee from the room?

12. Chapter 12: Gene says, "Phineas had thought of me as an extension of himself." Do you agree? Why or why not? Why does Gene consider, for a moment, stealing Dr. Stanpole's car? Why does he try to see Finny at the Infirmary? When he leaves and walks down past the gym and the water hole and playing fields, why does he feel that all of these possess a meaning that he can never understand? How does Finny surprise Gene the next day? Why "wouldn't [Finny] be any good in the war"? What does

Finny want so hard to believe? Does he believe it? "The rest of the day passed quickly." Until he returns to the Infirmary, how does the rest of the day seem to go for Gene? Why does Dr. Stanpole say, "This is something I think boys of your generation are going to see a lot of"? Does he simply mean death or something in addition to death? Discuss.

13. Chapter 13: How does Gene seem to feel about the army's takeover of the Far Common? Why does he believe he has just left the adolescence stage? How has he changed? Why is he unable to say anything about Phineas? Yet how is Finny "present in every moment of every day"? In conclusion, how was Finny different from all the others? Who was the enemy that he had helped Gene kill? To what extent do you think Gene is indeed "Phineas-filled," possessed of simplicity, harmony, and unity of character? Discuss. Returning finally to chapter 1, why does Gene return to Devon after fifteen years? What does he mean by, "So the more things remain the same, the more they change after all"?

WRITING ACTIVITIES

1. Make up the rules for a war game that Phineas might have created to pass the time during the summer session. Keep in mind his fertile imagination and his preference for sport in which the lines between winning and losing are fuzzily drawn.

2. After the death of Phineas, Gene "couldn't say anything or listen to anything about him." Speak for Gene; write an epitaph for Finny.

3. One of Finny's most compelling qualities is his irrepressibility. Try to identify and write down the aspects of his character and personality that contributed to this. Then make a list of Suggestions for Loving Life and Loving Living, using talents and qualities that Finny possessed as well as others you consider important.

4. Like Gene (who speaks of this in chapter 6), all of us are guilty at one time or another of failing to perceive and value experiences that are available to us. Write about a time in your life when you failed to take grateful advantage of a situation from which you might have learned and benefited.

5. "Now that Phineas was back it seemed time to start saying prayers again" (chapter 8). Write the prayers that Gene might have said that night.

6. Write the bylaws for the Super Suicide Society of the Summer Session.

7. Write a short critique (an analysis of some technical question concerning the writing of a novel or play). Address this question: In *A Separate Peace,* why are we never told Phineas's last name? Write at least a paragraph.

8. Seniors in high school often write semi-serious "wills" bequeathing to underclassmen certain of their more notable qualities or possessions. Write wills for Gene, Brinker, and Leper in which they leave as legacies what you consider their most (or perhaps least) admirable qualities.

9. If Phineas had kept a diary, write what his entries for the following days might have been. (The entries should reflect Finny's interests and concerns.)

   a. the day he invented blitzball
   b. the day after he fell from the tree
   c. the day after Gene visited him at home
   d. one other day of your choice, a day important to Finny

OTHER ACTIVITIES

1. Design and write an advertising brochure or flyer promoting Devon School. Include illustrations and text. For the former, refer to Gene's descriptions of the campus in chapter 1 and elsewhere.

2. "Around Devon we had gaits of every description." Pantomime the different ways of walking Gene refers to, including his "West Point stride" and the styles mentioned halfway through chapter 8. Make a special effort to capture Finny's "continuous flowing balance, so that he had seemed to drift along with no effort at all, relaxation on the move." Finish by discussing how the way one walks can convey subtle and not-so-subtle meanings.

3. Using pen and ink or watercolors, draw or paint the tree by the river as seen by Gene on the damp and forlorn afternoon in chapter 1 when he returns to Devon.

4. In chapter 12, Gene says, "Phineas had thought of me as an extension of himself." In chapter 13, he feels that he himself is "Phineas-filled." Using any medium of your choice (mobile, clay, collage, or other), create an artistic representation of the blended or mirrored identities of Gene and Finny.

5. For Phineas, the Summer Olympic Games of 1944 were very important, an event of peaceful competition in a world gone awry. In his games, Gene won every gold medal. Keeping the values of Phineas in mind, design the medal that he would have wanted to award Gene.

6. As a member of Devon's Golden Fleece Debating Society, debate with other students the following proposition: Wars are invariably caused by the older, wealthier, and more powerful elements of society who seek to broaden and strengthen their influence.

7. Imagine that Phineas accompanies Gene to see Leper in chapter 10. With two or three other students, role-play the scene that might have taken place in Leper's house.

SELECTED TEACHING RESOURCES

Media Aids

Cassettes (5)

A Separate Peace. 6.5 hours. Recorded Books.

Video

A Separate Peace. 104 min., Clearvue/eav, Perma-Bound, and Perfection Learning Corporation, 1972.

Printed Materials

Articles

Alley, Douglas. "Teaching Emerson through *A Separate Peace.*" *English Journal* 70 (January 1981): 19–21.

Ellis, James. "*A Separate Peace*: The Fall from Innocence." *English Journal* 53 (May 1964): 313–318.

Ely, Sister M. Amanda. "The Adult Image in Three Novels of Adolescent Life." *English Journal* 56 (November 1967): 1127–1131.

Greiling, Franziska Lynne. "The Theme of Freedom in *A Separate Peace.*" *English Journal* 56 (December 1967): 1269–1272.

Mengeling, Marvin E. "*A Separate Peace*: Meaning and Myth." *English Journal* 58 (December 1969): 1322–1329.

Thompson, C. Lamar. "Themes in *A Separate Peace.*" *Clearing House* 46 (November 1971): 188–189.

Witherington, Paul. "*A Separate Peace*: A Study in Structural Ambiguity." *English Journal* 54 (December 1965): 795–800.

Books

Bryant, Hallman Bell. *"A Separate Peace": The War Within.* Boston: Twayne Publishers, 1990.

Howes, Alan B. *Teaching Literature to Adolescents: Novels.* Glenview, IL: Scott, Foresman, 1972. An interview with John Knowles, pp. 146–155.

Teaching Aids

A Separate Peace. Contemporary Classics series. Perfection Learning Corporation.

A Separate Peace. Literature Unit Plans. Teacher's Pet Publications.

A Separate Peace. Novel Unit Guide and Perma-Guide. Perma-Bound.

A Separate Peace. Novel/Drama Curriculum Units. The Center for Learning.

A Separate Peace. Novel-Ties. Learning Links.

A Separate Peace. React series. Sundance.

Tests

A Separate Peace. Essay and objective versions. Perfection Learning Corporation.

Macbeth

William Shakespeare

Play: available in paperback from several publishing companies.

SUMMARY

Returning from battle, Macbeth and Banquo meet three wild witches who hail the former by his title, thane of Glamis, and by the titles thane of Cawdor and King, while Banquo is advised that he will never be king but that he will father kings. Two noblemen arrive shortly and declare Macbeth thane of Cawdor. For his part, Macbeth sees no hope of becoming king since the king's son Malcolm has been declared heir. With the encouragement of Lady Macbeth, however, he plots and executes the murder of the king by stabbing him in his sleep. When the king's sons flee, Macbeth attempts to lay the crime on them. Because he is troubled by the witches' prophecy for Banquo, Macbeth then arranges Banquo's murder, but the victim's ghost returns to haunt his killer and Banquo's son Fleance escapes. Macbeth then returns to the witches, who warn him of Macduff, another nobleman, but assure Macbeth that he cannot be harmed by any man born of woman and that he will never be vanquished "until / Great Birham Wood to high Dunsinane Hill / Shall come against him." Although Macbeth believes the witches, he sends out spies, and when Macduff escapes, Macbeth has his wife and children slain. Distraught by the memory of the evil that has been done, Lady Macbeth walks in her sleep and approaches mental collapse. Macbeth, however, is absorbed with his preparations to battle Malcolm's forces. Following a report of Lady Macbeth's death, a messenger observes an army advancing with protective branches and informs Macbeth that Birham Wood is coming to Dunsinane. Still Macbeth clings to the words of the witches and realizes he is defeated only when he faces Macduff, who informs him that he "was from his mother's womb / untimely ripped." Macduff kills Macbeth and carries his head to Malcolm, who is hailed as the new king.

APPRAISAL

Long a fixture in the English curriculum of the public schools, *Macbeth* continues to be an absorbing tale for each new generation of students. Its appeal stems from its supernatural tone and gripping portrayal of characters whose overwhelming desires for power and revenge prompt them to commit bloody crimes. The play is usually taught in the twelfth grade.

THEMES

ambition, the lust for power, evil and treachery, fate, guilt

LITERARY CONCEPTS

tragedy, blank verse, characterization, conflict, resolution, soliloquy, imagery, comic relief, irony, structure, tone, metaphor, simile, aside

RELATED READING

Several of Shakespeare's other plays, including *Hamlet*, *Othello*, and *King Lear*, provide character studies of rulers whose downfalls are brought about by their own defects in character. A number of Greek dramas, such as *Oedipus Rex* by Sophocles, present similar portraits of a king's decline. Contemporary works that explore ruthless leaders include *The Emperor Jones* by Eugene O'Neill and *All the King's Men* by Robert Penn Warren.

READING PROBLEMS AND OPPORTUNITIES

Shakespeare's plays have long presented students with the most difficult reading challenges of their high school years. Although *Macbeth* is no exception, the play (which is Shakespeare's shortest) can be taught and taught well. One secret lies in not belaboring the task. A month or more wading through endless translations of passages will sufficiently motivate most students to avoid ever reading or viewing any work of Shakespeare for the rest of their lives. In high school anthologies and even paperback editions, archaic words and phrases are explained in footnotes. Beyond these, a number of words can be used for vocabulary study, including the following (act and scene numbers are in parentheses):

harbinger (1:4),	*bounteous* (3:1),	*redress* (4:2),
frieze (1:6),	*malevolence* (3:6),	*avarice* (4:3),
cherubim (1:7),	*deftly* (4:1),	*agitation* (5:1),
adage (1:7),	*potent* (4:1),	*speculative* (5:4), and
multitudinous (2:2),	*vanquished* (4:1),	*equivocation* (5:5).
verities (3:1, 3:3),	*pernicious* (4:1, 4:3),	

INITIATING ACTIVITIES

1. With your classmates, brainstorm the characteristics of some of the current American and world political leaders. Your qualities should include the positive as well as the negative. Examine your class list when it is completed and divide it into two parts—characteristics of good leaders and characteristics of bad leaders. From these lists, write profiles of a good political leader and a poor one. Save these lists and descriptions for later use.

2. Discuss with your classmates the credibility of fortune-tellers, psychics, and horoscopes. Consider these questions: Can individuals predict the future? Are horoscopes accurate? What scientific or rational evidence exists for suggesting that such prophesies are accurate? How can horoscopes and fortune-tellers affect people's lives? Is there danger in believing such predictions? Why or why not? (*Note*: You may wish to bring to class a copy of a horoscope or a newspaper like *National Enquirer*, which often features predictions by psychics.)

Discussion Questions

1. Act 1, scene 1: What do the three witches plan to do? What might they mean by the line "Fair is foul, and foul is fair"?

2. Act 1, scene 2: What does the wounded sergeant report regarding Macbeth's performance? How does King Duncan reward Macbeth? Why does he choose this method?

3. Act 1, scene 3: What is Banquo's first impression of the three weird women? What do the witches predict for Banquo and Macbeth? Why doesn't Macbeth believe what they tell him? Why does he change his mind? What do Macbeth's asides reveal about his changing attitude?

4. Act 1, scene 4: What does this scene reveal about the relationship between Banquo and Duncan? Between Macbeth and Duncan? Why is Macbeth troubled over Malcolm's being named the Prince of Cumberland?

5. Act 1, scene 5: How does Lady Macbeth learn of her husband's good fortune? Why does she have misgivings about his abilities to see the witches' prophecies carried out? Why does she request that the spirits "unsex" her? What advice does she give Macbeth regarding his behavior when the king arrives? Why does she feel it is necessary to give this advice?

6. Act 1, scenes 6 and 7: How does Lady Macbeth greet Duncan and his retinue? Why is the king not suspicious of her? Of Macbeth? Why does Macbeth vacillate as he considers killing Duncan? How is Lady Macbeth able to persuade him to carry out the deed? Why does Macbeth then admonish her to "bring forth men-children only"?

7. Act 2, scene 1: Why is Banquo troubled and unable to sleep? When Banquo asks Macbeth about the three weird sisters, Macbeth says, "I think not of them." What is the irony of this response? Why does Macbeth see a vision of a dagger before him? What is the significance of the ringing of the bell?

8. Act 2, scene 2: What does Lady Macbeth fear at first? Why is Macbeth concerned that he could not say "Amen"? What does Lady Macbeth advise him to do? Why? Why does Macbeth fear returning the daggers? Is it consistent with Lady Macbeth's character that she agrees to return the daggers? Why or why not? Imagine this scene on the stage. How would Macbeth deliver his lines in this scene? How would you describe his appearance and actions?

9. Act 2, scene 3: What was Shakespeare's purpose in including the scene with the drunken porter? Why does he appear at this time? How does the weather foretell the evil deeds that have transpired? Macduff seeks to shield Lady Macbeth from the details of the murder, saying, "O gentle lady, 'Tis not for you to hear what I can speak." Explain the irony here. What action does Macbeth take on seeing the sleeping grooms? How does he rationalize this foul deed? What do Malcolm and Donalbain plan to do? Do you think they are wise to choose this course of action? Why or why not?

10. Act 2, scene 4: Besides the servants whom Macbeth killed, who else is suspected of the murder of Duncan? Why?

11. Act 3, scenes 1 and 2: In the opening soliloquy, Banquo expresses his fears about Macbeth's actions. What are those fears? Cite examples of exaggerated politeness used by Macbeth and his wife to cover their true feelings. How does Macbeth convince the murderers to kill Banquo? Why is he so determined that Fleance be killed also? What fears still plague Macbeth? How does Lady Macbeth seek to console and counsel her husband?

12. Act 3, scenes 3 and 4: In what way do the murderers succeed in their mission? In what way do they fail? What is Macbeth's reaction to the news of their deeds? What are his reactions to the appearance of Banquo's ghost? How does Lady Macbeth try to make excuses for her husband's behavior? Why do the lords accept her explanations? What is she finally forced to do? How does Macbeth know of Macduff's activities? What plans does Macbeth make? Why does he make these plans?

13. Act 3, scene 5: Why does Hecate chide the three witches? What does she predict that Macbeth will do? How does she know this?

14. Act 3, scene 6: Identify parts of the conversation between Lennox and the Lord that provide information about the type of ruler that Macbeth has become. What hopes do these two have that conditions may improve?

15. Act 4, scene 1: What is the purpose of the opening segment of this scene in which the witches prepare their brew? What is the first apparition that Macbeth sees? Why does he discount the warning in the first apparition when he sees the second? Why does he feel confident and secure after the third apparition? What causes Macbeth to seek further views of the future despite the witches' warning? What plan for revenge against Macduff does Macbeth devise? Why does he decide to do this?

16. Act 4, scene 2: Lady Macduff condemns her husband for leaving the country. Do you think Macduff was wise to leave? Why or why not? What would you have done in his place? Why does Ross try to defend Macduff? Why doesn't Lady Macduff leave after the messenger brings a warning? What does she say about the state of the world? Compare this to the witches' statement "Fair is foul, and foul is fair." Is Macduff's son courageous or foolish? Why?

17. Act 4, scene 3: What evils do Malcolm and Macduff attribute to Macbeth? What assistance is England offering so that Malcolm may save Scotland from Macbeth? What moves Macduff to take on Macbeth as a personal adversary?

18. Act 5, scene 1: Review the speeches made by Lady Macbeth during her sleepwalking scene and trace the references to people and events that she mentions to actual events in the play. How has her mind warped some of these events? Why does the doctor say that Lady Macbeth has need of the divine rather than a physician? Why does he dare not say what he is thinking?

19. Act 5, scene 2: According to Caithness and Angus, what is Macbeth's current mental state? What is the only source of his strength?

20. Act 5, scene 3: What regrets does Macbeth express regarding his life? In what ways is he unrealistic in his demands that the physician heal his wife? What loyalty or lack of loyalty does the doctor express for the king?

21. Act 5, scenes 4, 5, and 6: Why does Malcolm instruct his soldiers to cut branches from the trees? What is Macbeth's response to the death of his wife? Does his speech indicate that he has little feeling for her? Discuss. Why does his courage begin to wane?

22. Act 5, scenes 7 and 8: Why does Macbeth's encounter with young Siward continue to reinforce his belief in the prophecy of the witches? Why does he warn Macduff to turn back? Does this action suggest that he is beginning to show remorse for his past deeds? Why or why not? How is Macduff able to kill Macbeth? Do you believe that Macbeth was courageous in the end? Why or why not? Why is Siward pleased with the death of his son? What plans does Malcolm have to bind up the wounds of Scotland and begin his new reign?

WRITING ACTIVITIES

1. Review the lists you made for Initiating Activity #1. In addition, read over act 4, scene 3, which includes a discussion of the qualities of a ruler. Write an essay on Macbeth as a leader. Discuss both his good and bad qualities and quote appropriate lines from the play to support your views.

2. Throughout the play Shakespeare presents a contrast between black and white, darkness and light. (For example, see the description of Macbeth in act 4, scene 3.) In a well-organized paper, explore the dramatist's use of these motifs and explain how they underscore theme and help to unify the action.

3. Write a newspaper account of the battle that takes place in act 5. Because the play focuses on only a few characters and their actions, you will need to fill in details based on inferences drawn from the dialogue.

4. Is Lady Macbeth a feminist? Write a brief paper arguing your position. Support your viewpoint with specific references to the play.

5. Write a eulogy for Duncan. In preparation, review act 1, scenes 2, 4, and 6, and act 2, scenes 3 and 4 for clues to his character and his interaction with other characters.

6. Prepare the speech that Macbeth might have delivered to his men prior to the siege of Dunsinane Castle by Malcolm's forces. Write at least two pages.

7. You are Macduff. Write the letter you send to your wife and children from England justifying your actions and reaffirming your love for your family.

8. Shakespeare does not include stage directions in his plays. Choose one scene from *Macbeth* and revise it by adding directions having to do with gestures, movement, and vocal qualities. One good possibility for revision is act 1, scene 5.

9. Conduct some research on witchcraft in England during the sixteenth and seventeenth centuries. Then write a paper discussing Shakespeare's use of witchcraft in the play. Among questions to consider: How would the reaction of the audience in Shakespeare's time to the witches differ from the reaction of an audience today?

10. You are the Doctor of Physic in act 5, scene 1. Using modern language, write a psychological report on Lady Macbeth based on your observations.

OTHER ACTIVITIES

1. Using the stage directions you wrote for Writing Activity #8, enact the scene with several of your classmates.

2. Several film and television versions of *Macbeth* have been produced, some with effective musical soundtracks. Prepare a tape of music to use as background for a particular scene in the play. Keep in mind the usefulness of music in reinforcing tone.

3. "Hang out our banners on the outward walls," orders Macbeth. Design a banner to fly over Dunsinane Castle. Use materials that might have been available at the time (e.g., coarsely woven cloth). Make sure the banner reflects Macbeth's character and values through color and design.

4. Design a coat of arms for the House of Macbeth, Banquo, or Macduff. Your design should reflect the family's Scottish heritage as well as its particular achievements and values.

5. Prepare two or three posters that Macbeth's subjects might have used to make known their grievances against the king.

6. Using collage, clay, or perhaps some form of mixed media, create an artistic representation of one of the following familiar lines from *Macbeth* (act and scene numbers are in parentheses):

   a. "Fair is foul, and foul is fair." (1:1)
   b. "It will have blood; they say, blood will have blood." (4:3)
   c. "Something wicked this way comes." (4:1)
   d. "I have supped full with horrors." (5:5)
   e. "Life's but a walking shadow . . . / . . . a tale / Told by an idiot, full of sound and fury / Signifying nothing." (5:5)

SELECTED TEACHING RESOURCES

Media Aids

Cassettes (2)

Macbeth. Perfection Learning Corporation.

Cassettes (3)

Macbeth. 130 min., Anthony Quayle version. Clearvue/eav.

CD-ROM

Macbeth CD-ROM. Macintosh version. Clearvue/eav.

Internet

Gray, Terry A. 1997. *Mr. William Shakespeare and the Internet.* 1995-1997. Available: http://www.palomar.edu/Library/shake.html (Accessed: March 1, 1997).
This site contains numerous links to wonderful homepages devoted to Shakespeare, several on the teaching of Shakespeare.

Videos

Macbeth. 89 min., b & w. Perma-Bound and Perfection Learning Corporation, 1948.

Macbeth. 148 min. BBC version with Nicol Williamson. Ambrose Video Publishing, Inc., n.d.

Macbeth. 151 min., color. Clearvue/eav, n.d.

Macbeth, 1: The Politics of Power. 28 min., color. Britannica, n.d.

Macbeth, 2: The Themes of Macbeth. 28 min., color. Britannica, n.d.

Macbeth, 3: The Secret'st Man. 33 min., color. Britannica, n.d.

Trevor Nunn's Macbeth with the Royal Shakespeare Company. 150 min., color. Films for the Sciences and Humanities, n.d.

Printed Materials

Abridged Text

Macbeth. Shakespeare for Young People series (text shortened, language unchanged). Learning Links.

Articles

Bartling, Charles E. "On Teaching *Macbeth* and Shakespeare." *English Journal* 49 (January 1960): 38–39.

Calitri, Charles. "*Macbeth* and the Reluctant Reader." *English Journal* 48 (May 1959): 254–261.

Gleason, Marian. "As We Three Meet Again." *English Journal* 56 (October 1967): 1005–1006.

Hall, Evelyn W. "Color Him Red." *English Journal* 56 (April 1967): 564–565.

Books

Evans, Bertrand. *Teaching Shakespeare in the High School.* New York: Macmillan, 1966.

Howes, Alan B. *Teaching Literature to Adolescents: Plays.* Glenview, IL.: Scott, Foresman, 1968.

O'Brien, Peggy, ed. *Shakespeare Set Free: Teaching "Romeo and Juliet," "Macbeth," and "A Midsummer Night's Dream."* Washington, D.C.: The Folger Library, 1993. (Available from Perma-Bound.)

Parry, Martin. "The Tragedy of *Macbeth*." In *Teaching Shakespeare,* edited by Arthur Mizener, 13–47. New York: New American Library, 1969.

Parallel Text

Macbeth. Features original text and contemporary paraphrase side-by-side. Perfection Learning Corporation.

Posters

Macbeth. Set of five, 17" x 22", color. Perfection Learning Corporation and Sundance.

Teaching Aids

Macbeth. Insight series, React series, and Classroom Classics series. Sundance.

Macbeth. Literature Unit Plans. Teacher's Pet Publications.

Macbeth. Novel Unit Guide, Perma-Guide, and Student Packet. Perma-Bound.

Macbeth. Novel/Drama Curriculum Units. The Center for Learning.

Macbeth. Masterprose series. Perfection Learning Corporation.

Tests

Macbeth. Essay, objective, and alternative assessment versions. Perfection Learning Corporation.

Appendix A

DIAMANTES

Several response guides include an activity requiring students to write a diamante poem. A diamante is a diamond-shaped poem based on contrasts. Although there are variations, the most common pattern produces a seven-line poem with the following form:

Line 1—one word, usually a noun

Line 2—two adjectives that describe the noun

Line 3—three participles (*-ing*, *-ed*, *-en*) also describing the noun

Line 4—four nouns that provide a transition from the word in line 1 to the word in line 7; or a long phrase that provides the transition

Line 5—three participles that describe the noun in line 7

Line 6—two adjectives that describe the noun in line 7

Line 7—a noun that contrasts with line 1

Fire

orange and yellow

licking, leaping, lighting

caught between desire and indifference

staring, glaring, glistening

silver and blue

Ice

Appendix B

COMPANIES

Agency for Instructional Technology
Box A
Bloomington, IN 47402-0120
1-800-457-4509

Aims Media
9710 DeSoto Avenue
Chatsworth, CA 91311

Ambrose Video Publishing, Inc.
1290 Avenue of the Americas, Suite 2245
New York, NY 10104
1-800-526-4663

Bantam Doubleday Dell Audio Publishing
1540 Broadway
New York, NY 10036

Britannica
310 S. Michigan Avenue
Chicago, IL 60604
1-800-554-9862

The Center for Learning
Teachers/Authors/Publishers
P.O. Box 910
Villa Maria, PA 16155
1-800-767-9090 (Operator 18)

Christopher-Gordon Publishers, Inc.
480 Washington Street
Norwood, MA 02062

Clearvue/eav
6465 N. Avondale Avenue
Chicago, IL 60631-1996
1-800-CLEARVU

Corporation for Public Broadcasting
The Annenberg/CPB Project
901 E Street, NW
Washington, D.C. 20004-2037

Films for the Humanities & Sciences
P.O. Box 2053
Princeton, NJ 08543-2053

Films Incorporated Video
5547 N. Ravenswood Avenue
Chicago, IL 60640
1-800-343-4312

The Folger Library
201 E. Capitol Street, SE
Washington, D.C. 20003

Harper Audio
Division of HarperCollins Publishers, Inc.
10 E. 53rd Street
New York, NY 10022

J. Weston Walch, Publisher
321 Valley Street
P.O. Box 658
Portland, ME 04104-0658
1-800-341-6094

Learning Links
2300 Marcus Avenue
Dept. A96
New Hyde Park, NY 11042

Listening Library, Inc.
One Park Avenue
Old Greenwich, CT 06385

Lucerne Media
37 Ground Pine Road
Morris Plains, NJ 07959
1-800-341-2293

Media Guild
11722 Sorrento Valley Road
San Diego, CA 92121

PBS Video
1320 Braddock Place
Alexandria, VA 22314

Penguin Highbridge Audio
375 Hudson Street
New York, NY 10014

Penguin Electronics
375 Hudson Street
New York, NY 10014
1-800-253-6476

Perma-Bound
617 E. Vandalia Road
Jacksonville, IL 62650
1-800-637-6581

Perfection Learning Corporation
1000 N. Second Avenue
Logan, IA 51546-1099
1-800-831-4190

Rainbow Educational Media
4540 Preslyn Drive
Raleigh, NC 27604-3177
1-800-331-4047

Random House Audio
201 E. 50th Street
New York, NY 10022

Recorded Books, Inc.
270 Skipjack Road
Prince Frederick, MD 20678

Sundance
P.O. Box 1326
Newtown Road
Littleton, MA 01460
1-800-343-8204

Teacher's Pet Publications
11504 Hammock Point
Berlin, MD 21811

Thomas S. Klise Company
P.O. Box 317
Waterford, CT 06385

University of California Ext. Media Center
2176 Shattuck Avenue
Berkeley, CA 94704

Author / Title Index

About the Authors

Albert B. Somers is professor of education at Furman University in Greenville, SC. A native of North Carolina, Dr. Somers earned a B.A. in English and an M.A. in education from the University of North Carolina at Chapel Hill, and a Ph.D. in English education from Florida State University. His professional experience includes teaching high school English, working as an English language arts consultant at district and state levels, and teaching English and education in college. With Dr. Worthington, he has co-authored *Response Guides for Teaching Children's Books*, and *Candles and Mirrors*, in addition to *Novels and Plays*.

Janet Evans Worthington is the director of the Center for Lifelong Learning at Plattsburgh State University of New York, Plattsburgh. She holds a B.A. in English from the University of Chicago, an M.A. from the University of Iowa, and a Ph.D. in English education from Florida State University. Her career has included teaching at both secondary and college levels. She has written numerous articles on teaching English, and is co-author of *Response Guides for Teaching Children's Books*, and *Candles and Mirrors* with Albert B. Somers, and *Practical Robotics* with Bill Burns. Dr. Worthington is the mother of three children.

From *Teacher Ideas Press*

WHAT A NOVEL IDEA! Projects and Activities for Young Adult Literature
Katherine Wiesolek Kuta

Designed around the new language arts standards (reading, writing, representing, viewing, speaking, and listening), these stimulating activities for novels create opportunities for students to develop skills and become better readers, writers, and speakers. **Grades 7–12**.
ca.160p. 8½x11 paper ISBN 1-56308-479-1

MYSTERY AND DETECTION: Thinking and Problem Solving with the Sleuths
Jerry D. Flack

Turn your classroom into a real Scotland Yard! This unique resource ties in dozens of problem-solving and enrichment activities with mystery and sleuthing. It is divided into topical chapters on language arts, art, social studies, future studies, and crime and punishment. **Grades 5–9** *(Adaptable to other grades)*.
Gifted Treasury Series; Jerry D. Flack, Ed.
xx, 246p. 8½x11 paper ISBN 0-87287-815-5

STAGINGS: Short Scripts for Middle and High School Students
Joan Garner

These original, skill-specific scripts were designed around the guidelines for the theatre discipline of the National Standards for Arts Education. Simple and affordable to produce, the nine plays make up this resource that *Booklist* calls "A must purchase for drama and literature studies." **Grades 6–12**.
xiii, 233p. 8½x11 paper ISBN 1-56308-343-4

DRAMA THAT DELIVERS
Nancy Duffy Hery

Eight reproducible plays allow students to address sensitive issues such as suicide, alchoholism, divorce, anger, and peer pressure through drama and role-playing. Participants consider difficult problems and make choices in the decision for what happens at the plays' endings. **Grades 6–12**.
xi, 113p. 8½x11 paper ISBN 1-56308-429-5

READERS THEATRE FOR YOUNG ADULTS: Scripts and Script Development
Kathy Howard Latrobe and Mildred Knight Laughlin

"Highly recommended" by *Curriculum Review*, this unique teaching tool helps students develop a thorough understanding of theme, character, and drama. Twelve reproducible scripts from the classics serve as examples of the readers theatre format. In addition, the authors have selected 30 contemporary novels and have identified a scene from each that is suitable for adaptation to readers theatre. **Grades 7–12**.
xi, 130p. 8½x11 paper ISBN 0-87287-743-4

For a FREE catalog or to place an order, please contact:

Teacher Ideas Press
Dept. B52 · P.O. Box 6633 · Englewood, CO 80155-6633
1-800-237-6124, ext. 1 · Fax: 303-220-8843 · E-mail: lu-books@lu.com

Check out the TIP Web site!
www.lu.com/tip